V. I. Lenin

On Workers' Control
and the Nationalization of Industry

Fredonia Books
Amsterdam, The Netherlands

On Workers' Control and the Nationalization
of Industry

by
Vladimir Ilyich Ulyanov (Lenin)

ISBN: 1-58963-923-5

Copyright © 2002 by Fredonia Books

Reprinted from the 1970 edition

Fredonia Books
Amsterdam, The Netherlands
http://www.fredoniabooks.com

CONTENTS

From the DRAFT AND EXPLANATION
OF A PROGRAMME
FOR THE SOCIAL-DEMOCRATIC PARTY[1]

Draft Programme

A. 1. Big factories are developing in Russia with ever-growing rapidity, ruining the small handicraftsmen and peasants, turning them into propertyless workers, and driving ever-increasing numbers of the people to the cities, factory and industrial villages and townlets.

2. This growth of capitalism signifies an enormous growth of wealth and luxury among a handful of factory owners, merchants and landowners, and a still more rapid growth of the poverty and oppression of the workers. The improvements in production and the machinery introduced in the big factories, while facilitating a rise in the productivity of social labour, serve to strengthen the power of the capitalists over the workers, to increase unemployment and with it to accentuate the defenceless position of the workers.

3. But while carrying the oppression of labour by capital to the highest pitch, the big factories are creating a special class of workers which is enabled to wage a struggle against capital, because their very conditions of life are destroying all their ties with their own petty production, and, by uniting the workers through their common labour and transferring them from factory to factory, are welding masses of working folk together. The workers are beginning a struggle against the capitalists, and an intense urge for unity is appearing among them. Out of the isolated revolts of the workers is growing the struggle of the Russian working class.

4. This struggle of the working class against the capitalist class is a struggle against all classes who live by the labour of others, and against all exploitation. It can only end in the passage of political power into the hands of the working class, the transfer of all the land, instruments, factories, machines, and mines to the whole of society for the organisation of socialist production, under which all that is produced by the workers and all improvements in production must benefit the working people themselves.

5. The movement of the Russian working class is, according to its character and aims, part of the international (Social-Democratic) movement of the working class of all countries....

Explanation of the Programme

... What, however, is the domination of the capitalist class over the entire mass of working folk based on? It is based on the fact that all the factories, mills, mines, machines, and instruments of labour are in the hands of the capitalists, are their private property; on the fact that they possess enormous quantities of land (of all the land in European Russia, more than one-third belongs to landed proprietors, who do not number half a million). The workers possess no instruments of labour or materials, and so they have to sell their labour-power to the capitalists, who only pay the workers what is necessary for their keep, and place all the surplus produced by labour in their pockets; thus they pay for only part of the working time they use, and appropriate the rest. The entire increase in wealth resulting from the combined labour of the masses of workers or from improvements in production goes to the capitalist class, while the workers, who toil from generation to generation, remain propertyless proletarians. That is why there is only one way of ending the exploitation of labour by capital, and that is to abolish the private ownership of the instruments of labour, to hand over all the factories, mills, mines, and also all the big estates, etc., to the whole of society and to conduct socialist production in common, directed by the workers themselves. The articles

produced by labour in common will then go to benefit the
working people themselves, while the surplus they produce
over and above their keep will serve to satisfy the needs
of the workers themselves, to secure the full development
of all their capabilities and equal rights to enjoy all the
achievements of science and art. That is why the programme
states that the struggle between the working class and the
capitalists can end only in this way. To achieve that,
however, it is necessary that political power, i.e., the power
to govern the state, should pass from the hands of a
government which is under the influence of the capitalists
and landowners, or from the hands of a government directly
made up of elected representatives of the capitalists, into
the hands of the working class.

Such is the ultimate aim of the struggle of the working
class, such is the condition for its complete emancipation. . . .

Written in prison. *Draft
Programme*—after December 9
(21), 1895; *Explanation of the
Programme* in June-July 1896

First published in 1924 in   *Collected Works*, Vol. 2,
Proletarskaya Revolutsia No. 3   pp. 95-96, 107-08

From the Pamphlet TO THE RURAL POOR

An Explanation for the Peasants of What the Social-Democrats Want[2]

Money has everywhere become the ruling power. All the goods produced by human labour are exchanged for money. With money you can buy anything. With money you can even buy a man, that is to say, force a man who owns nothing to work for another who has money. Formerly, land used to be the ruling power—that was the case under the serf-owning system: whoever possessed land possessed power and authority. Today, however, money, capital, has become the ruling power. With money you can buy as much land as you like. Without money you will not be able to do much even if you have land: you must have money to buy a plough or other implements, to buy livestock, to buy clothes and other town-made goods, not to speak of paying taxes. For the sake of money nearly all the landlords have mortgaged their estates to the banks. To get money the government borrows from rich people and bankers all over the world, and pays hundreds of millions of rubles yearly in interest on these loans.

For the sake of money everyone today is waging a fierce war against everyone else. Each tries to buy cheap and to sell dear, each tries to get ahead of the other, to sell as many goods as possible, to undercut the other, to conceal from him a profitable market or a profitable contract. In this general scramble for money the little man, the petty artisan or the small peasant, fares worse than all: he is always left behind by the rich merchant or the rich

10

peasant. The little man never has any reserves; he lives from hand to mouth; each difficulty or accident compels him to pawn his last belongings or to sell his livestock at a trifling price. Once he has fallen into the clutches of a kulak or of a usurer he very rarely succeeds in escaping from the net, and in most cases he is utterly ruined. Every year tens and hundreds of thousands of small peasants and artisans lock up their cottages, surrender their holdings to the commune *gratis* and become wage-workers, farm-hands, unskilled workers, proletarians. But the rich grow richer and richer in this struggle for money. They pile up millions and hundreds of millions of rubles in the banks and make profit not only with their own money, but also with the money deposited in the banks by others. The little man who deposits a few score or a few hundred rubles in a bank or a savings-bank receives interest at the rate of three or four kopeks to the ruble; but the rich make millions out of these scores and use these millions to increase their turnover and make ten and twenty kopeks to the ruble.

That is why the Social-Democratic workers say that the only way to put an end to the poverty of the people is to change the existing order from top to bottom, throughout the country, and to establish a *socialist order*, in other words, to take the estates from the big landowners, the factories from the factory owners, and money capital from the bankers, to abolish their *private property* and turn it over to the whole working people throughout the country. When that is done the workers' labour will be made use of not by rich people living on the labour of others, but by the workers themselves and by those elected by them. The fruits of common labour and the advantages from all improvements and machinery will then benefit all the working people, all the workers. Wealth will then grow at a still faster rate because the workers will work better for themselves than they did for the capitalists; the working day will be shorter; the workers' standard of living will be higher; all their conditions of life will be completely changed.

But it is not an easy matter to change the existing order throughout the country. That requires a great deal of effort, a long and stubborn struggle. All the rich, all the property-owners, all the *bourgeoisie** will defend their riches with all their might. The officials and the army will rise to defend all the *rich class*, because the government itself is in the hands of the rich class. The workers must rally as one man for the struggle against all those who live on the labour of others; the workers themselves must unite and help to unite all the poor in a single *working class*, in a single *proletarian class*. The struggle will not be easy for the working class, but it will certainly end in the workers' victory because the bourgeoisie, or those who live on the labour of others, are an insignificant minority of the population, while the working class is the vast majority. The workers against the property-owners means millions against thousands.

The workers in Russia are already beginning to unite for this great struggle in a single workers' Social-Democratic Party. Difficult as it is to unite in secret, hiding from the police, nevertheless, the organisation is growing and gaining strength. When the Russian people have won political liberty, the work of uniting the working class, the cause of socialism, will advance much more rapidly, more rapidly than it is advancing among the German workers.

Written in March 1903

<table>
<tr><td>First published as a separate pamphlet in May 1903, in Geneva, by the League of Russian Social-Democracy Abroad</td><td>Collected Works,
Vol. 6, pp. 374-77</td></tr>
</table>

---

* Bourgeois means a property-owner. The bourgeoisie are all the property-owners taken together. A big bourgeois is the owner of big property. A petty bourgeois is the owner of small property. The words bourgeoisie and proletariat mean the same as property-owners and workers, the rich and the poor, or those who live on the labour of others and those who work for others for wages.

Although the socialist proletariat was split up into numerous sects, the Commune was a splendid example of the unanimity with which the proletariat was able to accomplish the democratic tasks which the bourgeoisie could only proclaim. Without any particularly complex legislation, in a simple, straightforward manner, the proletariat, which had seized power, carried out the democratisation of the social system, abolished the bureaucracy, and made all official posts elective.

But two mistakes destroyed the fruits of the splendid victory. The proletariat stopped half-way: instead of setting about "expropriating the expropriators", it allowed itself to be led astray by dreams of establishing a higher justice in the country united by a common national task; such institutions as the banks, for example, were not taken over, and Proudhonist[4] theories about a "just exchange", etc., still prevailed among the socialists. The second mistake was excessive magnanimity on the part of the proletariat: instead of destroying its enemies it sought to exert moral influence on them; it underestimated the significance of direct military operations in civil war, and instead of launching a resolute offensive against Versailles that would have crowned its victory in Paris, it tarried and gave the Versailles government time to gather the dark forces and prepare for the bloodsoaked week of May.

But despite all its mistakes the Commune was a superb example of the great proletarian movement of the nineteenth century. Marx set a high value on the historic significance of the Commune—if, during the treacherous attempt by the Versailles gang to seize the arms of the Paris proletariat, the workers had allowed themselves to be disarmed without a fight, the disastrous effect of the demoralisation, that this weakness would have caused in the proletarian movement, would have been far, far greater than the losses suffered by the working class in the battle to defend its arms.[5] The sacrifices of the Commune, heavy as they were, are made up for by its significance for the general struggle of the proletariat: it stirred the socialist movement throughout Europe, it demonstrated the strength of civil war, it dispelled patriotic illusions, and destroyed the naïve belief in any efforts of the bourgeoisie for common national aims. The Commune taught the European proletariat to pose concretely the tasks of the socialist revolution.

Zagranichnaya Gazeta No. 2,
March 23, 1908

Collected Works,
Vol. 13, pp. 476-77

THE TAYLOR SYSTEM—MAN'S ENSLAVEMENT
BY THE MACHINE

Capitalism cannot be at a standstill for a single moment. It must forever be moving forward. Competition, which is keenest in a period of crisis like the present, calls for the invention of an increasing number of new devices to reduce the cost of production. But the domination of capital converts all these devices into instruments for the further exploitation of the workers.

The Taylor system is one of these devices.

Advocates of this system recently used the following techniques in America.

An electric lamp was attached to a worker's arm, the worker's movements were photographed and the movements of the lamp studied. Certain movements were found to be "superfluous" and the worker was made to avoid them, i.e., to work more intensively, without losing a second for rest.

The layout of new factory buildings is planned in such a way that not a moment will be lost in delivering materials to the factory, in conveying them from one shop to another, and in dispatching the finished products. The cinema is systematically employed for studying the work of the best operatives and increasing its intensity, i.e., "speeding up" the workers.

For example, a mechanic's operations were filmed in the course of a whole day. After studying the mechanic's movements the efficiency experts provided him with a bench high enough to enable him to avoid losing time in bending down. He was given a boy to assist him. This boy had to hand up each part of the machine in a definite and most efficient way. Within a few days the mechanic performed the work of assembling the given type of machine in *one-fourth* of the time it had taken before!

What an enormous gain in labour productivity!... But the worker's pay is not increased fourfold, but only half as much again, at the very most, and *only for a short period* at that. As soon as the workers get used to the new system their pay is cut to the former level. The capitalist obtains an enormous profit, but the workers toil four times as hard as before and wear down their nerves and muscles four times as fast as before.

A newly engaged worker is taken to the factory cinema where he is shown a "model" performance of his job; the worker is made to "catch up" with that performance. A week later he is taken to the cinema again and shown pictures of his own performance, which is then compared with the "model".

All these vast improvements are introduced *to the detriment* of the workers, for they lead to their still greater oppression and exploitation. Moreover, this rational and efficient distribution of labour is confined *to each factory*.

The question naturally arises: What about the distribution of labour in society as a whole? What a vast amount of labour is wasted at present owing to the disorganised and chaotic character of capitalist production as a whole! How much time is wasted as the raw materials pass to the factory through the hands of hundreds of buyers and middlemen, while the requirements of the market are unknown! Not only time, but the actual products are wasted and damaged. And what about the waste of time and labour in delivering the finished goods to the consumers through a host of small middlemen who, too, cannot know the requirements of their customers and perform not only a host of superfluous movements, but also make a host of superfluous purchases, journeys, and so on and so forth!

Capital organises and rationalises labour within the factory for the purpose of increasing the exploitation of the workers and increasing profit. In social production as a whole, however, chaos continues to reign and grow, leading to crises when the accumulated wealth cannot find purchasers, and millions of workers starve because they are unable to find employment.

The Taylor system—without its initiators knowing or wishing it—is preparing the time when the proletariat will take over all social production and appoint its own workers' committees for the purpose of properly distributing and rationalising all social labour. Large-scale production, machinery, railways, telephone—all provide thousands of opportunities to cut by three-fourths the working time of the organised workers and make them four times better off than they are today.

And these workers' committees, assisted by the workers' unions, will be able to apply these principles of rational distribution of social labour when the latter is freed from its enslavement by capital.

Put Pravdy No. 35, March 13, 1914
Signed: *M.M.*

Collected Works,
Vol. 20, pp. 152-54

From the Article KARL MARX

A Brief Biographical Sketch
with an Exposition of Marxism

Socialism

From the foregoing it is evident that Marx deduces the inevitability of the transformation of capitalist society into socialist society wholly and exclusively from the economic law of the development of contemporary society. The socialisation of labour, which is advancing ever more rapidly in thousands of forms and has manifested itself very strikingly, during the half-century since the death of Marx, in the growth of large-scale production, capitalist cartels, syndicates and trusts, as well as in the gigantic increase in the dimensions and power of finance capital, provides the principal material foundation for the inevitable advent of socialism. The intellectual and moral motive force and the physical executor of this transformation is the proletariat, which has been trained by capitalism itself. The proletariat's struggle against the bourgeoisie, which finds expression in a variety of forms ever richer in content, inevitably becomes a political struggle directed towards the conquest of political power by the proletariat ("the dictatorship of the proletariat"). The socialisation of production cannot but lead to the means of production becoming the property of society, to the "expropriation of the expropriators". A tremendous rise in labour productivity, a shorter working day, and the replacement of the remnants, the ruins, of small-scale, primitive and disunited production by collective and improved labour—such are the direct consequences of this transformation. Capitalism breaks for all time the ties between agriculture and industry, but at the same time,

18

through its highest development, it prepares new elements of those ties, a union between industry and agriculture based on the conscious application of science and the concentration of collective labour, and on a redistribution of the human population (thus putting an end both to rural backwardness, isolation and barbarism, and to the unnatural concentration of vast masses of people in big cities).

Written July-November 1914

First published in
Proletarskaya Revolutsia
No. 6-7 (18-19), 1923

Collected Works,
Vol. 21, pp. 71-72

From REPLY TO P. KIEVSKY
(Y. PYATAKOV)

Capitalism in general, and imperialism in particular, turn democracy into an illusion—though at the same time capitalism engenders democratic aspirations in the masses, creates democratic institutions, aggravates the antagonism between imperialism's denial of democracy and the mass striving for democracy. Capitalism and imperialism can be overthrown only by economic revolution. They cannot be overthrown by democratic transformations, even the most "ideal". But a proletariat not schooled in the struggle for democracy is incapable of performing an economic revolution. Capitalism cannot be vanquished without *taking over the banks*, without repealing *private ownership* of the means of production. These revolutionary measures, however, cannot be implemented without organising the entire people for democratic administration of the means of production captured from the bourgeoisie, without enlisting the entire mass of the working people, the proletarians, semi-proletarians and small peasants, for the democratic organisation of their ranks, their forces, their participation in state affairs. Imperialist war may be said to be a triple negation of democracy (*a*. every war replaces "rights" by violence; *b*. imperialism as such is the negation of democracy; *c*. imperialist war fully equates the republic with the monarchy), but the awakening and growth of socialist revolt against imperialism are *indissolubly* linked with the growth of democratic resistance and unrest. Socialism leads to the withering away of *every* state, consequently also of every democracy, but socialism can be implemented only *through* the dictatorship of the proletariat, which combines violence against the bourgeoisie, i.e., the minority of the population, with *full* development of democracy, i.e., the genuinely equal and genuinely universal participation of the *entire* mass of the population in all *state* affairs and in all the complex problems of abolishing capitalism.

It is in these "contradictions" that Kievsky, having forgotten the Marxist teaching on democracy, got himself confused. Figuratively speaking, the war has so oppressed his thinking that he uses the agitational slogan "break out of imperialism" to replace all thinking, just as the cry "get out of the colonies" is used to replace analysis of what, properly speaking, is the *meaning*—economically and politically—of the civilised nations "getting out of the colonies".

The Marxist solution of the problem of democracy is for the proletariat to *utilise all* democratic institutions and aspirations in its class struggle against the bourgeoisie in order to prepare for its overthrow and assure its own victory. Such utilisation is no easy task. To the Economists, Tolstoyans, etc., it often seems an unpardonable concession to "bourgeois" and opportunist views, just as to Kievsky defence of national self-determination "in the epoch of finance capital" seems an unpardonable concession to bourgeois views. Marxism teaches us that to "fight opportunism" by renouncing utilisation of the democratic institutions created and distorted by the bourgeoisie of the *given*, capitalist, society is to *completely surrender* to opportunism!

The slogan of *civil war* for socialism indicates the quickest way out of the imperialist war and *links* our struggle against the war with our struggle against opportunism. It is the only slogan that correctly takes into account both wartime peculiarities—the war is dragging out and threatening to grow into a whole "epoch" of war—and the general character of our activities as distinct from opportunism with its pacifism, legalism and adaptation to one's "own" bourgeoisie. In addition, civil war against the bourgeoisie is a *democratically* organised and *democratically* conducted war of the propertyless mass against the propertied minority. But civil war, like every other, must inevitably replace rights by violence. However, violence in the name of the interests and rights of the majority is of a different nature: it tramples on the "rights" of the exploiters, the bourgeoisie, it is *unachievable* without democratic organisation of the army and the "rear". Civil war forcibly expropriates, immediately and first of all, the banks, factories, railways, the big estates, etc. But *in order* to expropriate all this, we shall have to introduce election of all officials and officers by the people, *completely merge* the army conducting the war against the bourgeoisie with the mass of the population, completely democratise administration of the food supply, the production and distribution of food, etc. The object of civil war is to seize the banks, factories, etc., destroy all possibility of resistance by the bourgeoisie, destroy *its* armed forces. But that aim cannot be achieved *either* in its purely military, *or* economic, *or* political aspects, unless we, during the war, simultaneously introduce and extend democracy among *our* armed forces and in *our* "rear". We tell the masses now (and they instinctively feel that we are right): "They are deceiving you in making you fight for imperialist capitalism in a war disguised by the great slogans of democracy. You must, you shall wage a *genuinely* democratic war *against* the bourgeoisie for the achievement of genuine democracy and socialism." The present war unites and "merges" nations into coalitions by means of violence and financial dependence. In our civil war against the bourgeoisie, *we* shall unite and merge the nations *not* by the force of the ruble, *not* by the force of the truncheon, not by violence, but by *voluntary* agreement and solidarity of the working people against the exploiters. For the bourgeoisie the proclamation of equal rights for all nations has become a deception. For us it will be the truth that will facilitate and accelerate the winning over of all nations. Without effectively organised *democratic* relations between nations—and, consequently, without freedom of secession—civil war of the workers and working people generally of all nations against the bourgeoisie is *impossible*.

Through utilisation of bourgeois democracy to socialist and consistently democratic organisation of the proletariat against the bourgeoisie and against opportunism. There is no other path. There is *no* other way out. Marxism, just as life itself, knows no other way out. In this path we must include free secession and free merging of nations, we must not fight shy of them, not fear that they will "defile" the "purity" of our economic aims.

Written August-September 1916

First published in
Proletarskaya Revolutsia
No. 7, 1929

Collected Works,
Vol. 23, pp. 24-27

TO ARTHUR SCHMID

Dear Comrade,

Will you allow me to suggest an amicable agreement?

I must admit that yesterday I paid insufficient attention to one very important point in your arguments.[6] Namely, the idea that the peculiarity of Switzerland lies, among other things, in her greater degree of democracy (the referendum), and that this peculiarity should be made use of *also* for propaganda purposes. This idea is very important and, in my opinion, completely correct.

Could we not apply this idea in such a way that our differences (which are probably very insignificant) should disappear? For example:

If we put the question for the referendum *only* in this way—for complete elimination or against?—we shall get a mixture of pacifist (bourgeois-pacifist, etc.) and socialist votes for it, i.e., we shall get not a clarification of a socialist consciousness but a darkening of it, not the application of the idea and the policy of *class struggle* to this particular question (namely, the question of militarism) but the renunciation of the point of view of the class struggle on the question of militarism.

But if we put the question for the referendum in this way—for the expropriation of large capitalist enterprises in industry and agriculture, *as the only way* of completely eliminating militarism, or against expropriation?

If we put it like that, we shall be saying in our practical

policy the same thing that we all recognise theoretically, namely, that the complete elimination of militarism is thinkable and realisable only in connection with the elimination of capitalism.

Consequently there should be approximately the following formulation: (1) we demand the *immediate* expropriation of large enterprises, perhaps in the form of a direct Federal property and income tax, with such high, revolutionarily-high, rates for large properties that the capitalists will, in fact, be expropriated.

(2) We declare that such a socialist transformation of Switzerland is economically possible already today, directly, and, in consequence of the unbearably high cost of living, is urgently necessary as well, and that for the political effecting of such a transformation Switzerland needs not a bourgeois but a proletarian government, which would rely not on the bourgeoisie but on the broad masses of hired workers and small people, and that the revolutionary mass struggle which we see beginning, for example, in the mass strikes and street demostrations in Zurich, and which is recognised by the Aarau decision,[7] pursues *exactly* that purpose—to put a *real* end in that way to the intolerable position of the masses.

(3) We declare that such a transformation of Switzerland *will quite inevitably arouse* imitation and the most resolute enthusiastic support on the part of the working class and the mass of the exploited in *all* civilised countries, and that *only* in connection with such a transformation will *the complete elimination of militarism* for which we strive, and for which at present particularly wide masses in Europe are instinctively thirsting, become not an empty phrase, not an amiable wish, but a genuine, practically achievable and politically self-explanatory measure.

What do you think of this?

Do you not consider that, if the question is put in this way (both in practical agitation and in parliamentary speeches and proposals for a legislative initiative and for a referendum), we shall avoid *the* danger that bourgeois and "socialist" pacifists will falsely understand and misinterpret our anti-militarist slogan in the sense that we suppose it possible to completely abolish militarism in *bourgeois Switzerland*, in her *imperialist* environment,

without a socialist revolution (which, of course, is nonsense
that we all unanimously repudiate).

With Party greetings,

N. Lenin

Wl. Uljanow.
Spiegelgasse 14^{II} (bei Kammerer). Zürich I.

Written December 1, 1916
Sent to Winterthur
(Switzerland)

First published in 1931   *Collected Works,*
in *Lenin Miscellany XVII*   Vol. 35, pp. 256-58

LETTERS FROM AFAR[8]

Fifth Letter
The Tasks Involved in the Building
of the Revolutionary
Proletarian State
(*Excerpt*)

In the preceding letters, the immediate tasks of the revolutionary proletariat in Russia were formulated as follows: (1) to find the surest road to the next stage of the revolution, or to the second revolution, which (2) must transfer political power from the government of the landowners and capitalists (the Guchkovs, Lvovs, Milyukovs, Kerenskys) to a government of the workers and poorest peasants. (3) This latter government must be organised on the model of the Soviets of Workers' and Peasants' Deputies, namely, (4) it must smash, completely eliminate, the old state machine, the army, the police force and bureaucracy (officialdom), that is common to *all* bourgeois states, and substitute for this machine (5) not only a mass organisation, but a universal organisation of the entire armed people. (6) *Only* such a government, of "such" a class composition ("revolutionary-democratic dictatorship of the proletariat and peasantry") and such organs of government ("proletarian militia") *will be capable* of successfully carrying out the extremely difficult and absolutely urgent *chief* task of the moment, namely: to achieve *peace*, not an imperialist peace, not a deal between the imperialist powers concerning the division of the booty by the capitalists and their governments, but a really lasting and democratic peace, which cannot be achieved without a proletarian revolution in a number of countries. (7) In Russia the victory of the proletariat can be achieved in the very near future *only* if, from the very first step, the workers are supported by the vast majority of the peasants fighting for the confiscation of the landed estates (and for the nationalisation of all the land, if we assume that the agrarian programme of the "104" is still essentially the agrarian programme of the *peasantry*[9]). (8) In connection with such a peasant revolution, and on its basis, the proletariat can and must, in alliance with the *poorest* section of the peasantry, take further steps towards *control* of the production and distribution of the basic products, towards the introduction of "universal labour service", etc. These steps are dictated, with absolute inevitability, by the conditions created by the war, which in many respects will become still more acute in the postwar period. In their entirety and in their development these steps will mark the *transition to socialism*, which cannot be achieved in Russia directly, at one stroke, without transitional measures, but is quite achievable and urgently necessary as a result of such transitional measures. (9) In this connection, the task of immediately organising special Soviets of Workers' Deputies in the *rural districts,* i.e., Soviets of agricultural *wage*-workers *separate* from the Soviets of the other peasant deputies, comes to the forefront with extreme urgency.

Such, briefly, is the programme we have outlined, based on an appraisal of the class forces in the Russian and world revolution, and also on the experience of 1871 and 1905....

Written March 26 (April 8), 1917

First published in the magazine
Bolshevik No. 3-4, 1924

Collected Works,
Vol. 23, pp. 340-41

From the FAREWELL LETTER
TO THE SWISS WORKERS[10]

To the Russian proletariat has fallen the great honour of *beginning* the series of revolutions which the imperialist war has made an objective inevitability. But the idea that the Russian proletariat is the chosen revolutionary proletariat among the workers of the world is absolutely alien to us. We know perfectly well that the proletariat of Russia is *less* organised, *less* prepared and *less* class-conscious than the proletariat of other countries. It is not its special qualities, but rather the special conjuncture of historical circumstances that *for a certain, perhaps very short, time* has made the proletariat of Russia the vanguard of the revolutionary proletariat of the whole world.

Russia is a peasant country, one of the most backward of European countries. Socialism *cannot* triumph there *directly* and *immediately*. But the peasant character of the country, the vast reserve of land in the hands of the nobility, *may*, to judge from the experience of 1905, give tremendous sweep to the bourgeois-democratic revolution in Russia and *may* make our revolution the *prologue* to the world socialist revolution, a *step* toward it.

Our Party was formed and developed in the struggle for these ideas, which have been fully confirmed by the experience of 1905 and the spring of 1917, in the uncompromising struggle against all the other parties; and we shall continue to fight for these ideas.

In Russia, socialism cannot triumph directly and immediately. But the peasant mass *can* bring the inevitable and matured agrarian upheaval to the point of *confiscating* all the immense holdings of the nobility. This has always been our slogan and it has now again been advanced in St. Petersburg by the Central Committee of our Party and by *Pravda*, our Party's newspaper. The proletariat will fight for *this* slogan, without closing its eyes to the inevitability of cruel class conflicts between the agricultural labourers and the poorest peasants closely allied with them, on the one hand, and the *rich peasants*, whose position has been strengthened by Stolypin's agrarian "reform" (1907-14),[11] on the other. The fact should not be overlooked that the 104 peasant deputies in the First (1906) and Second (1907) Dumas introduced a revolutionary agrarian bill demanding the nationalisation of all lands and their disposal by local committees elected on the basis of complete democracy.

Such a revolution would not, in itself, be socialism. But it would give a great impetus to the world labour movement. It would immensely strengthen the position of the socialist proletariat in Russia and its influence on the agricultural labourers and the poorest peasants. It would enable the city proletariat to develop, on the strength of this influence, such revolutionary organisations as the Soviets of Workers' Deputies, to replace the old instruments of oppression employed by bourgeois states, the army, the police, the bureaucracy; to carry out—under pressure of the unbearably burdensome imperialist war and its consequences—a series of revolutionary measures to *control* the production and distribution of goods.

Published in German in the
magazine *Jugend-Internationale*
No. 8, May 1, 1917

First published in Russian
in the newspaper *Yedinstvo*
No. 145, September 21, 1917

Collected Works,
Vol. 23, pp. 371-72

From THE TASKS OF THE PROLETARIAT
IN OUR REVOLUTION

Draft Platform for the Proletarian Party[12]

Nationalisation of the Banks
and Capitalist Syndicates

15. Under no circumstances can the party of the proletariat set itself the aim of "introducing" socialism in a country of small peasants so long as the overwhelming majority of the population has not come to realise the need for a socialist revolution.

But only bourgeois sophists, hiding behind "near-Marxist" catchwords, can deduce from this truth a justification of the policy of postponing immediate revolutionary measures, the time for which is fully ripe; measures which *have been* frequently *resorted to during the war by a number of bourgeois states*, and which are absolutely indispensable in order to combat impending total economic disorganisation and famine.

Such measures as the nationalisation of the land, of all the banks and capitalist syndicates, or, at least, the *immediate* establishment of the *control* of the Soviets of Workers' Deputies, etc., over them—measures which do not in any way constitute the "introduction" of socialism —must be absolutely insisted on, and, whenever possible, carried out in a revolutionary way. Without such measures, which are only steps towards socialism, and which are perfectly feasible economically, it will be impossible to heal the wounds caused by the war and to avert the impending collapse; and the party of the revolutionary proletariat will

never hesitate to lay hands on the fabulous profits of the
capitalists and bankers, who are enriching themselves on
the war in a particularly scandalous manner.

Written April 10 (23), 1917

Published September 1917
as a pamphlet by Priboi
Publishers (Petrograd)
Signed: *N. Lenin*

Collected Works,
Vol. 24, pp. 73-74

THE SEVENTH (APRIL) ALL-RUSSIA CONFERENCE OF THE R.S.D.L.P.(B.)[13]
APRIL 24-29 (MAY 7-12), 1917

1

From the REPORT ON THE CURRENT SITUATION
APRIL 24 (MAY 7)

What, then, are the tasks of the revolutionary proletariat? The main flaw, the main error, in all the socialists' arguments is that this question is put in too general a form, as the question of the transition to socialism. What we should talk about, however, are concrete steps and measures. Some of them are ripe, and some are not. We are now at a transition stage. Clearly, we have brought to the fore new forms, unlike those in bourgeois states. The Soviets of Workers' and Soldiers' Deputies are a form of state which does not exist and never did exist in any country. This form represents the first steps towards socialism and is inevitable at the beginning of a socialist society. This is a fact of decisive importance. The Russian revolution has created the Soviets. No bourgeois country in the world has or can have such state institutions. No socialist revolution can be operative with any other state power than this. The Soviets must take power not for the purpose of building an ordinary bourgeois republic, nor for the purpose of making a direct transition to socialism. This cannot be. What, then, is the purpose? The Soviets must take power in order to make the first concrete steps towards this transition, steps that can and should be made. In this respect fear is the worst enemy. The masses must be urged to take these steps immediately, otherwise the power of the Soviets will have no meaning and will give the people nothing.

I shall now attempt to answer the question as to what concrete measures we can suggest to the people without running counter to our Marxist convictions.

Why do we want the power to pass to the Soviets of Workers' and Soldiers' Deputies?

The first measure the Soviets must carry out is the nationalisation of the land. All the peoples are talking about nationalisation. Some say it is a most utopian measure; nevertheless, everybody comes to accept it, because landownership in Russia is so complicated that the only way out is to remove all boundary lines dividing the land and make it the property of the state. Private ownership of land must be abolished. That is the task confronting us, because the majority of the people are in favour of it. To accomplish it we need the Soviets. This measure cannot be carried out with the help of the old government officials.

The second measure. We cannot be for "introducing" socialism—this would be the height of absurdity. We must preach socialism. The majority of the population in Russia are peasants, small farmers who can have no idea of socialism. But what objections can they have to a bank being set up in each village to enable them to improve their farming? They can say nothing against it. We must put over these practical measures to the peasants in our propaganda, and make the peasants realise that they are necessary.

Quite another thing is the Sugar Syndicate. This is a clear fact. Here our proposal must be direct and practical: these already fully developed syndicates must be taken over by the state. If the Soviets intend to assume power, it is only for such ends. There is no other reason why they should do so. The alternative is: either the Soviets develop further, or they die an ignominious death as in the case of the Paris Commune. If it is a bourgeois republic that is needed, this can very well be left to the Cadets.

I shall conclude by referring to a speech which impressed me most. I heard a coal miner deliver a remarkable speech. Without using a single bookish word, he told us how they had made the revolution. Those miners were not concerned with the question as to whether or not they should have a president. They seized the mine, and the important question to them was how to keep the cables intact so that production might not be interrupted. Then came the question of bread, which was scarce, and the miners also agreed on the method of obtaining it. Now that is a real programme of the revolution, not derived from books. That is what I call really winning power locally.

Nowhere is the bourgeoisie so well established as in Petrograd. Here the capitalists have the power in their hands. But throughout the country, the peasants, without pursuing any socialist tasks, are carrying out purely practical measures. I think that only this programme of the revolutionary movement indicates the true path of the revolution. We are for these measures being started on with the greatest caution and circumspection. But it is only these measures that must be carried out; we should go ahead in this direction only. There is no other way out. Unless this is done the Soviets will be broken up and will die an ignominious death. But if the revolutionary proletariat should actually win power, it will only be for the sake of going forward. And to go forward means to take definite steps to get us out of the war—words alone won't do it. The complete success of these steps is only possible by world revolution, if the revolution kills the war, if the workers of the whole world support the revolution. Taking power is, therefore, the only practical measure and the only way out.

First published
in 1921 in N. Lenin
(V. Ulyanov), *Works*,
Vol. XIV. Part 2

Collected Works,
Vol. 24, pp. 241-43

2

From the RESOLUTION ON THE CURRENT SITUATION

Operating as it does in one of the most backward countries of Europe amidst a vast population of small peasants, the proletariat of Russia cannot aim at immediately putting into effect socialist changes.

But it would be a grave error, and in effect even a complete desertion to the bourgeoisie, to infer from this that the working class must support the bourgeoisie, or that it must keep its activities within limits acceptable to the petty bourgeoisie, or that the proletariat must renounce its leading role in the matter of explaining to the people the urgency of taking a number of practical steps towards socialism for which the time is now ripe.

These steps are: first, nationalisation of the land. This measure, which does not directly go beyond the framework of the bourgeois system, would, at the same time, be a heavy blow at private ownership of the means of production, and as such would strengthen the influence of the socialist proletariat over the semi-proletariat in the countryside.

The next steps are the establishment of state control over all banks, and their amalgamation into a single central bank; also control over the insurance agencies and big capitalist syndicates (for example, the Sugar Syndicate, the Coal Syndicate, the Metal Syndicate, etc.), and the gradual introduction of a more just progressive tax on incomes and properties. Economically, these measures are timely; technically, they can be carried out immediately; politically,

36

they are *likely* to receive the support of the overwhelming majority of the peasants, who have everything to gain by these reforms.

The Soviets of Workers', Soldiers', Peasants', and other Deputies, which now cover Russia with a dense and growing network, could also introduce, parallel with the above measures, universal labour conscription, for on the one hand the character of the Soviets guarantees that all these new reforms will be introduced only when an overwhelming majority of the people has clearly and firmly realised the practical need for them; on the other hand, their character guarantees that the reforms will not be sponsored by the police and officials, but will be carried out by way of voluntary participation of the organised and armed masses of the proletariat and peasantry in the management of their own affairs.

All these and other similar measures can and should be not only discussed and prepared for enforcement on a national scale in the event of all power passing to the proletarians and semi-proletarians, but also implemented by the local revolutionary organs of power of the whole people when the opportunity arises.

Great care and discretion should be exercised in carrying out the above measures; a solid majority of the population must be won over and this majority must be clearly convinced of the country's practical preparedness for any particular measure. This is the direction in which the class-conscious vanguard of the workers must focus its attention and efforts, because it is the bounden duty of these workers to help the peasants find a way out of the present debacle.

Supplement to
Soldatskaya Pravda No. 13,
May 16 (3), 1917

Collected Works,
Vol. 24, pp. 311-12

INEVITABLE CATASTROPHE
AND EXTRAVAGANT PROMISES

(Article One)

The inevitable debacle, the catastrophe of unprecedented dimensions that is facing us is of such importance that we must dwell on this question again and again if we are to fully grasp its implications. In the last issue of *Pravda* we said that the *programme* of the Executive Committee of the Soviet of Workers' and Soldiers' Deputies no longer differs *in any way* from that of "terrible" Bolshevism.[14]

Today we must point out that the programme of the Menshevik Minister Skobelev goes even *further* than Bolshevism. Here is the programme, as reported in the ministerial paper, *Rech*[15]:

"The Minister [Skobelev] declared that '... the country's economy is on the brink of disaster. We must intervene in all fields of economic life, as there is no money in the Treasury. We must improve the condition of the working masses, and to do that we must take the profits from the tills of the businessmen and bankers'. (*Voice in the audience*: 'How?') 'By ruthless taxation of property,' replied the Minister of Labour Skobelev. 'It is a method known to the science of finance. The rate of taxation on the propertied classes must be increased to one hundred per cent of their profits.' (*Voice in the audience*: 'That means everything.') 'Unfortunately,' declared Skobelev, 'many corporations have already distributed their dividends among the shareholders, and we must therefore levy a progressive personal tax on the propertied classes. We will go even further, and, if the capitalists wish to preserve the bourgeois method of business, let them work without interest, so as not to lose their clients.... We must introduce compulsory labour service for the shareholders, bankers and factory owners, who are in a rather slack mood because the incentive that formerly stimulated them to work is now lacking.... We must force the shareholders to submit to the state; they, too, must be subject to labour service.'"

We advise the workers to read and reread this programme, to discuss it and go into the matter of its practicability.

The important thing is the conditions necessary for its fulfilment, and the taking of immediate steps towards its fulfilment.

This programme in itself is an excellent one and coincides with the Bolshevik programme, except that in one particular it goes even *further* than our programme, namely, it promises to "take the profits from the tills of the bankers" to the extent of "one hundred per cent".

Our Party is much more moderate. Its resolution demands much less than this, namely, the mere establishment of control over the banks and the "gradual [just listen, the Bolsheviks are for gradualness!] introduction of a more just progressive tax on incomes and properties".[16]

Our Party is more moderate than Skobelev.

Skobelev dispenses immoderate, nay, extravagant promises, *without understanding the conditions required for their practical realisation*.

That is the crux of the matter.

It is *impossible* not only to realise Skobelev's programme, but even to make any serious efforts towards its realisation, either arm in arm with ten ministers from the party of the landowners and capitalists, or with the bureaucratic, official-ridden machine to which the government of the capitalists (plus a few Mensheviks and Narodniks) is perforce limited.

Less promises, Citizen Skobelev, and more practicalness. Less rhetoric and more understanding as to *how* to get down to *business*.

And get down to business we can and should immediately, without a day's delay, if we are to save the country from an inevitable and terrible catastrophe. But the whole thing is that the "new" Provisional Government *does not want* to get down to business; and even if it wanted to, it *could not*, for it is fettered by a thousand chains which safeguard the interests of capital.

We can and should in a single day call upon the people to get down to business; we can and should in a single day issue a decree *immediately* convening:

1) Councils and conventions of bank employees, both of individual banks and on a national scale, to work out

immediate practical measures for amalgamating all banks and banking houses into a single State Bank, and exercising precise control over all banking operations, the results of such control to be published forthwith;

2) Councils and conventions of employees of all syndicates and trusts to work out measures for control and accountancy; the results of such control to be published forthwith;

3) This decree should grant the right of control not only to the Soviets of Workers', Soldiers', and Peasants' Deputies, but also to councils of the workers at every large factory, as well as to the representatives of every large political party (those parties should be regarded as large parties which, for example, on May 12 put forward independent lists of candidates in not less than two Petrograd districts); all ledgers and documents to be open to control;

4) The decree should call upon all shareholders, directors and members of the boards of all companies to publish the names of all shareholders owning stock to an amount of not less than 10,000 (or 5,000) rubles, together with a list of stocks and companies in which these persons are "interested"; false statements (made to the controlling bodies of the bank and other employees) shall be punished by confiscation of all property and by imprisonment for a term of not less than five years;

5) The decree should call upon the people to establish immediately, through the local organs of self-government, universal labour service, for the control and enforcement of which a universal people's militia should be established (in the rural districts directly, in the cities through the workers' militia).

Without universal labour service, the country *cannot be saved* from ruin; and without a people's militia, universal labour service cannot be effected. This will be obvious to everyone who has not reached a state of ministerial insanity or has not had his brain turned by putting too much trust in ministerial eloquence.

Every person is *bound* to stand for such measures if he really wishes to save tens of millions from ruin and disaster.

In the next article we shall deal with the question of the gradual introduction of a more equitable system of taxation, and also what should be done to advance from among the people and gradually place in ministerial positions really gifted organisers (both from among the workers and the capitalists) who have given a good account of themselves in this kind of work.

(Article Two)

When Skobelev, with ministerial *élan*, talked himself into taking one hundred per cent of the capitalists' profits, he furnished us with a specimen of claptrap. This kind of phrase-mongering is always used in bourgeois parliamentary republics to hoodwink the people.

But here we have something worse than mere phrase-mongering. "If the capitalists wish to preserve the bourgeois method of business, let them work without interest, so as not to lose their clients," Skobelev said. This sounds like a "terrible" threat to the capitalists; but in fact, it is an attempt (unconscious probably on the part of Skobelev, but certainly conscious on the part of the capitalists) to *make safe the rule* of almighty capital by a temporary sacrifice of profits.

The workers are taking "too much", say the capitalists; let us make them responsible without giving them either power or the opportunity to effectively control production. Let us sacrifice our profits for a time; by "preserving the bourgeois method of business and not losing our clients", we shall hasten the collapse of this transitory stage in industry, we shall disorganise it in every possible way and lay the blame on the workers.

That such is the plan of the capitalists is proved by the facts. The colliery owners in the South are actually disorganising production, are *"deliberately neglecting and disorganising it"* (see *Novaya Zhizn* for May 16 reporting statements made by a *workers' delegation*[17]). The picture is clear: *Rech* is lying brazenly when it puts the blame on the workers. The colliery owners are "deliberately disorganising production"; and Skobelev sings his song: "If the capitalists wish to preserve the bourgeois method of business, let them work without interest." The position is clear.

It is to the *advantage* of the capitalists and the bureaucrats to make "extravagant promises", diverting people's attention away from the *main thing*, namely, the transfer of real control to the workers.

The workers must sweep aside all high-sounding phrases, promises, declarations, project-mongering by bureaucrats in the centre, who are ever ready to draw up spectacular plans, rules, regulations, and standards. Down with all this lying! Down with all this hullabaloo of bureaucratic and bourgeois project-mongering which has everywhere ended in smoke! Down with this habit of shelving things! The workers must demand the *immediate* establishment of *genuine* control, to be exercised by the *workers themselves*.

That is the most important condition of success, success in averting catastrophe. If that is lacking, all else is sheer deception. If we have it, we need not be in a hurry to "take one hundred per cent of the profits". We can and should be more moderate; we should *gradually* introduce a more equitable system of taxation; we shall differentiate between the small and large shareholders; we shall take *very little* from the former, and a great deal (but *not* necessarily all) from the latter *only*. The number of large shareholders is insignificant; but the role they play, like the wealth they possess, is *tremendous*. It may safely be said that if one were to draw up a list of the *five or even three thousand* (or perhaps even one thousand) of Russia's wealthiest men, or if one were to trace (by means of control exercised from *below*, by bank, syndicate, and other employees) all the threads and ties of their finance capital, their banking connections, there would be revealed the whole complexus of capitalist domination, the vast body of wealth amassed at the expense of the labour of others, all the essential roots of "control" over the social production and distribution of goods.

It is *this* control that must be handed over to the workers. It is this complexus, these roots, that the interests of capital require to be concealed from the people. Better forego for a time "all" our profits, or ninety-nine per cent of our income, than disclose to the people these roots of our power—thus reason the capitalist class and its unconscious servant, the government official.

Under no circumstances shall *we* relinquish our right, our demand that this citadel of finance capital be disclosed to the people, that it be placed under workers' control—thus reasons the class-conscious worker. And every passing day will prove the correctness of this reasoning to growing masses of the poor, to a growing majority of the people, to a growing number of sincere people who are honestly seeking a way to avert disaster.

This citadel of finance capital has to be taken if all those phrases and projects for averting disaster are not to remain sheer deception. As far as individual capitalists, or even most of the capitalists, are concerned, the proletariat has no intention of "taking their last shirt from them" (as Shulgin has been "scaring" himself and his friends), has no intention of taking "everything" from them. On the contrary, it intends to put them on useful and honourable jobs—under the control of the workers.

The most useful and indispensable job for the people at this moment of impending catastrophe is that of *organisation*. Marvels of proletarian organisation—that is our slogan now, and will become our slogan and our demand doubly so when the proletariat is in power. Without the organisation of the masses it will be absolutely impossible either to introduce universal labour service, which is absolutely essential, or establish any at all serious control over the banks and syndicates and over the production and distribution of goods.

That is why it is necessary to begin, and begin immediately, with a workers' militia, in order that we may proceed gradually, but firmly and intelligently, to the creation of a people's militia and the replacement of the police and the standing army by the universally armed people. That is why it is necessary to advance talented organisers from among *all* sections of society, from among *all* classes, not excepting the capitalists, who *at present* have more of the required experience. There are many such talents among the people. Such forces lie dormant among the peasantry and the proletariat for lack of application. They must be advanced from below in the course of practical work, such as the efficient elimination of queues in a given district, skilful organisation of house committees, domestic servants, and model farms, proper management of factories that have been taken over by the workers, and so on and so forth. When these have been advanced from below in the

43

course of practical work, and their abilities tested in practice, they should all be promoted to "ministers"—not in the old sense of the term, not in the sense of giving them portfolios, but by appointing them national instructors, travelling organisers, assistants in the business of establishing *everywhere* the strictest order, the greatest economy in human labour, the strictest comradely discipline.

That is what the party of the proletariat must preach to the people as the means of averting disaster. That is what it must start carrying out now in part in those localities where it is gaining power. That is what it must carry out in full when it assumes state power.

RESOLUTION ON MEASURES TO COPE
WITH ECONOMIC DISORGANISATION[18]

1. The complete disruption of Russia's economic life has now reached a point where catastrophe is unavoidable, a catastrophe of such appalling dimensions that a number of essential industries will be brought to a standstill, the farmer will be prevented from conducting farming on the necessary scale, and railway traffic will be interrupted with a consequent stoppage of grain deliveries to the industrial population and the cities, involving millions of people. What is more, the break-down has already started, and has affected various industries. Only by the greatest exertion of all the nation's forces and the adoption of a number of immediate revolutionary measures, both in the local areas and at the centre of government, can this debacle be effectively coped with.

2. Neither by bureaucratic methods, i.e., the setting up of institutions in which the capitalists and officials preponderate, nor by preserving the profits of the capitalists, their supreme rule in industry, their supremacy over finance capital, and their commercial secrets as regards their banking, commercial, and industrial transactions, can the disaster be averted. This has been amply proved by the partial effects of the crisis as revealed in a number of industries.

3. The only way to avert disaster is to establish effectual workers' control over the production and distribution of goods. For the purpose of such control it is necessary, first of all, that the workers should have a majority of not less than three-fourths of all the votes in all the decisive insti-

tutions and that the owners who have not withdrawn from their business and the engineering staffs should be enlisted without fail; secondly, that shop committees, the central and local Soviets of Workers', Soldiers' and Peasants' Deputies, as well as the trade unions, should have the right to participate in this control, that all commercial and bank books be open to their inspection, and that the management supply them with all the necessary information; third, that a similar right should be granted to representatives of all the major democratic and socialist parties.

4. Workers' control, which the capitalists in a number of conflict cases have already accepted, should, by means of various well-considered measures introduced gradually but without any delay, be developed into full regulation of the production and distribution of goods by the workers.

5. Workers' control should similarly be extended to all financial and banking operations with the aim of discovering the true financial state of affairs; such control to be participated in by councils and conventions of bank, syndicate and other employees, which are to be organised forthwith.

6. To save the country from disaster the workers and peasants must first of all be inspired with absolute and positive assurance, conveyed by deeds and not by words, that the governing bodies both in the local areas and at the centre will not hesitate to hand over to the people the bulk of the profits, incomes, and property of the great banking, financial, commercial, and industrial magnates of capitalist economy. Unless this measure is carried out, it is futile to demand or expect real revolutionary measures or any real revolutionary effort on the part of the workers and peasants.

7. In view of the break-down of the whole financial and monetary system and the impossibility of rehabilitating it while the war is on, the aim of the state organisation should be to organise on a broad, regional, and subsequently country-wide, scale the exchange of agricultural implements, clothes, boots and other goods for grain and other farm products. The services of the town and rural co-operative societies should be widely enlisted.

8. Only when these measures have been carried out will it be possible and necessary to introduce general and com-

pulsory labour service. This measure, in turn, calls for the establishment of a workers' militia, in which the workers are to serve without pay after their regular eight-hour day; this to be followed by the introduction of a nation-wide people's militia in which the workers and other employees shall be paid by the capitalists. Only such a workers' militia and the people's militia that will grow out of it could and should introduce universal compulsory labour service, not by bureaucratic means and in the interests of the capitalists, but to save the country from the impending debacle. Only such a militia could and should introduce real revolutionary discipline and get the whole people to make that supreme effort necessary for averting disaster. Only universal compulsory labour service is capable of ensuring the maximum economy in the expenditure of labour-power.

9. Among the measures aimed at saving the country from disaster, one of the most important tasks is that of engaging a large labour force in the production of coal and raw materials, and for work in the transport services. No less important is it that the workers employed in producing ammunition should be gradually switched over to producing goods necessary for the country's economic rehabilitation.

10. The systematic and effective implementation of all these measures is possible only if all the power in the state passes to the proletarians and semi-proletarians.

Sotsial-Demokrat No. 64,   *Collected Works,*
May 25 (June 7), 1917   Vol. 24, pp. 513-15

SPEECH MADE AT THE FIRST PETROGRAD CONFERENCE OF SHOP COMMITTEES[19] MAY 31 (JUNE 13), 1917

Brief Newspaper Report

Comrade Avilov's resolution shows a complete disregard for the class stand. B. V. Avilov would seem to have made up his mind in this resolution to collect together and concentrate all the faults common to all the resolutions of the petty-bourgeois parties.

Avilov's resolution starts with the postulate, by now indisputable to any socialist, that capitalism's robber economy has reduced Russia to complete economic and industrial ruin, but then goes on to propose the hazy formula of control of industry by "the state authorities" with the co-operation of the broad democratic mass.

Everybody nowadays is having a good deal to say about control. Even people who used to scream "murder" at the very mention of the word "control" now admit that control is necessary.

By using the term "control" in the abstract, however, they want to reduce the idea of control to naught.

The coalition government, which "socialists" have now joined, has done nothing yet in the way of putting this control into effect, and therefore it is quite understandable that the shop committees are demanding real workers' control, and not control on paper.

In dealing with the idea of control and the question of when and by whom this control is to be effected, one must not for a single moment forget the class character of the modern state, which is merely an organisation of class rule. A similar class analysis should be applied to the concept "revolutionary democracy", and this analysis should be based on the actual balance of social forces.

Avilov's resolution starts with a promise to give everything, but ends, in effect, with a proposition to leave everything as it was. There is not a shadow of revolutionism in the whole resolution.

In revolutionary times of all times it is necessary accurately to analyse the question as to the very essence of the state, as to whose interests it shall protect, and as to how it should be constructed in order effectively to protect the interests of the working people. In Avilov's resolution this has not been dealt with at all.

Why is it that our new coalition government, which "socialists" have now joined, has not carried out control in the course of three months, and, what is more, in the conflict between the colliery owners and the workers of Southern Russia, the government has openly sided with the capitalists?

For control over industry to be effectively carried out it must be a *workers' control* with a workers' majority in all the leading bodies, and the management must give an account of its actions to all the authoritative workers' organisations.

Comrades, workers, see that you get real control, not fictitious control, and reject in the most resolute manner all resolutions and proposals for establishing such a fictitious control existing only on paper.

Pravda No. 73,
June 16 (3), 1917

Collected Works,
Vol. 24, pp. 556-57

ECONOMIC DISLOCATION
AND THE PROLETARIAT'S STRUGGLE AGAINST IT

We are publishing in this issue the resolution on economic measures for combating dislocation, passed by the Conference of Factory Committees.*

The main idea of the resolution is to indicate the conditions for *actual* control over the capitalists and production in contrast to the empty *phrases* about control used by the bourgeoisie and the petty-bourgeois officials. The bourgeoisie are lying when they allege that the systematic measures taken by the state to ensure threefold or even tenfold profits for the capitalists are "control". The petty bourgeoisie, partly out of naïveté, partly out of economic interest, trust the capitalists and the capitalist state, and content themselves with the most meaningless bureaucratic projects for control. The resolution passed by the workers lays special emphasis on the *all-important* thing, that is, on what is to be done 1) to prevent the actual "preservation" of capitalist profits; 2) to tear off the veil of commercial secrecy; 3) to give the workers a majority in the control agencies; 4) to ensure that the organisation (of control and direction), being "nation-wide" organisation, is directed by the Soviets of Workers', Soldiers' and Peasants' Deputies *and not by the capitalists*.

Without this, all talk of control and regulation is either sheer bunkum or even outright deception of the people.

Now it is against this truth, as plain as can be to every politically-conscious and thinking worker, that the leaders of our petty bourgeoisie, the Narodniks and Mensheviks

---

* See pp. 45-47 of this book.—*Ed.*

(*Izvestia*,[20] *Rabochaya Gazeta*[21]), are up in arms. Unfortunately, those who write for *Novaya Zhizn*, and who have repeatedly wavered between us and them, have this time sunk to the same level.

Comrades Avilov and Bazarov try to cover up their descent into the swamp of petty-bourgeois credulity, compromise, and bureaucratic project-making by Marxist-sounding arguments. Let us look into these arguments.

We *Pravda* people are said to be deviating from Marxism to syndicalism just because we defend the resolution of the Organising Bureau (approved by the Conference). Shame on you, Comrades Avilov and Bazarov! Such carelessness (or such trickery) is fit only for *Rech* and *Yedinstvo*[22]! We suggest nothing like the ridiculous transfer of the railways to the railwaymen, or the tanneries to the tanners. What we do suggest is *workers' control*, which should develop into complete regulation of production and distribution by the workers, into "nation-wide organisation" of the exchange of grain for manufactured goods, etc. (with the "services of urban and rural co-operative societies widely enlisted"). What we suggest is "the transfer of *all* state power to the Soviets of Workers', Soldiers' and Peasants' Deputies".

Only people who had not read the resolution right through, or who cannot read at all, could, with clear conscience, find any syndicalism in it.

And only pedants, who understand Marxism as Struve and all liberal bureaucrats "understood" it, can assert that "skipping state capitalism is utopian" and that "in our country, too, the very type of regulation should retain its state-capitalist character".

Take the Sugar Syndicate or the state railways in Russia or the oil barons, etc. What is that but state capitalism? How can you "skip" *what already exists*?

The point is that people who have turned Marxism into a kind of stiffly bourgeois doctrine *evade* the specific issues posed by reality, which in Russia has in practice produced a combination of the syndicates in industry and the small-peasant farms in the countryside. They evade these specific issues by advancing pseudo-intellectual, and in fact utterly meaningless, arguments about a "permanent revolution", about "introducing" socialism, and other nonsense.

Let us get down to business! Let us have fewer excuses and keep closer to practical matters! Are the profits made from war supplies, profits amounting to 500 per cent or more, to be left intact? Yes or no? Is commercial secrecy to be left intact? Yes or no? Are the workers to be enabled to exercise control? Yes or no?

Comrades Avilov and Bazarov give no answer to these practical questions. By using "Struvean" arguments sounding "near-Marxist", they unwittingly stoop to the level of accomplices of the bourgeoisie. The bourgeoisie want nothing better than to answer the people's queries about the scandalous profits of the war supplies deliverers, and about economic dislocation, with "learned" arguments about the "utopian" character of socialism.

These arguments are ridiculously stupid, for what makes socialism objectively impossible is the *small-scale* economy which we by no means presume to expropriate, or even to regulate or control.

What we are trying to make something real instead of a *bluff* is the "state regulation" of which the Mensheviks, the Narodniks and all bureaucrats (who have carried Comrades Avilov and Bazarov with them) talk in order to dismiss the matter, making projects to *safeguard* capitalist profits and orating to preserve commercial secrecy. This is the point, worthy near-Marxists, and not the "introduction" of socialism!

Not regulation of and control over the workers by the capitalist class, but *vice versa*. This is the point. Not confidence in the "state", fit for a Louis Blanc, but demand for a state led by the proletarians and semi-proletarians— that is how we must *combat economic dislocation*. Any other solution is sheer bunkum and deception.

Pravda No. 73,
June 17 (4), 1917

Collected Works,
Vol. 25, pp. 43-45

HOW THE CAPITALISTS CONCEAL
THEIR PROFITS

Concerning the Issue of Control

How much they talk about control! And how *little* it all means. How they dodge the issue by resorting to general phrases, grandiloquent turns of speech, and solemn "projects" doomed for ever to remain projects only.

Now the issue is that unless commercial and bank secrecy is abolished, and unless a law is immediately passed making the books of commercial firms open to the trade unions, all phrases on control and all projects for it will be so much meaningless verbiage.

Here is a small but instructive illustration. A comrade who is a bank employee has sent us the following information showing how profits are concealed in official reports.

On May 7, 1917, *Vestnik Finansov*[23] No. 18 published a report of the Petrograd Loan and Discount Bank. The report gives the bank's net profit as 13,000,000 rubles (the exact figure is 12,960,000; we shall use round numbers in the text and give exact figures in parentheses).

On closer scrutiny, a well-informed person will see at once that that is *not the whole profit at all* and that a considerable part of the profit is cleverly concealed under other items, so that no "tax", "compulsory loan" and, in general, no financial measure will ever bring it out unless commercial and bank secrecy is completely abolished. Indeed, the amount of 5,500,000 rubles is given as reserve capital. Profits are quite often entered for concealment as so-called reserves, or reserve capital. If I am a millionaire who has made a profit of 17,000,000 rubles and wants to reserve 5,000,000, I only have to enter this 5,000,000 as "reserve capital" to do the trick! In this way I *dodge* all the various laws on "state control", "state taxation of profits" and so on.

Again, the report indicates slightly less than 1,000,000 rubles (825,000) as money made in interest and commissions. "The question is," writes the bank employee, "what are the sums that generally constitute the bank's profit, since the money made in interest is not listed under profits??"

Moreover, the sum of 300,000 rubles, listed as remaining profit made in previous years, *is not included in the total profits*! Together, then, with the foregoing item, we have more than another sweet million in profit hidden away. Similarly, the sum of 224,000 rubles of "unpaid dividends to shareholders" *is missing* in the total profit, although everyone knows that dividends are paid out of net profits.

Furthermore, the report lists the sum of 3,800,000 rubles as "carry-overs". "Whoever has not taken a direct part in the business will find it hard to establish what these carry-overs are," the comrade writes. "One thing is certain: in preparing a report, one can easily conceal a part of the profit by listing it under 'carry-overs' and then transferring it to 'where it belongs'."

To sum up. The profit has been listed as 13,000,000 rubles, but, in point of fact, it must be somewhere between 19 and 24 million, or almost 80 per cent profit on a basic capital of 30 million.

Isn't it obvious that the government's threats to the capitalists, the government's promises to the workers, the government's Bills and laws aimed at taking 90 per cent of the profits of the big capitalists are useless, absolutely useless, as long as there is commercial and bank secrecy?

Pravda No. 94,
July 12 (June 29), 1917

Collected Works,
Vol. 25, pp. 139-40

From THE IMPENDING CATASTROPHE
AND HOW TO COMBAT IT[24]

Famine Is Approaching

Unavoidable catastrophe is threatening Russia. The railways are incredibly disorganised and the disorganisation is progressing. The railways will come to a standstill. The delivery of raw materials and coal to the factories will cease. The delivery of grain will cease. The capitalists are deliberately and unremittingly sabotaging (damaging, stopping, disrupting, hampering) production, hoping that an unparalleled catastrophe will mean the collapse of the republic and democracy, and of the Soviets and proletarian and peasant associations generally, thus facilitating the return to a monarchy and the restoration of the unlimited power of the bourgeoisie and the landowners.

The danger of a great catastrophe and of famine is imminent. All the newspapers have written about this time and again. A tremendous number of resolutions have been adopted by the parties and by the Soviets of Workers', Soldiers' and Peasants' Deputies—resolutions which admit that a catastrophe is unavoidable, that it is very close, that extreme measures are necessary to combat it, that "heroic efforts" by the people are necessary to avert ruin, and so on.

Everybody says this. Everybody admits it. Everybody has decided it is so.

Yet nothing is being done.

Six months of revolution have elapsed. The catastrophe is even closer. Unemployment has assumed a mass scale. To think that there is a shortage of goods in the country,

55

the country is perishing from a shortage of food and labour, although there is a sufficient quantity of grain and raw materials, and yet in such a country, at so critical a moment, there is mass unemployment! What better evidence is needed to show that after six months of revolution (which some call a great revolution, but which so far it would perhaps be fairer to call a rotten revolution), in a democratic republic, with an abundance of unions, organs and institutions which proudly call themselves "revolutionary-democratic", absolutely *nothing* of any importance has actually been done to avert catastrophe, to avert famine? We are nearing ruin with increasing speed. The war will not wait and is causing increasing dislocation in every sphere of national life.

Yet the slightest attention and thought will suffice to satisfy anyone that the ways of combating catastrophe and famine are available, that the measures required to combat them are quite clear, simple, perfectly feasible, and fully within reach of the people's forces, and that these measures are *not* being adopted *only* because, *exclusively* because, their realisation would affect the fabulous profits of a handful of landowners and capitalists.

And, indeed, it is safe to say that every single speech, every single article in a newspaper of any trend, every single resolution passed by any meeting or institution quite clearly and explicitly recognises the chief and principal measure of combating, of averting, catastrophe and famine. This measure is control, supervision, accounting, regulation by the state, introduction of a proper distribution of labour-power in the production and distribution of goods, husbanding of the people's forces, the elimination of all wasteful effort, economy of effort. Control, supervision and accounting are the prime requisites for combating catastrophe and famine. This is indisputable and universally recognised. And it is just what *is not being done* from fear of encroaching on the supremacy of the landowners and capitalists, on their immense, fantastic and scandalous profits, profits derived from high prices and war contracts (and, directly or indirectly, nearly everybody is now "working" for the war), profits about which everybody knows and which everybody sees, and over which everybody is sighing and groaning.

And absolutely nothing is being done to introduce such control, accounting and supervision by the state as would be in the least effective....

Control Measures Are Known to All and Easy to Take

One may ask: aren't methods and measures of control extremely complex, difficult, untried and even unknown? Isn't the delay due to the fact that although the statesmen of the Cadet Party, the merchant and industrial class, and the Menshevik and Socialist-Revolutionary parties have for six months been toiling in the sweat of their brow, investigating, studying and discovering measures and methods of control, still the problem is incredibly difficult and has not yet been solved?

Unfortunately, this is how they are trying to present matters to hoodwink the ignorant, illiterate and downtrodden muzhiks and the Simple Simons who believe everything and never look into things. In reality, however, even tsarism, even the "old regime", when it set up the War Industries Committees, *knew* the principal measure, the chief method and way to introduce control, namely, by uniting the population according to profession, purpose of work, branch of labour, etc. But tsarism *feared* the union of the population and therefore did its best to restrict and artificially hinder this generally known, very easy and quite practical method and way of control.

All the belligerent countries, suffering as they are from the extreme burdens and hardships of the war, suffering —in one degree or another—from economic chaos and famine, have long ago outlined, determined, applied and tested a *whole series* of control measures, which consist almost invariably in uniting the population and in setting up or encouraging unions of various kinds, in which state representatives participate, which are under the supervision of the state, etc. All these measures of control are known to all, much has been said and written about them, and the laws passed by the advanced belligerent powers relating to control have been translated into Russian or expounded in detail in the Russian press.

If our state really *wanted* to exercise control in a business-like and earnest fashion, if its institutions had not condemned themselves to "complete inactivity" by their servility to the capitalists, all the state would have to do would be to draw freely on the rich store of control measures which are already known and have been used in the past. The only obstacle to this—an obstacle concealed from the eyes of the people by the Cadets, Socialist-Revolutionaries and Mensheviks—was, and still is, that control would bring to light the fabulous profits of the capitalists and would cut the ground from under these profits.

To explain this most important question more clearly (a question which is essentially equivalent to that of the programme of *any* truly revolutionary government that would wish to save Russia from war and famine), let us enumerate these principal measures of control and examine each of them.

We shall see that all a government would have had to do, if its name of revolutionary-democratic government were not merely a joke, would have been to decree, in the very first week of its existence, the adoption of the principal measures of control, to provide for strict and severe punishment to be meted out to capitalists who fraudulently evaded control, and to call upon the population itself to exercise supervision over the capitalists and see to it that they scrupulously observed the regulations on control—and control would have been introduced in Russia long ago.

These principal measures are:

(1) Amalgamation of all banks into a single bank, and state control over its operations, or nationalisation of the banks.

(2) Nationalisation of the syndicates, i.e., the largest, monopolistic capitalist associations (sugar, oil, coal, iron and steel, and other syndicates).

(3) Abolition of commercial secrecy.

(4) Compulsory syndication (i.e., compulsory amalgamation into associations) of industrialists, merchants and employers generally.

(5) Compulsory organisation of the population into con-

sumers' societies, or encouragement of such organisation, and the exercise of control over it.

Let us see what the significance of each of these measures would be if carried out in a revolutionary-democratic way.

Nationalisation of the Banks

The banks, as we know, are centres of modern economic life, the principal nerve centres of the whole capitalist economic system. To talk about "regulating economic life" and yet evade the question of the nationalisation of the banks means either betraying the most profound ignorance or deceiving the "common people" by florid words and grandiloquent promises with the deliberate intention of not fulfilling these promises.

It is absurd to control and regulate deliveries of grain, or the production and distribution of goods generally, without controlling and regulating bank operations. It is like trying to snatch at odd kopeks and closing one's eyes to millions of rubles. Banks nowadays are so closely and intimately bound up with trade (in grain and everything else) and with industry that without "laying hands" on the banks nothing of any value, nothing "revolutionary-democratic", can be accomplished.

But perhaps for the state to "lay hands" on the banks is a very difficult and complicated operation? They usually try to scare philistines with this very idea—that is, the capitalists and their defenders try it, because it is to their advantage to do so.

In reality, however, nationalisation of the banks, which would not deprive any "owner" of a single kopek, presents absolutely no technical or cultural difficulties, and is being delayed *exclusively* because of the vile greed of an insignificant handful of rich people. If nationalisation of the banks is so often confused with the confiscation of private property, it is the bourgeois press, which has an interest in deceiving the public, that is to blame for this widespread confusion.

The ownership of the capital wielded by and concentrated in the banks is certified by printed and written certificates called shares, bonds, bills, receipts, etc. Not a single one of these certificates would be invalidated or altered if the banks were nationalised, i.e., if all the banks were amalgamated into a single state bank. Whoever owned fifteen rubles on a savings account would continue to be the owner of fifteen rubles after the nationalisation of the banks; and whoever had fifteen million rubles would continue after the nationalisation of the banks to have fifteen million rubles in the form of shares, bonds, bills, commercial certificates and so on.

What, then, is the significance of nationalisation of the banks?

It is that no effective control of any kind over the individual banks and their operations is possible (even if commercial secrecy, etc., were abolished) because it is impossible to keep track of the extremely complex, involved and wily tricks that are used in drawing up balance sheets, founding fictitious enterprises and subsidiaries, enlisting the services of figureheads, and so on, and so forth. Only the amalgamation of all banks into one, which in itself would imply no change whatever in respect of ownership, and which, we repeat, would not deprive any owner of a single kopek, would make it *possible* to exercise real control—provided, of course, all the other measures indicated above were carried out. Only by nationalising the banks *can* the state *put itself in a position* to know where and how, whence and when, millions and billions of rubles flow. And only control over the banks, over the centre, over the pivot and chief mechanism of capitalist circulation, would make it possible to organise real and not fictitious control over all economic life, over the production and distribution of staple goods, and organise that "regulation of economic life" which otherwise is inevitably doomed to remain a ministerial phrase designed to fool the common people. Only control over banking operations, provided they were concentrated in a single state bank, would make it possible, if certain other easily-practicable measures were adopted, to organise the effective collection of income tax in such a way as to prevent the concealment of property and incomes; for at present the income tax is very largely a fiction.

Nationalisation of the banks has only to be decreed and

it would be carried out by the directors and employees themselves. No special machinery, no special preparatory steps on the part of the state would be required, for this is a measure that can be effected by a single decree, "at a single stroke". It was made economically feasible by capitalism itself once it had developed to the stage of bills, shares, bonds and so on. *All* that is required is to *unify accountancy*. And if the revolutionary-democratic government were to decide that immediately, by telegraph, meetings of managers and employees should be called in every city, and conferences in every region and in the country as a whole, for the immediate amalgamation of all banks into a single state bank, this reform would be carried out in a few weeks. Of course, it would be the managers and the higher bank officials who would offer resistance, who would try to deceive the state, delay matters, and so on, for these gentlemen would lose their highly remunerative posts and the opportunity of performing highly profitable fraudulent operations. *That is the heart of the matter.* But there is not the slightest technical difficulty in the way of the amalgamation of the banks; and if the state power were revolutionary not only in word (i.e., if it did not fear to do away with inertia and routine), if it were democratic not only in word (i.e., if it acted in the interests of the majority of the people and not of a handful of rich men), it would be enough to decree confiscation of property and imprisonment as the penalty for managers, board members and big shareholders for the slightest delay or for attempting to conceal documents and accounts. It would be enough, for example, to organise the poorer employees *separately* and to reward them for detecting fraud and delay on the part of the rich for nationalisation of the banks to be effected as smoothly and rapidly as can be.

The advantages accruing to the whole people from nationalisation of the banks—*not* to the workers especially (for the workers have little to do with banks) but to the mass of peasants and small industrialists—would be enormous. The saving in labour would be gigantic, and, assuming that the state would retain the former number of bank employees, nationalisation would be a highly important step towards making the use of the banks universal, towards increasing the number of their branches, putting their operations within easier reach, etc., etc. The availability of credit on easy terms for the *small* owners, for the peasants, would increase immensely. As to the state, it would for the first time be in a position first to *review* all the chief monetary operations, which would be unconcealed, then to *control* them, then to *regulate* economic life, and finally to *obtain* millions and billions for major state transactions, without paying the capitalist gentlemen sky-high "commissions" for their "services". That is the reason —and the only reason—why all the capitalists, all the bourgeois professors, all the bourgeoisie, and all the Plekhanovs, Potresovs and Co., who serve them, are prepared to fight tooth and nail against nationalisation of the banks and invent thousands of excuses to prevent the adoption of this very easy and very pressing measure, although *even* from the standpoint of the "defence" of the country, i.e., from the military standpoint, this measure would provide a gigantic advantage and would tremendously enhance the "military might" of the country.

The following objection might be raised: why do such advanced states as Germany and the U.S.A. "regulate economic life" so magnificently without even thinking of nationalising the banks?

Because, we reply, *both* these states are not merely capitalist, but also imperialist states, although one of them is a monarchy and the other a republic. As such, they carry out the reforms they need by reactionary-bureaucratic methods, whereas we are speaking here of revolutionary-democratic methods.

This "little difference" is of major importance. In most cases it is "not the custom" to think of it. The term "revolutionary democracy" has become with us (especially among the Socialist-Revolutionaries and Mensheviks) almost a conventional phrase, like the expression "thank God", which is also used by people who are not so ignorant as to believe in God; or like the expression "honourable citizen", which is sometimes used even in addressing staff members of *Dyen*[25] or *Yedinstvo*, although nearly everybody guesses that these newspapers have been founded and are maintained by the capitalists in the interests of the capitalists, and that there is therefore very little "honourable" about the pseudo-socialists contributing to these newspapers.

If we do not employ the phrase "revolutionary democracy" as a stereotyped ceremonial phrase, as a conventional epithet, but *reflect* on its meaning, we find that to be a democrat means reckoning in reality with the interests of the majority of the people and not the minority, and that to be a revolutionary means destroying everything harmful and obsolete in the most resolute and ruthless manner.

Neither in America nor in Germany, as far as we know, is any claim laid by either the government or the ruling classes to the name "revolutionary democrats", to which our Socialist-Revolutionaries and Mensheviks lay claim (and which they prostitute).

In Germany there are only *four* very large private banks of national importance. In America there are only *two*. It is easier, more convenient, more profitable for the financial magnates of those banks to unite privately, surreptitiously, in a reactionary and not a revolutionary way, in a bureaucratic and not a democratic way, bribing government officials (this is the general rule both in America *and in Germany*), and preserving the private character of the banks in order to preserve secrecy of operations, to milk the state of millions upon millions in "super-profits", and to make financial frauds possible.

Both America and Germany "regulate economic life" in such a way as to create conditions of *war-time penal servitude* for the workers (and partly for the peasants) and a *paradise* for the bankers and capitalists. Their regulation consists in "squeezing" the workers to the point of starvation, while the capitalists are guaranteed (surreptitiously, in a reactionary-bureaucratic fashion) profits *higher* than before the war.

Such a course is quite possible in republican-imperialist Russia too. Indeed, it is the course being followed not only by the Milyukovs and Shingaryovs, but also by Kerensky in partnership with Tereshchenko, Nekrasov, Bernatsky, Prokopovich and Co., who *also uphold*, in a reactionary-bureaucratic manner, the "inviolability" of the banks and their sacred right to fabulous profits. So let us better tell the *truth*, namely, that in republican Russia they want to regulate economic life in a reactionary-bureaucratic manner, but "often" find it difficult to do so owing to the existence of the "Soviets", which Kornilov No. 1 did not manage to disband, but which Kornilov No. 2 will try to disband....

That would be the truth. And this simple if bitter truth is more useful for the enlightenment of the people than the honeyed lies about "our", "great", "revolutionary" democracy.

* * *

Nationalisation of the banks would greatly facilitate the simultaneous nationalisation of the insurance business, i.e., the amalgamation of all the insurance companies into one, the centralisation of their operations, and state control over them. Here, too, congresses of insurance company employees could carry out this amalgamation immediately and without any great effort, provided a revolutionary-democratic government decreed this and ordered directors and big shareholders to effect the amalgamation without the slightest delay and held every one of them strictly accountable for it. The capitalists have invested hundreds of millions of rubles in the insurance business; the work is all done by the employees. The amalgamation of this business would lead to lower insurance premiums, would provide a host of facilities and conveniences for the insured and would make it possible to increase their number without increasing expenditure of effort and funds. Absolutely nothing but the inertia, routine and self-interest of a handful of holders of remunerative jobs are delaying this reform, which, among other things, would enhance the country's defence potential by economising national labour and creating a number of highly important opportunities to "regulate economic life" not in word, but in deed.

Nationalisation of the Syndicates

Capitalism differs from the old, pre-capitalistic systems of economy in having created the closest interconnection and interdependence of the various branches of the economy. Were this not so, incidentally, no steps towards socialism would be technically feasible. Modern capitalism, under which the banks dominate production, has carried this interdependence of the various branches of the economy to the utmost. The banks and the more important branches of industry and commerce have become inseparably merged. This means, on the one hand, that it is impossible to nationalise the banks alone, without proceeding to create a state monopoly of commercial and industrial syndicates (sugar, coal, iron, oil, etc.), and without nationalising them. It means, on the other hand, that if carried out in earnest, the regulation of economic activity would demand the simultaneous nationalisation of the banks and the syndicates.

Let us take the sugar syndicate as an example. It came into being under tsarism, and at that time developed into a huge capitalist combine of splendidly equipped refineries. And, of course, this combine, thoroughly imbued with the most reactionary and bureaucratic spirit, secured scandalously high profits for the capitalists and reduced its employees to the status of humiliated and downtrodden slaves lacking any rights. Even at that time the state controlled and regulated production—in the interests of the rich, the magnates.

All that remains to be done here is to transform reactionary-bureaucratic regulation into revolutionary-democratic regulation by simple decrees providing for the summoning of a congress of employees, engineers, directors and shareholders, for the introduction of uniform accountancy, for control by the workers' unions, etc. This is an exceedingly simple thing, yet it has not been done! Under what is a democratic republic, the regulation of the sugar industry *actually* remains reactionary-bureaucratic; everything remains as of old—the dissipation of national labour, routine and stagnation, and the enrichment of the Bobrinskys and Tereshchenkos. Democrats and not bureaucrats, the workers and other employees and not the "sugar barons", should be called upon to exercise independent initiative—and this could and should be done in a few days, at a single stroke, if only the Socialist-Revolutionaries and Mensheviks did not befog the minds of the people by plans for "association" with these very sugar barons, for the very association with the wealthy from which the "complete inaction" of the government in the matter of regulating economic life follows with absolute inevitability, and of which it is a consequence.*

Take the oil business. It was to a vast extent "socialised" by the earlier development of capitalism. Just a couple of oil barons wield millions and hundreds of millions of rubles, clipping coupons and raking in fabulous profits from a "business" which is *already* actually, technically and socially organised on a national scale and is *already* being conducted by hundreds and thousands of employees, engineers, etc. Nationalisation of the oil industry could be effected *at once* by, and is imperative for, a revolutionary-democratic state, especially when the latter suffers from an acute crisis and when it is essential to economise national labour and to increase the output of fuel at all costs. It is clear that here bureaucratic control can achieve nothing, can change nothing, for the "oil barons" can cope with the Tereshchenkos, the Kerenskys, the Avksentyevs and the Skobelevs as easily as they coped with the tsar's ministers—by means of delays, excuses and promises, and by bribing the bourgeois press directly or indirectly (this is called "public opinion", and the Kerenskys and Avksentyevs "reckon" with it), by bribing officials (left by the Kerenskys and Avksentyevs in their old jobs in the old state machinery which remains intact).

If anything real is to be done bureaucracy must be abandoned for democracy, and in a truly revolutionary way, i.e., war must be declared on the oil barons and shareholders, the confiscation of their property and punishment by imprisonment must be decreed for delaying nationalisation of the oil business, for concealing incomes or accounts, for sabotaging production, and for failing to take steps to increase production. The initiative of the workers and other employees must be drawn on; *they* must be immediately summoned to conferences and congresses; a certain proportion of the profits must be assigned to *them*, provided they institute overall control and increase production. Had

---

* These lines had been written when I learnt from the newspapers that the Kerensky government is introducing a sugar monopoly, and, of course, is introducing it in a reactionary-bureaucratic way, without congresses of workers and other employees, without publicity, and without curbing the capitalists!

these revolutionary-democratic steps been taken at once, immediately, in April 1917, Russia, which is one of the richest countries in the world in deposits of liquid fuel, could, using water transport, have done a very great deal during this summer to supply the people with the necessary quantities of fuel.

Neither the bourgeois nor the coalition Socialist-Revolutionary-Menshevik-Cadet government has done anything at all. Both have confined themselves to a bureaucratic playing at reforms. They have not dared to take a single revolutionary-democratic step. Everything has remained as it was under the tsars—the oil barons, the stagnation, the hatred of the workers and other employees for their exploiters, the resulting chaos, and the dissipation of national labour—only the *letterheads* on the incoming and outgoing papers in the "republican" offices have been changed!

Take the coal industry. It is technically and culturally no less "ripe" for nationalisation, and is being no less shamelessly managed by the robbers of the people, the coal barons, and there are a number of most striking *facts* of direct sabotage, direct *damage* to and stoppage of production by the industrialists. Even the ministerial *Rabochaya Gazeta* of the Mensheviks has admitted these facts. And what do we find? Absolutely nothing has been done, except to call the old, reactionary-bureaucratic meetings "on a half-and-half basis"—an equal number of workers and bandits from the coal syndicate! Not a single revolutionary-democratic step has been taken, not a shadow of an attempt has been made to establish the only control which is real—control from *below*, through the employees' union, through the workers, and by using terror against the coal industrialists who are ruining the country and bringing production to a standstill! How can this be done when we are "all" in favour of the "coalition"—if not with the Cadets, then with commercial and industrial circles. And coalition means leaving power in the hands of the capitalists, letting them go unpunished, allowing them to hamper affairs, to blame everything on the workers, to intensify the chaos and *thus* pave the way for a new Kornilov revolt!

Abolition of Commercial Secrecy

Unless commercial secrecy is abolished, either control over production and distribution will remain an empty promise, only needed by the Cadets to fool the Socialist-Revolutionaries and Mensheviks, and by the Socialist-Revolutionaries and Mensheviks to fool the working classes, or control can be exercised only by reactionary-bureaucratic methods and means. Although this is obvious to every unprejudiced person, and although *Pravda* persistently demanded the abolition of commercial secrecy* (and was suppressed largely for this reason by the Kerensky government which is subservient to capital), neither our republican government nor the "authorised bodies of revolutionary democracy" have even thought of this *first step* to real control.

This is the very key to all control. Here we have the most sensitive spot of capital, which is robbing the people and sabotaging production. And this is exactly why the Socialist-Revolutionaries and Mensheviks are afraid to do anything about it.

The usual argument of the capitalists, one reiterated by the petty bourgeoisie without reflection, is that in a capitalist economy the abolition of commercial secrecy is in general absolutely impossible, for private ownership of the means of production, and the dependence of the individual undertakings on the market render essential the "sanctity" of commercial books and commercial operations, including, of course, banking operations.

Those who in one form or another repeat this or similar arguments allow themselves to be deceived and themselves deceive the people by shutting their eyes to two fundamental, highly important and generally known facts of modern economic activity. The first fact is the existence of large-scale capitalism, i.e., the peculiar features of the economic system of banks, syndicates, large factories, etc. The second fact is the war.

It is modern large-scale capitalism, which is everywhere becoming monopoly capitalism, that deprives commercial secrecy of every shadow of reasonableness, turns it into hypocrisy and into an instrument exclusively for concealing financial swindles and the fantastically high profits of big

* See pp. 53-54 of this book.—*Ed.*

capital. Large-scale capitalist economy, by its very technical nature, is socialised economy, that is, it both operates for millions of people and, directly or indirectly, unites by its operations hundreds, thousands and tens of thousands of families. It is not like the economy of the small handicraftsman or the middle peasant who keep no commercial books at all and who would therefore not be affected by the abolition of commercial secrecy!

As it is, the operations conducted in large-scale business are known to hundreds or more persons. Here the law protecting commercial secrecy does not serve the interests of production or exchange, but those of speculation and profit-seeking in their crudest form, and of direct fraud, which, as we know, in the case of joint-stock companies is particularly widespread and very skilfully concealed by reports and balance-sheets, so compiled as to deceive the public.

While commercial secrecy is unavoidable in small commodity production, i.e., among the small peasants and handicraftsmen, where production itself is not socialised but scattered and disunited, in large-scale capitalist production, the protection of commercial secrecy means protection of the privileges and profits of literally a handful of people *against* the interest of the whole people. This has already been recognised by the law, inasmuch as provision is made for the publication of the accounts of joint-stock companies. But *this* control, which has already been introduced in all advanced countries, as well as in Russia, is a reactionary-bureaucratic control which does not open the eyes of the *people* and which *does not allow the whole truth* about the operations of joint-stock companies to become known.

To act in a revolutionary-democratic way, it would be necessary to immediately pass another law abolishing commercial secrecy, compelling the big undertakings and the wealthy to render the fullest possible accounts, and investing every group of citizens of substantial democratic numerical strength (1,000 or 10,000 voters, let us say) with the right to examine *all* the records of any large undertaking. Such a measure could be fully and easily effected by a simple decree. It *alone* would allow full scope for *popular* initiative in control, through the office employees' unions, the workers' unions and all the political parties, and it alone would make control effective and democratic.

Add to this the war. The vast majority of commercial and industrial establishments are now working not for the "free market", but *for the government*, for the war. This is why I have already stated in *Pravda* that people who counter us with the argument that socialism cannot be introduced are liars, and barefaced liars at that, because it is not a question of introducing socialism now, directly, overnight, but of *exposing plunder of the state*.[26]

Capitalist "war" economy (i.e., economy directly or indirectly connected with war contracts) is systematic and legalised *plunder*, and the Cadet gentry, who, together with the Mensheviks and Socialist-Revolutionaries, are opposing the abolition of commercial secrecy, are nothing but *aiders and abettors of plunder*.

The war is now costing Russia fifty million rubles *a day*. These fifty million go mostly to army contractors. Of these fifty, at least five million *daily*, and probably ten million or more, constitute the "honest income" of the capitalists, and of the officials who are in one way or another in collusion with them. The very large firms and banks which lend money for war contracts transactions thereby make fantastic profits, and do so by plundering the state, for no other epithet can be applied to this defrauding and plundering of the people "on the occasion of" the hardships of war, "on the occasion of" the deaths of hundreds of thousands and millions of people.

"Everybody" knows about these scandalous profits made on war contracts, about the "letters of guarantee" which are concealed by the banks, about who benefits by the rising cost of living. It is smiled on in "society". Quite a number of precise references are made to it *even* in the bourgeois press, which as a general rule keeps silent about "unpleasant" facts and avoids "ticklish" questions. Everybody knows about it, yet everybody keeps silent, everybody tolerates it, everybody puts up with the government, which prates eloquently about "control" and "regulation"!!

The revolutionary democrats, were they real revolutionaries and democrats, would immediately pass a law abolishing commercial secrecy, compelling contractors and merchants to render accounts public, forbidding them to abandon their field of activity without the permission of the authorities, imposing the penalty of confiscation of property and shooting* for concealment and for deceiving the people, organising verification and control *from below*, democratically, by the people themselves, by unions of workers and other employees, consumers, etc.

Our Socialist-Revolutionaries and Mensheviks fully deserve to be called scared democrats, for on this question they repeat what is said by all the scared philistines, namely, that the capitalists will "run away" if "too severe" measures are adopted, that "we" shall be unable to get along without the capitalists, that the British and French millionaires, who are, of course, "supporting" us, will most likely be "offended" in their turn, and so on. It might be thought that the Bolsheviks were proposing something unknown to history, something that has never been tried before, something "utopian", while, as a matter of fact, even 125 years ago, in France, people who were real "revolutionary democrats", who were really convinced of the just and defensive character of the war they were waging, who really had popular support and were sincerely convinced of this, were able to establish *revolutionary* control over the rich and to achieve results which earned the admiration of the world. And in the century and a quarter that have since elapsed, the development of capitalism, which resulted in the creation of banks, syndicates, railways and so forth, has greatly facilitated and simplified the adoption of measures of really democratic control by the workers and peasants over the exploiters, the landowners and capitalists.

In point of fact, the whole question of control boils down to who controls whom, i.e., which class is in control and which is being controlled. In our country, in republican Russia, with the help of the "authorised bodies" of supposedly revolutionary democracy, it is the landowners and capitalists who are still recognised to be, and still are, the controllers. The inevitable result is the capitalist robbery that arouses universal indignation among the people, and

---

* I have already had occasion to point out in the Bolshevik press that it is right to argue against the death penalty only when it is applied by the exploiters against the *mass* of the working people with the purpose of maintaining exploitation.[27] It is hardly likely that any revolutionary government whatever could do without applying the death penalty to the *exploiters* (i.e., the landowners and capitalists).

the economic chaos that is being artificially kept up by the capitalists. We must resolutely and irrevocably, not fearing to break with the old, not fearing boldly to build the new, pass to control *over* the landowners and capitalists *by* the workers and peasants. And this is what our Socialist-Revolutionaries and Mensheviks fear worse than the plague.

Compulsory Association

Compulsory syndication, i.e., compulsory association, of the industrialists, for example, is already being practised in Germany. Nor is there anything new in it. Here, too, through the fault of the Socialist-Revolutionaries and Mensheviks, we see the utter stagnation of republican Russia, whom these none-too-respectable parties "entertain" by dancing a quadrille with the Cadets, or with the Bublikovs, or with Tereshchenko and Kerensky.

Compulsory syndication is, on the one hand, a means whereby the state, as it were, expedites capitalist development, which everywhere leads to the organisation of the class struggle and to a growth in the number, variety and importance of unions. On the other hand, compulsory "unionisation" is an indispensable precondition for any kind of effective control and for all economy of national labour.

The German law, for instance, binds the leather manufacturers of a given locality or of the whole country to form an association, on the board of which there is a representative of the state for the purpose of control. A law of this kind does not directly, i.e., in itself, affect property relations in any way; it does not deprive any owner of a single kopek and does not predetermine whether the control is to be exercised in a reactionary-bureaucratic or a revolutionary-democratic form, direction or spirit.

Such laws can and should be passed in our country immediately, without wasting a single week of precious time; it should be left to *social conditions themselves* to determine the more specific forms of enforcing the law, the speed with which it is to be enforced, the methods of supervision over ıts enforcement, etc. In this case, the state requires no special machinery, no special investigation, nor preliminary enquiries for the passing of such a law. All that is required is the determination to break with certain private interests of the capitalists, who are "not accustomed" to such interference and have no desire to forfeit the super-profits which are ensured by the old methods of management and the absence of control.

No machinery and no "statistics" (which Chernov wanted to substitute for the revolutionary initiative of the peasants) are required to *pass* such a law, inasmuch as its implementation must be made the duty of the manufacturers or indusrialists themselves, of the *available* public forces, under the control of the available public (i.e., non-government, non-bureaucratic) forces too, which, however, must consist by all means of the so-called "lower estates", i.e., of the oppressed and exploited classes, which in history have always proved to be immensely *superior* to the exploiters in their capacity for heroism, self-sacrifice and comradely discipline.

Let us assume that we have a really revolutionary-democratic government and that it decides that the manufacturers and industrialists in every branch of production who employ, let us say, not less than two workers shall immediately amalgamate into uyezd and gubernia associations. Responsibility for the strict observance of the law is laid in the first place on the manufacturers, directors, board members, and big shareholders (for they are the real leaders of modern industry, its real masters). They shall be regarded as deserters from military service, and punished as such, if they do not work for the immediate implementation of the law, and shall bear mutual responsibility, one answering for all, and all for one, with the whole of their property. Responsibility shall next be laid on all office employees, who shall also form *one* union, and on all workers and their trade union. The purpose of "unionisation" is to institute the fullest, strictest and most detailed accountancy, but chiefly to *combine operations* in the purchase of raw materials, the sale of products, and the *economy* of national funds and forces. When the separate establishments are amalgamated into a single syndicate, this economy can attain tremendous proportions, as economic science teaches us and as is shown by the example of all syndicates, cartels and trusts. And it must be repeated that this unionisation will not in itself alter property relations one iota and will not deprive any owner of a single kopek. This circumstance must be strongly stressed, for the bourgeois press constantly "frightens" small and medium proprietors by asserting that socialists in general, and the Bolsheviks in particular, want to "expropriate" them—a deliberately false assertion, as socialists do not intend to, cannot and will not expropriate the small peasant *even if there is a fully socialist* revolution. All the time we are speaking *only* of the immediate and urgent measures, which have already been introduced in Western Europe and which a democracy that is at all consistent ought to introduce immediately in our country to combat the impending and inevitable catastrophe.

Serious difficulties, both technical and cultural, would be encountered in amalgamating the small and very small proprietors into associations, owing to the extremely small proportions and technical primitiveness of their enterprises and the illiteracy or lack of education of the owners. But precisely such enterprises could be exempted from the law (as was pointed out above in our hypothetical example). Their non-amalgamation, let alone their belated amalgamation, could create no serious obstacle, for the part played by the huge number of small enterprises in the sum total of production and their importance to the economy as a whole are *negligible*, and, moreover, they are often in one way or another dependent on the big enterprises.

Only the big enterprises are of decisive importance; and here the technical and cultural means and forces for "unionisation" *do exist*; what is lacking is the firm, determined initiative of a *revolutionary* government which should be ruthlessly severe towards the exploiters to set these forces and means in motion.

The poorer a country is in technically trained forces, and in intellectual forces generally, the more *urgent* it is to decree compulsory association as early and as resolutely as possible and to begin with the bigger and biggest enterprises when putting the decree into effect, for it is association that will *economise* intellectual forces and make it possible to use them *to the full* and to distribute them more correctly. If, after 1905, even the Russian peasants in their out-of-the-way districts, under the tsarist government, in face of the thousands of obstacles raised by that government, were able to make a tremendous forward stride in the creation of all kinds of associations, it is clear that the amalgamation of large- and medium-scale industry and trade could be effected in several months, if not earlier, provided compulsion to this end were exercised by a really revolutionary-democratic government relying on the support, participation, interest and advantage of the "lower ranks", the democracy, the workers and other employees, and calling upon *them* to exercise control.

Regulation of Consumption

The war has compelled all the belligerent and many of the neutral countries to resort to the regulation of consumption. Bread cards have been issued and have become customary, and this has led to the appearance of other ration cards. Russia is no exception and has also introduced bread cards.

Using this as an example, we can draw, perhaps, the most striking comparison of all between reactionary-bureaucratic methods of combating a catastrophe, which are confined to minimum reforms, and revolutionary-democratic methods, which, to justify their name, must directly aim at a violent rupture with the old, obsolete system and at the achievement of the speediest possible progress.

The bread card—this typical example of how consumption is regulated in modern capitalist countries—aims at, and achieves (at best), one thing only, namely, distributing available supplies of grain to give everybody his share. A maximum limit to consumption is established, not for all foodstuffs by far, but only for principal foodstuffs, those of "popular" consumption. And that is all. There is no intention of doing anything else. Available supplies of grain are calculated in a bureaucratic way, then divided on a per capita basis, a ration is fixed and introduced, and there the matter ends. Luxury articles are not affected, for they are "anyway" scarce and "anyway" so dear as to be beyond the reach of the "people". And so, in *all* the belligerent countries without exception, *even* in Germany, which evidently, without fear of contradiction, may be said to be a model of the most careful, pedantic and strict regulation of consumption—*even* in Germany we find that the rich constantly *get around* all "rationing". This, too, "everybody" knows and "everybody" talks about with a smile; and in the German socialist papers, and sometimes even in the bourgeois papers, despite the fierce military stringency of the German censorship, we constantly find items and reports about the "menus" of the rich, saying how the wealthy can obtain white bread in any quantity at a certain health resort (visited, on the plea of illness, by everybody who has plenty of money), and how the wealthy substitute choice and rare articles of luxury for articles of popular consumption.

A reactionary capitalist state which *fears* to undermine the pillars of capitalism, of wage slavery, of the economic supremacy of the rich, which *fears* to encourage the initiative of the workers and the working people generally, which *fears* to provoke them to a more exacting attitude—*such* a state will be quite content with bread cards. Such a state does not for a moment, in any measure it adopts, lose sight of the *reactionary* aim of strengthening capitalism, preventing its being undermined, and confining the "regulation of economic life" in general, and the regulation of consumption in particular, to such measures as are absolutely essential to feed the people, *and makes no attempt* whatsoever at real regulation of consumption by exercising *control over the rich* and laying the *greater part* of the burden in wartime on those who are better off, who are privileged, well fed and overfed in peace-time.

The reactionary-bureaucratic solution to the problem with which the war has confronted the peoples confines itself to bread cards, to the equal distribution of "popular" foodstuffs, of those absolutely essential to feed the people, without retreating one little bit from bureaucratic and reactionary ideas, that is, from the aim of *not* encouraging the initiative of the poor, the proletariat, the mass of the people ("demos"), of *not* allowing *them* to exercise control over the rich, and of leaving *as many* loopholes *as possible* for the rich to compensate themselves with articles of luxury. And a great number of loopholes are left in *all* countries, we repeat, even in Germany—not to speak of

76

Russia; the "common people" starve while the rich visit health resorts, supplement the meagre official ration by all sorts of "extras" obtained on the side, and do *not* allow *themselves* to be controlled.

In Russia, which has only just made a revolution against the tsarist regime in the name of liberty and equality, in Russia, which, as far as its actual political institutions are concerned, has at once become a democratic republic, what particularly strikes the people, what particularly arouses popular discontent, irritation, anger and indignation is that *everybody* sees the easy way in which the wealthy get around the bread cards. They do it very easily indeed. "From under the counter", and for a very high price, especially if one has "*pull*" (which only the rich have), one can obtain anything, and in large quantities, too. It is the people who are starving. The regulation of consumption is confined within the narrowest bureaucratic-reactionary limits. The government has not the slightest intention of putting regulation on a really revolutionary-democratic footing, is not in the least concerned about doing so.

"Everybody" is suffering from the queues but—but the rich send their servants to stand in the queues, and even engage special servants for the purpose! And that is "democracy"!

At a time when the country is suffering untold calamities, a revolutionary-democratic policy would not confine itself to bread cards to combat the impending catastrophe but would add, firstly, the compulsory organisation of the whole population in consumers' societies, for otherwise control over consumption cannot be fully exercised; secondly, labour service for the rich, making them perform without pay secretarial and similar duties for these consumers' societies; thirdly, the equal distribution among the population of absolutely all consumer goods, so as really to distribute the burdens of the war equitably; fourthly, the organisation of control in such a way as to have the poorer classes of the population exercise control over the consumption of the rich.

The establishment of real democracy in this sphere and the display of a real revolutionary spirit in the organisation of control by the most needy classes of the people would be a very great stimulus to the employment of all available intellectual forces and to the development of the truly revolutionary energies of the entire people. Yet now the ministers of republican and revolutionary-democratic Russia, exactly like their colleagues in all other imperialist countries, make pompous speeches about "working in common for the good of the people" and about "exerting every effort", but the people see, feel and sense the hypocrisy of this talk.

The result is that no progress is being made, chaos is spreading irresistibly, and a catastrophe is approaching, for our government cannot introduce war-time penal servitude for the workers in the Kornilov, Hindenburg, general imperialist way—the traditions, memories, vestiges, habits and institutions of the *revolution* are still too much alive among the people; our government does not want to take any really serious steps in a revolutionary-democratic direction, for it is thoroughly infected and thoroughly enmeshed by its dependence on the bourgeoisie, its "coalition" with the bourgeoisie, and its fear to encroach on their real privileges.

Government Disruption of the Work of the Democratic Organisations

We have examined various ways and means of combating catastrophe and famine. We have seen everywhere that the contradictions between the democrats, on the one hand, and the government and the bloc of the Socialist-Revolutionaries and Mensheviks which is supporting it, on the other, are irreconcilable. To prove that these contradictions exist in reality, and not merely in our exposition, and that their irreconcilability is *actually* borne out by conflicts affecting the people as a whole, we have only to recall two very typical "results" and lessons of the six months' history of our revolution.

The history of the "reign" of Palchinsky is one lesson. The history of the "reign" and fall of Peshekhonov is the other.

The measures to combat catastrophe and hunger described above boil down to the all-round encouragement (even to the extent of compulsion) of "unionisation" of the population, and primarily the democrats, i.e., the majority of the population, or, above all, the oppressed classes, the workers and peasants, especially the poor peasants. And this is the path which the population itself spontaneously began to adopt in order to cope with the unparalleled difficulties, burdens and hardships of the war.

Tsarism did everything to hamper the free and independent "unionisation" of the population. But after the fall of the tsarist monarchy, democratic organisations began to spring up and grow rapidly all over Russia. The struggle against the catastrophe began to be waged by spontaneously arising democratic organisations—by all sorts of committees of supply, food committees, fuel councils, and so on and so forth.

And the most remarkable thing in the whole six months' history of our revolution, as far as the question we are examining is concerned, is that a *government* which calls itself republican and revolutionary, and which is *supported* by the Mensheviks and Socialist-Revolutionaries in the name of the "authorised bodies of revolutionary democracy", *fought* the democratic organisations and *defeated them*!!

By this fight, Palchinsky earned extremely wide and very sad notoriety all over Russia. He acted behind the government's back, without coming out publicly (just as the Cadets generally preferred to act, willingly pushing forward Tsereteli "for the people", while they themselves arranged all the important business on the quiet). Palchinsky hampered and thwarted every serious measure taken by the spontaneously created democratic organisations, for no serious measure could be taken without "injuring" the excessive profits and wilfulness of the Kit Kityches. And Palchinsky was in fact a loyal defender and servant of the Kit Kityches. Palchinsky went so far—and this fact was reported in the newspapers—as simply to *annul* the orders of the spontaneously created democratic organisations!

The whole history of Palchinsky's "reign"—and he "reigned" for many months, and just when Tsereteli, Skobelev and Chernov were "ministers"—was a monstrous scandal from beginning to end; the will of the people and the decisions of the democrats were frustrated to *please* the capitalists and meet their filthy greed. Of course, only a negligible part of Palchinsky's "feats" could find its way into the press, and a full investigation of the manner in which he *hindered* the struggle against famine can be made only by a truly democratic government of the proletariat when it gains power and submits all the actions of Palchinsky and his like, without concealing anything, *to the judgement* of the people.

It will perhaps be argued that Palchinsky was an exception, and that after all he was removed.... But the fact is that Palchinsky was not the exception but the *rule*, that the situation has in no way improved with his removal, that his place has been taken by the same kind of Palchinskys with different names, and that all the *"influence"* of the capitalists, and the entire policy of *frustrating the struggle against hunger to please the capitalists*, has remained intact. For Kerensky and Co. are only a screen for defence of the interests of the capitalists.

The most striking proof of this is the resignation of Peshekhonov, the Food Minister. As we know, Peshekhonov is a very, very moderate Narodnik. But in the organisation of food supply he wanted to work honestly, in contact with and supported by the democratic organisations. The *experience* of Peshekhonov's work and his *resignation* are all the more interesting because this extremely moderate Narodnik, this member of the Popular Socialist Party, who was ready to accept any compromise with the bourgeoisie, was nevertheless compelled to resign! For the Kerensky government, to please the capitalists, landowners and kulaks, had *raised* the fixed prices of grain!

This is how M. Smith describes this "step" and its significance in the newspaper *Svobodnaya Zhizn*[28] No. 1, of September 2:

"Several days before the government decided to raise the fixed prices, the following scene was enacted in the national Food Committee: Rolovich, a Right-winger, a stubborn defender of the interests of private trade and a ruthless opponent of the grain monopoly and state interference in economic affairs, publicly announced with a smug smile that he understood the fixed grain prices would shortly be raised.

"The representative of the Soviet of Workers' and Soldiers' Deputies replied by declaring that he knew nothing of the kind, that as long as the revolution in Russia lasted such an act could not take place, and that at any rate the government could not take such a step without first consulting the authorised democratic bodies—the

Economic Council and the national Food Committee. This statement was supported by the representative of the Soviet of Peasants' Deputies.

"But, alas, reality introduced a very harsh amendment to this counter-version! It was the representative of the wealthy elements and not the representatives of the democrats who turned out to be right. He proved to be excellently informed of the preparations for an attack on democratic rights, although the democratic representatives indignantly denied the very possibility of such an attack."

And so, both the representative of the workers and the representative of the peasants explicitly state their opinion in the name of the vast majority of the people, yet the Kerensky government acts contrary to that opinion, in the interests of the capitalists!

Rolovich, a representative of the capitalists, turned out to be excellently informed behind the backs of the democrats—just as we have always observed, and now observe, that the bourgeois newspapers, *Rech* and *Birzhevka*,[29] are best informed of the doings in the Kerensky government.

What does this possession of excellent information show? Obviously, that the capitalists have their "channels" and *virtually* hold power in their own hands. Kerensky is a figurehead which they use as and when they find necessary. The interests of tens of millions of workers and peasants turn out to have been sacrificed to the profits of a handful of the rich.

And how do our Socialist-Revolutionaries and Mensheviks react to this outrage to the people? Did they address an appeal to the workers and peasants, saying that after this, prison was the only place for Kerensky and his colleagues?

God forbid! The Socialist-Revolutionaries and Mensheviks, through their Economic Department, confined themselves to adopting the impressive resolution to which we have already referred! In this resolution they declare that the raising of grain prices by the Kerensky government is "a *ruinous* measure which deals a *severe blow* both at the food supply and at the whole economic life of the country", and that these ruinous measures have been taken in direct "*violation*" of the law!!

Such are the results of the policy of compromise, of flirting with Kerensky and desiring to "spare" him!

The government violates the law by adopting, in the interests of the rich, the landowners and capitalists, a measure which *ruins* the whole business of control, food supply and the stabilisation of the extremely shaky finances, yet the Socialist-Revolutionaries and Mensheviks continue to talk about an understanding with commercial and industrial circles, continue to attend conferences with Tereshchenko and to spare Kerensky, and confine themselves to a paper resolution of protest, which the government very calmly pigeonholes!!

This reveals with great clarity the fact that the Socialist-Revolutionaries and Mensheviks have betrayed the people and the revolution, and that the Bolsheviks are becoming the real leaders of the masses, *even* of the Socialist-Revolutionary and Menshevik masses.

For only the winning of power by the proletariat, headed by the Bolshevik Party, can put an end to the outrageous actions of Kerensky and Co. and *restore* the work of democratic food distribution, supply and other organisations, which Kerensky and his government are *frustrating*.

The Bolsheviks are acting—and this can be very clearly seen from the above example—as the representatives of the interests of the *whole* people, which are to ensure food distribution and supply and meet the most urgent needs of the workers *and peasants*, despite the vacillating, irresolute and truly treacherous policy of the Socialist-Revolutionaries and Mensheviks, a policy which has brought the country to an act as shameful as this raising of grain prices!

Financial Collapse and Measures
to Combat It

There is another side to the problem of raising the fixed grain prices. This raising of prices involves a new chaotic increase in the issuing of paper money, a further increase in the cost of living, increased financial disorganisation and the approach of financial collapse. Everybody admits that the issuing of paper money constitutes the worst form of compulsory loan, that it most of all affects the conditions of the workers, of the poorest section of the population, and that it is the chief evil engendered by financial disorder.

And it is to this measure that the Kerensky government, supported by the Socialist-Revolutionaries and Mensheviks, is resorting!

There is no way of effectively combating financial disorganisation and inevitable financial collapse except that of revolutionary rupture with the interests of capital and that of the organisation of really democratic control, i.e., control from "below", control by the workers and the poor peasants *over* the capitalists, a way to which we referred throughout the earlier part of this exposition.

Large issues of paper money encourage profiteering, enable the capitalists to make millions of rubles, and place tremendous difficulties in the way of a very necessary expansion of production, for the already high cost of materials, machinery, etc., is rising further by leaps and bounds. What can be done about it when the wealth acquired by the rich through profiteering is being concealed?

An income tax with progressive and very high rates for larger and very large incomes might be introduced. Our government has introduced one, following the example of other imperialist governments. But it is largely a fiction, a dead letter, for, firstly, the value of money is falling faster and faster, and, secondly, the more incomes are derived from profiteering and the more securely commercial secrecy is maintained, the greater their concealment.

Real and not nominal control is required to make the tax real and not fictitious. But control over the capitalists is impossible if it remains bureaucratic, for the bureaucracy is itself bound to and interwoven with the bourgeoisie by thousands of threads. That is why in the West-European imperialist states, monarchies and republics alike, financial order is obtained solely by the introduction of "labour service", which creates *war-time penal servitude* or *war-time slavery* for the workers.

Reactionary-bureaucratic control is the only method known to imperialist states—not excluding the democratic republics of France and America—of foisting the burdens of the war on to the proletariat and the working people.

The basic contradiction in the policy of our government is that, in order not to quarrel with the bourgeoisie, not to destroy the "coalition" with them, the government has to introduce reactionary-bureaucratic control, which it calls "revolutionary-democratic" control, deceiving the people at every step and irritating and angering the masses who have just overthrown tsarism.

Yet only revolutionary-democratic measures, only the organisation of the oppressed classes, the workers and peasants, the masses, into unions would make it possible to establish a most effective control *over the rich* and wage a most successful fight against the concealment of incomes.

An attempt is being made to encourage the use of cheques as a means of avoiding excessive issue of paper money. This measure is of no significance as far as the poor are concerned, for anyway they live from hand to mouth, complete their "economic cycle" in one week and return to the capitalists the few meagre coppers they manage to earn. The use of cheques might have great significance as far as the rich are concerned. It would enable the state, especially in conjunction with such measures as nationalisation of the banks and abolition of commercial secrecy, *really to control* the incomes of the capitalists, really to impose taxation on them, and really to "democratise" (and at the same time bring order into) the financial system.

But this is hampered by the fear of infringing the privileges of the bourgeoisie and destroying the "coalition" with them. For unless truly revolutionary measures are adopted and compulsion is very seriously resorted to, the capitalists will not submit to any control, will not make known their budgets, and will not surrender their stocks of paper money for the democratic state to "keep account" of.

The workers and peasants, organised in unions, by nationalising the banks, making the use of cheques legally compulsory for all rich persons, abolishing commercial secrecy, imposing confiscation of property as a penalty for concealment of incomes, etc., might with extreme ease make control both effective and universal—control, that is, over the rich, and such control as would *secure the return* of paper money *from those* who have it, *from those* who conceal it, *to the treasury*, which issues it.

This requires a revolutionary dictatorship of the democracy, headed by the revolutionary proletariat; that is, it requires that the democracy should become revolutionary *in fact*. That is the crux of the matter. But that is just what is not wanted by our Socialist-Revolutionaries and Mensheviks, who are deceiving the people by displaying the *flag* of "revolutionary democracy" while they are in fact supporting the reactionary-bureaucratic policy of the bourgeoisie, who, as always, are guided by the rule: "*Après nous le déluge*"—after us the deluge!

We usually do not even notice how thoroughly we are permeated by anti-democratic habits and prejudices regarding the "sanctity" of bourgeois property. When an engineer or banker publishes the income and expenditure of a worker, information about his wages and the productivity of his labour, this is regarded as absolutely legitimate and fair. Nobody thinks of seeing it as an intrusion into the "private life" of the worker, as "spying or informing" on the part of the engineer. Bourgeois society regards the labour and earnings of a wage-worker as *its* open book, any bourgeois being entitled to peer into it at any moment, and at any moment to expose the "luxurious living" of the worker, his supposed "laziness", etc.

Well, and what about reverse control? What if the unions of employees, clerks and *domestic servants* were invited by a *democratic* state to verify the income and expenditure of capitalists, to publish information on the subject and to assist the government in combating concealment of incomes?

What a furious howl against "spying" and "informing" would be raised by the bourgeoisie! When "masters" control servants, or when capitalists control workers, this is considered to be in the nature of things; the private life of the working and exploited people is *not* considered inviolable. The bourgeoisie are entitled to call to account any "wage slave" and at any time to make public his income and expenditure. But if the oppressed attempt to control the oppressor, to show up *his* income and expenditure, to expose *his* luxurious living even in war-time, when his luxurious living is directly responsible for armies at the front starving and perishing—oh, no, the bourgeoisie will not tolerate "spying" and "informing"!

It all boils down to the same thing: the rule of the bourgeoisie *is irreconcilable* with truly-revolutionary true democracy. We cannot be revolutionary democrats in the twentieth century and in a capitalist country *if we fear* to advance towards socialism.

Can We Go Forward If We Fear
to Advance Towards Socialism?

What has been said so far may easily arouse the following objection on the part of a reader who has been brought up on the current opportunist ideas of the Socialist-Revolutionaries and Mensheviks. Most measures described here, he may say, are *already* in effect socialist and not democratic measures!

This current objection, one that is usually raised (in one form or another) in the bourgeois, Socialist-Revolutionary and Menshevik press, is a reactionary defence of backward capitalism, a defence decked out in a Struvean garb. It seems to say that we are not ripe for socialism, that it is too early to "introduce" socialism, that our revolution is a bourgeois revolution and therefore we must be the menials of the bourgeoisie (although the great bourgeois revolutionaries in France 125 years ago made their revolution a great revolution by exercising *terror* against all oppressors, landowners and capitalists alike!).

The pseudo-Marxist lackeys of the bourgeoisie, who have been joined by the Socialist-Revolutionaries and who argue in this way, do not understand (as an examination of the theoretical basis of their opinion shows) what imperialism is, what capitalist monopoly is, what the state is, and what revolutionary democracy is. For anyone who understands this is bound to admit that there can be no advance except towards socialism.

Everybody talks about imperialism. But imperialism is merely monopoly capitalism.

That capitalism in Russia has also become monopoly capitalism is sufficiently attested by the examples of the Produgol, the Prodamet, the Sugar Syndicate, etc. This Sugar Syndicate is an object-lesson in the way monopoly capitalism develops into state-monopoly capitalism.

And what is the state? It is an organisation of the ruling class—in Germany, for instance, of the Junkers and capitalists. And therefore what the German Plekhanovs (Scheidemann, Lensch, and others) call "war-time socialism" is in fact war-time state-monopoly capitalism, or, to put it more simply and clearly, war-time penal servitude for the workers and war-time protection for capitalist profits.

Now try to *substitute* for the Junker-capitalist state, for the landowner-capitalist state, a *revolutionary-democratic* state, i.e., a state which in a revolutionary way abolishes *all* privileges and does not fear to introduce the fullest democracy in a revolutionary way. You will find that, given a really revolutionary-democratic state, state-monopoly capitalism inevitably and unavoidably implies a step, and more than one step, towards socialism!

For if a huge capitalist undertaking becomes a monopoly, it means that it serves the whole nation. If it has become a state monopoly, it means that the state (i.e., the armed organisation of the population, the workers and peasants above all, provided there is *revolutionary* democracy) directs the whole undertaking. In whose interest?

Either in the interest of the landowners and capitalists, in which case we have not a revolutionary-democratic, but a reactionary-bureaucratic state, an imperialist republic.

Or in the interest of revolutionary democracy—and then *it is a step towards socialism*.

For socialism is merely the next step forward from state-capitalist monopoly. Or, in other words, socialism is merely state-capitalist monopoly *which is made to serve the interests of the whole people* and has to that extent *ceased* to be capitalist monopoly.

There is no middle course here. The objective process of development is such that it is *impossible* to advance from *monopolies* (and the war has magnified their number, role and importance tenfold) without advancing towards socialism.

Either we have to be revolutionary democrats in fact, in which case we must not fear to take steps towards socialism.

Or we fear to take steps towards socialism, condemn them in the Plekhanov, Dan or Chernov way, by arguing that our revolution is a bourgeois revolution, that socialism cannot be "introduced", etc., in which case we inevitably sink to the level of Kerensky, Milyukov and Kornilov, i.e., we in a *reactionary-bureaucratic* way suppress the "revolutionary-democratic" aspirations of the workers and peasants.

There is no middle course.

And therein lies the fundamental contradiction of our revolution.

It is impossible to stand still in history in general, and in war-time in particular. We must either advance or retreat. It is *impossible* in twentieth-century Russia, which has won a republic and democracy in a revolutionary way, to go forward without *advancing* towards socialism, without taking *steps* towards it (steps conditioned and determined by the level of technology and culture: large-scale machine production cannot be "introduced" in peasant agriculture nor abolished in the sugar industry).

But to fear to advance *means* retreating—which the Kerenskys, to the delight of the Milyukovs and Plekhanovs, and with the foolish assistance of the Tseretelis and Chernovs, are actually doing.

The dialectics of history is such that the war, by extraordinarily expediting the transformation of monopoly capitalism into state-monopoly capitalism, has *thereby* extraordinarily advanced mankind towards socialism.

Imperialist war is the eve of socialist revolution. And this not only because the horrors of the war give rise to proletarian revolt—no revolt can bring about socialism unless the economic conditions for socialism are ripe—but because state-monopoly capitalism is a complete *material* preparation for socialism, the *threshold* of socialism, a rung on the ladder of history between which and the rung called socialism *there are no intermediate rungs*.

* * *

Our Socialist-Revolutionaries and Mensheviks approach the question of socialism in a doctrinaire way, from the standpoint of a doctrine learnt by heart but poorly understood. They picture socialism as some remote, unknown and dim future.

But socialism is now gazing at us from all the windows of modern capitalism; socialism is outlined directly, *practically*, by every important measure that constitutes a forward step on the basis of this modern capitalism.

What is universal labour conscription?

It is a step forward on the basis of modern monopoly capitalism, a step towards the regulation of economic life as a whole, in accordance with a certain general plan, a step towards the economy of national labour and towards the prevention of its senseless wastage by capitalism.

In Germany it is the Junkers (landowners) and capitalists who are introducing universal labour conscription, and therefore it inevitably becomes war-time penal servitude for the workers.

But take the same institution and think over its significance in a revolutionary-democratic state. Universal labour conscription, introduced, regulated and directed by the Soviets of Workers', Soldiers' and Peasants' Deputies, will *still not* be socialism, but it will *no longer* be capitalism. It will be a tremendous *step towards* socialism, a step from which, if complete democracy is preserved, there can no longer be any retreat back to capitalism, without unparalleled violence being committed against the masses.

The Struggle Against Economic Chaos—and the War

A consideration of the measures to avert the impending catastrophe brings us to another supremely important question, namely, the connection between home and foreign policy, or, in other words, the relation between a war of conquest, an imperialist war, and a revolutionary, proletarian war, between a criminal predatory war and a just democratic war.

All the measures to avert catastrophe we have described would, as we have already stated, greatly enhance the defence potential, or, in other words, the military might of the country. That, on the one hand. On the other hand, these measures cannot be put into effect without turning the war of conquest into a just war, turning the war waged by the capitalists in the interests of the capitalists into a war waged by the proletariat in the interests of all the working and exploited people.

And, indeed, nationalisation of the banks and syndicates, taken in conjunction with the abolition of commercial secrecy and the establishment of workers' control over the capitalists, would not only imply a tremendous saving of national labour, the possibility of economising forces and means, but would also imply an improvement in the conditions of the working *masses*, of the majority of the population. As everybody knows, economic organisation is of decisive importance in modern warfare. Russia has enough grain, coal, oil and iron; in this respect, we are in a better position than any of the belligerent European countries. And given a struggle against economic chaos by the measures indicated above, enlisting popular initiative in this struggle, improving the people's conditions, and nationalising the banks and syndicates, Russia could use her revolution and her democracy to raise the whole country to an incomparably higher level of economic organisation.

If instead of the "coalition" with the bourgeoisie, which is hampering every measure of control and sabotaging production, the Socialist-Revolutionaries and Mensheviks had in April effected the transfer of power to the Soviets and had directed their efforts not to playing at "ministerial leapfrog", not to bureaucratically occupying, side by side with the Cadets, ministerial, deputy-ministerial and similar posts, but to guiding the workers and peasants in *their* control *over* the capitalists, in their *war against* the capitalists, Russia would now be a country completely transformed economically, with the land in the hands of the peasants, and with the banks nationalised, i.e., would *to that extent* (and these are extremely important economic bases of modern life) be *superior* to all other capitalist countries.

The defence potential, the military might, of a country whose banks have been nationalised is *superior* to that of a country whose banks remain in private hands. The military might of a peasant country whose land is in the hands of peasant committees is *superior* to that of a country whose land is in the hands of landowners....

Written September 10-14
(23-27), 1917

Published at the end of
October 1917 in pamphlet form
by Priboi Publishers (Petrograd)

Collected Works, Vol. 25,
pp. 323-24, 327-61

From THE TASKS OF THE REVOLUTION

Struggle Against Famine
and Economic Ruin

5. The Soviet Government must immediately introduce workers' control of production and distribution on a nation-wide scale. Experience since May 6 has shown that in the absence of such control all the promises of reforms and attempts to introduce them are powerless, and famine, accompanied by unprecedented catastrophe, is becoming a greater menace to the whole country week by week.

It is necessary to nationalise the banks and the insurance business immediately, and also the most important branches of industry (oil, coal, metallurgy, sugar, etc.), and at the same time, to abolish commercial secrets and to establish unrelaxing supervision by the workers and peasants over the negligible minority of capitalists who wax rich on government contracts and evade accounting and just taxation of their profits and property.

Such measures, which do not deprive either the middle peasants, the Cossacks or the small handicraftsmen of a single kopek, are urgently needed for the struggle against famine and are absolutely just because they distribute the burdens of the war equitably. Only after capitalist plunder has been curbed and the deliberate sabotage of production has been stopped will it be possible to work for an improvement in labour productivity, introduce universal labour conscription and the proper exchange of grain for manufactured goods, and return to the Treasury thousands of millions in paper money now being hoarded by the rich.

Without such measures, the abolition of the landed estates without compensation is also impossible, for the major part of the estates is mortgaged to the banks, so that the interests of the landowners and capitalists are inseparably linked up....

Written in the first half of
September 1917

Published in *Rabochy Put*
Nos. 20-21, October 9 and 10
(September 26 and 27), 1917
Signed: *N. K.*

Collected Works,
Vol. 26, p. 65

The chief difficulty facing the proletarian revolution is the establishment on a country-wide scale of the most precise and most conscientious accounting and control, of *workers' control* of the production and distribution of goods.

When the writers of *Novaya Zhizn* argued that in advancing the slogan "workers' control" we were slipping into syndicalism, this argument was an example of the stupid school-boy method of applying "Marxism" without studying it, just *learning it by rote* in the Struve manner. Syndicalism either repudiates the revolutionary dictatorship of the proletariat, or else relegates it, as it does political power in general, to a back seat. We, however, put it in the forefront. If we simply say in unison with the *Novaya Zhizn* writers: *not* workers' control *but* state control, it is simply a bourgeois-reformist phrase, it is, in essence, a purely Cadet formula, because the Cadets have no objection to the workers *participating* in "state" control. The Kornilovite Cadets know perfectly well that such participation offers the bourgeoisie the best way of fooling the workers, the most subtle way of politically *bribing* all the Gvozdyovs, Nikitins, Prokopoviches, Tseretelis and the rest of that gang.

When we say: "workers' control", always *juxtaposing* this slogan to dictatorship of the proletariat, always putting it *immediately after* the latter, we thereby explain what kind of state we mean. The state is the organ of *class* domination. Of which class? If of the bourgeoisie, then it is the Cadet-Kornilov-"Kerensky" state which has been "Kornilovising" and "Kerenskyising" the working people of Russia for more than six months. If it is of the proletariat, if we are speaking of a proletarian state, *that is*, of the proletarian dictatorship, then workers' control *can* become the country-wide, all-embracing, omnipresent, most precise and most conscientious *accounting* of the production and distribution of goods.

This is the chief difficulty, the chief task that faces the proletarian, i.e., socialist, revolution. Without the Soviets, this task would be impracticable, at least in Russia. The Soviets *indicate* to the proletariat the organisational work which *can* solve this historically important problem.

This brings us to another aspect of the question of the state apparatus. In addition to the chiefly "oppressive" apparatus—the standing army, the police and the bureaucracy—the modern state possesses an apparatus which has extremely close connections with the banks and syndicates, an apparatus which performs an enormous amount of accounting and registration work, if it may be expressed this way. This apparatus must not, and should not, be smashed. It must be wrested from the control of the capitalists; the capitalists and the wires they pull must be *cut off*, *lopped off*, *chopped away from* this apparatus; it must be *subordinated* to the proletarian Soviets; it must be expanded, made more comprehensive, and nation-wide. And this *can* be done by utilising the achievements already made by large-scale capitalism (in the same way as the proletarian revolution can, in general, reach its goal only by utilising these achievements).

Capitalism has created an accounting *apparatus* in the shape of the banks, syndicates, postal service, consumers' societies, and office employees' unions. *Without big banks socialism would be impossible.*

The big banks *are* the "state apparatus" which we *need* to bring about socialism, and which we *take ready-made* from capitalism; our task here is merely to *lop off* what *capitalistically mutilates* this excellent apparatus, to make it *even bigger*, even more democratic, even more comprehensive. Quantity will be transformed into quality. A single State Bank, the biggest of the big, with branches in every rural district, in every factory, will constitute as much as nine-tenths of the *socialist* apparatus. This will be country-wide *book-keeping,* country-wide *accounting* of the production and distribution of goods, this will be, so to speak, something in the nature of the *skeleton* of socialist society.

We can "lay hold of" and "set in motion" this "state apparatus" (which is not fully a state apparatus under capitalism, but which will be so with us, under socialism) at one stroke, by a single decree, because the actual work of book-keeping, control, registering, accounting and counting is performed by *employees*, the majority of whom themselves lead a proletarian or semi-proletarian existence.

By a single decree of the proletarian government these employees can and must be transferred to the status of state employees, in the same way as the watchdogs of capitalism like Briand and other bourgeois ministers, by a single decree, transfer railwaymen on strike to the status of state employees. We shall need many more state employees of this kind, and more *can* be obtained, because capitalism has simplified the work of accounting and control, has reduced it to a comparatively simple system of *book-keeping*, which any literate person can do.

The conversion of the bank, syndicate, commercial, etc., etc., rank-and-file employees into state employees is quite feasible both technically (thanks to the preliminary work performed for us by capitalism, including finance capitalism) and politically, provided the *Soviets* exercise control and supervision.

As for the higher officials, of whom there are very few, but who gravitate towards the capitalists, they will have to be dealt with in the same way as the capitalists, i.e., "severely". Like the capitalists, they will offer *resistance*. This resistance will have to be *broken*, and if the immortally-naïve Peshekhonov, as early as June 1917, lisped like the infant that he was in state affairs, that "the resistance of the capitalists has been broken", this childish phrase, this childish boast, this childish swagger, *will be converted by the proletariat into reality*.

We can do this, for it is merely a question of breaking the resistance of an insignificant minority of the population, literally a handful of people, over each of whom the employees' unions, the trade unions, the consumers' societies and the Soviets will institute such *supervision* that every Tit Titych will be *surrounded* as the French were at Sedan.[30] We know these Tit Tityches by name: we only have to consult the lists of directors, board members, large shareholders, etc. There are several hundred, at most several thousand of them in the *whole* of Russia, and the proletarian state, with the apparatus of the Soviets, of the employees' unions, etc., will be able to appoint ten or even a hundred supervisers to each of them, so that instead of "breaking resistance" it may even be possible, by means of *workers' control* (over the capitalists), to make all resistance *impossible*.

The important thing will not be even the confiscation of the capitalists' property, but country-wide, all-embracing workers' control over the capitalists and their possible supporters. Confiscation alone leads nowhere, as it does not contain the element of organisation, of accounting for proper distribution. Instead of confiscation, we could easily impose a *fair* tax (even on the Shingaryov scale, for instance), taking care, of course, to preclude the possibility of anyone evading assessment, concealing the truth, evading the law. And this possibility can be *eliminated only* by the workers' control of the *workers' state*.

Compulsory syndication, i.e., compulsory amalgamation in associations under state control—this is what capitalism has prepared the way for, this is what has been carried out in Germany by the Junkers' state, this is what can be easily carried out in Russia by the Soviets, by the proletarian dictatorship, and this is what will *provide us with a "state apparatus"* that will be universal, up-to-date, and non-bureaucratic.*

* * *

The fourth plea of the counsels for the bourgeoisie is that the proletariat will not be able "to set the state apparatus in motion". There is nothing new in this plea compared with the preceding one. We could not, of course, either lay hold of or set in motion the old apparatus. The

---

* For further details of the meaning of compulsory syndication see my pamphlet: *The Impending Catastrophe and How to Combat It.* (See pp. 55-90 of this book).—*Ed.*

new apparatus, the Soviets, *has already* been set in motion by "a mighty burst of creative enthusiasm that stems from the people themselves". We only have to free it from the *shackles* put on it by the domination of the Socialist-Revolutionary and Menshevik leaders. This apparatus *is already* in motion; we only have to free it from the monstrous, petty-bourgeois impediments preventing it from going full speed ahead.

Two circumstances must be considered here to supplement what has already been said. In the first place, the new means of control have been created *not* by us, but by capitalism in its military-imperialist stage; and in the second place, it is important to introduce more democracy into the *administration* of a proletarian state.

The grain monopoly and bread rationing were introduced not by us, but by the capitalist state in the war. It had already introduced universal labour conscription within the framework of capitalism, which is war-time penal servitude for the workers. But here too, as in all its history-making activities, the proletariat takes its weapons from capitalism and does not "invent" or "create them out of nothing".

The grain monopoly, bread rationing and labour conscription in the hands of the proletarian state, in the hands of sovereign Soviets, will be the most powerful means of accounting and control, means which, applied to the capitalists, and to *the rich in general*, applied to them by the *workers*, will provide a force unprecedented in history for "setting the state apparatus in motion", for overcoming the resistance of the capitalists, for subordinating them to the proletarian state. These means of control and of *compelling people to work* will be more potent than the laws of the Convention and its guillotine. The guillotine *only* terrorised, only broke *active* resistance. *For us, this is not enough.*

For us, this is not enough. We must not only "terrorise" the capitalists, i.e., make them feel the omnipotence of the proletarian state and give up all idea of actively resisting it. We must also break *passive* resistance, which is undoubtedly more dangerous and harmful. We must not only break resistance of every kind. We must also *compel the capitalists to work* within the framework of the new state organisation. It is not enough to "remove" the capitalists; we must (after removing the undesirable and incorrigible "resisters") employ them *in the service of the new state*. This applies both to the capitalists and to the upper section of the bourgeois intellectuals, office employees, etc.

And we have the means to do this. The means and instruments for this have been placed in our hands by the capitalist state in the war. These means are the grain monopoly, bread rationing and labour conscription. "He who does not work, neither shall he eat"—this is the fundamental, the first and most important rule the Soviets of Workers' Deputies can and will introduce when they become the ruling power.

Every worker has a work-book. This book does not degrade him, although *at present* it is undoubtedly a document of capitalist wage-slavery, certifying that the workman belongs to some parasite.

The Soviets will introduce work-books *for the rich* and *then* gradually for the whole population (in a peasant country work-books will probably not be needed for a long time for the overwhelming majority of the peasants). The work-book will cease to be the badge of the "common herd", a document of the "lower" orders, a certificate of wage-slavery. It will become a document certifying that in the new society there are no longer any "workmen", nor, on the other hand, are there any longer men *who do not work*.

The rich will be obliged to get a work-book from the workers' or office employees' union with which their occupation is most closely connected, and every week, or other definite fixed period, they will have to get from that union a certificate to the effect that they are performing their work conscientiously; without this they will not be able to receive bread ration cards or provisions in general. The proletarian state will say: we need good organisers of banking and the amalgamation of enterprises (in this matter the capitalists have more experience, and it is easier to work with experienced people), and we need far, far more engineers, agronomists, technicians and scientifically trained specialists of every kind than were needed before. We shall give all these specialists work to which they are accustomed and which they can cope with; in all probability we shall introduce complete wage equality only gradually and shall pay these specialists higher salaries during the transition period. We shall place them, however, under comprehensive workers' control and we shall achieve the complete and absolute operation of the rule "He who does not work, neither shall he eat". We shall not invent the organisational form of the work, but take it ready-made from capitalism—we shall take over the banks, syndicates, the best factories, experimental stations, academies, and so forth; all that we shall have to do is to borrow the best models furnished by the advanced countries.

Of course, we shall not in the least descend to a utopia, we are not deserting the soil of most sober, practical reason when we say that the entire capitalist class will offer the most stubborn resistance, but this resistance will be broken by the organisation of the entire population in Soviets. Those capitalists who are exceptionally stubborn and recalcitrant will, of course, have to be punished by the confiscation of their whole property and by imprisonment. On the other hand, however, the victory of the proletariat will bring about *an increase* in the number of cases of the kind that I read about in today's *Izvestia* for example:

"On September 26, two engineers came to the Central Council of Factory Committees to report that a group of engineers had decided to form a union of socialist engineers. The Union believes that the present time is actually the beginning of the social revolution and places itself at the disposal of the working people, desiring, in defence of the workers' interests, to work in complete unity with the workers' organisations. The representatives of the Central Council of Factory Committees answered that the Council will gladly set up in its organisation an Engineers' Section which wil embody in its programme the main theses of the First Conference of Factory Committees on workers' control over production. A joint meeting of delegates of the Central Council of Factory Committees and of the initiative group of socialist engineers will be held within the next few days." (*Izvestia*, September 27, 1917.)

Written at the end of
September-October 1 (14), 1917

Published in October 1917 in
the magazine *Prosveshcheniye*
No. 1-2

Collected Works,
Vol. 26, pp. 104-11

1. *Workers' control* over the production, storage, purchase and sale of all products and raw materials shall be introduced in all industrial, commercial, banking, agricultural and other enterprises employing not less than five workers and office employees (together), or with an annual turnover of not less than 10,000 rubles.

2. Workers' control shall be exercised by all the workers and office employees of an enterprise, either directly, if the enterprise is small enough to permit it, or through their elected representatives, who shall be elected *immediately* at general meetings, at which minutes of the elections shall be taken and the names of those elected communicated to the government and to the local Soviets of Workers', Soldiers' and Peasants' Deputies.

3. Unless permission is given by the elected representatives of the workers and office employees, the suspension of work of an enterprise or an industrial establishment of state importance (see Clause 7), or any change in its operation, is strictly prohibited.

4. The elected representatives shall be given access to *all* books and documents and to *all* warehouses and stocks of materials, instruments and products, without exception.

5. The decisions of the elected representatives of the workers and office employees are binding upon the owners of enterprises and may be annulled only by trade unions and their congresses.

6. In all enterprises of state importance *all* owners and

all representatives of the workers and office employees elected for the purpose of exercising workers' control shall be answerable to the state for the maintenance of the strictest order and discipline and for the protection of property. Persons guilty of dereliction of duty, concealment of stocks, accounts, etc., shall be punished by the confiscation of the whole of their property and by imprisonment for a term of up to five years.

7. By enterprises of state importance are meant all enterprises working for defence, or in any way connected with the manufacture of articles necessary for the existence of the masses of the population.

8. More detailed rules on workers' control shall be drawn up by the local Soviets of Workers' Deputies and by conferences of factory committees, and also by committees of office employees at general meetings of their representatives.

Written October 26 or 27
(November 8 or 9), 1917

First published in 1929 in the
second and third editions of
Lenin's *Collected Works,*
Vol. XXII

Collected Works,
Vol. 26, pp. 264-65

TO THE POPULATION

Comrades—workers, soldiers, peasants and all working people!

The workers' and peasants' revolution has definitely triumphed in Petrograd, having dispersed or arrested the last remnants of the small number of Cossacks deceived by Kerensky. The revolution has triumphed in Moscow too. Even before the arrival of a number of troop trains dispatched from Petrograd, the officer cadets and other Kornilovites in Moscow signed peace terms—the disarming of the cadets and the dissolution of the Committee of Salvation.[32]

Daily and hourly reports are coming in from the front and from the villages announcing the support of the overwhelming majority of the soldiers in the trenches and the peasants in the uyezds for the new government and its decrees on peace and the immediate transfer of the land to the peasants. The victory of the workers' and peasants' revolution is assured because the majority of the people have already sided with it.

It is perfectly understandable that the landowners and capitalists, and the *top groups* of office employees and civil servants closely linked with the bourgeoisie, in a word, all the wealthy and those supporting them, react to the new revolution with hostility, resist its victory, threaten to close the banks, disrupt or bring to a standstill the work of the different establishments, and hamper the revolution in every way, openly or covertly. Every politically-conscious worker was well aware that we would inevitably encounter resistance of this kind. The entire Party press of the Bolsheviks has written about this on numerous occasions. Not for a single minute will the working classes be intimidated by this resistance; they will not falter in any way before the threats and strikes of the supporters of the bourgeoisie.

The majority of the people are with us. The majority of the working and oppressed people all over the world are with us. Ours is the cause of justice. Our victory is assured.

The resistance of the capitalists and the high-ranking employees will be smashed. Not a single person will be deprived of his property except under the special state law proclaiming nationalisation of the banks and syndicates. This law is being drafted. Not one of the working people will suffer the loss of a kopek; on the contrary, he will be helped. Apart from the strictest accounting and control, apart from levying the set taxes in full the government has no intention of introducing any other measure.

In support of these just demands the vast majority of the people have rallied around the Provisional Workers' and Peasants' Government.

Comrades, working people! Remember that now *you yourselves* are at the helm of state. No one will help you if you yourselves do not unite and take into *your* hands *all affairs* of the state. *Your* Soviets are from now on the organs of state authority, legislative bodies with full powers.

Rally around your Soviets. Strengthen them. Get on with the job yourselves; begin right at the bottom, do not wait for anyone. Establish the strictest revolutionary law and order, mercilessly suppress any attempts to create anarchy by drunkards, hooligans, counter-revolutionary officer cadets, Kornilovites and their like.

Ensure the strictest control over production and accounting of products. Arrest and hand over to the revolutionary courts all who dare to injure the people's cause, irrespective of whether the injury is manifested in sabotaging production (damage, delay and subversion), or in hoarding grain and products or holding up shipments of grain, disorganising the railways and the postal, telegraph and telephone services, or any resistance whatever to the great cause of peace, the cause of transferring the land to the peasants, of ensuring workers' control over the production and distribution of products.

Comrades, workers, soldiers, peasants and all working people! Take *all* power into the hands of *your* Soviets. Be watchful and guard like the apple of your eye your land, grain, factories, equipment, products, transport—all that from now onwards will be *entirely* your property, public property. Gradually, with the consent and approval of the majority of the peasants, in keeping with their *practical* experience and that of the workers, we shall go forward firmly and unswervingly to the victory of socialism—a victory that will be sealed by the advanced workers of the most civilised countries, bring the peoples lasting peace and liberate them from all oppression and exploitation.

November 5, 1917,
Petrograd

V. Ulyanov (Lenin),
Chairman of the Council of People's Commissars

Pravda No. 4
(evening edition),
November 19 (6), 1917

Collected Works,
Vol. 26, pp. 296-98

THESES FOR A LAW ON THE CONFISCATION OF APARTMENT AND TENEMENT HOUSES[33]

1) *All* land (urban) shall become the property of the nation.

2) Houses which are *systematically* let to tenants shall be confiscated and become the property of the nation.

3) Owners of houses that are *not* let to tenants shall, pending the decision of the Constituent Assembly, remain in possession without any change in their rights of ownership.

4) Several-months compensation (2 to 3 months) to owners of confiscated houses who can prove their...*

5) Rent shall be collected by (whom?) the *Soviets* (paid into the current accounts of the Soviets).

6) Building committees (the trade unions + building offices) shall take charge also of house supplies (fuel, etc.).

7) Rent payment to come in force immediately.

8) The building and house committees shall come into force gradually as and when they are set up by the trade unions and the Soviets.

9) The heating of the houses and their normal upkeep shall be the duty of the house committees and other institutions (trade unions, Soviets, fuel departments of the town council, etc.).

Written November 20
(December 3), 1917

First published in 1933 in
Lenin Miscellany XXI

Collected Works,
Vol. 42, p. 39

---

* The sentence is unfinished.—*Ed.*

TO A. G. SHLYAPNIKOV
AND F. E. DZERZHINSKY

Comrade Shlyapnikov and Comrade Dzerzhinsky

The bearer, Comrade Vorobyov, a delegate from the Urals, has excellent references from his local organisation. In the Urals, there is a most acute problem. The boards of the Urals works *here* (with offices in Petrograd) should be *arrested* immediately, threatened with (revolutionary) court proceedings for bringing about a crisis in the Urals, while all the works in the Urals should be *confiscated*. Draw up a draft decree as soon as possible.[34]

Lenin

Written at the end of November
(beginning of December), 1917

First published April 22, 1920
in the newspaper *Uralsky*
Rabochy (Yekaterinburg) No. 95

Collected Works,
Vol. 36, p. 459

REPORT ON THE ECONOMIC CONDITION
OF PETROGRAD WORKERS AND THE TASKS
OF THE WORKING CLASS, DELIVERED
AT A MEETING OF THE WORKERS' SECTION
OF THE PETROGRAD SOVIET OF WORKERS'
AND SOLDIERS' DEPUTIES
DECEMBER 4 (17), 1917

Newspaper Report

The Revolution of October 25 had shown the exceptional political maturity of the proletariat and its ability to stand firm in opposition to the bourgeoisie, said the speaker. The complete victory of socialism, however, would require a tremendous organisational effort filled with the knowledge that the proletariat must become the ruling class.

The proletariat was faced with the tasks of transforming the state system on socialist lines, for no matter how easy it would be to cite arguments in favour of a middle course such a course would be insignificant, the country's economic situation having reached a state that would rule out any middle course. There was no place left for half-measures in the gigantic struggle against imperialism and capitalism. The point at issue was—win or lose.

The workers should and did understand this; this was obvious because they had rejected half-way, compromise decisions. The more profound the revolution, the greater the number of active workers required to accomplish the replacement of capitalism by a socialist machinery. Even if there were no sabotage, the forces of the petty bourgeoisie would be inadequate. The task was one that could be accomplished only by drawing on the masses, only by the independent activity of the masses. The proletariat, therefore, should not think of improving its position at the moment, but should think of becoming the ruling class. It could not be expected that the rural proletariat would be clearly and firmly conscious of its own interests. Only the working class could be, and every proletarian, conscious of the great prospects, should feel himself to be a leader and carry the masses with him.

The proletariat should become the ruling class in the sense of being the leader of all who work; it should be the ruling class politically.

The prejudice that only the bourgeoisie could run the state must be fought against. The proletariat must take the rule of the state upon itself.

The capitalists were doing everything they could to complicate the tasks of the working class. And all working-class organisations—trade unions, factory committees and others—would have to conduct a determined struggle in the economic sphere. The bourgeoisie was spoiling every-thing, sabotaging everything, in order to wreck the work-ing-class revolution. And the tasks of organising produc-tion devolved entirely on the working class. They should do away, once and for all, with the prejudice that state affairs or the management of banks and factories were beyond the power of the workers. All this could be solved only by tremendous day-to-day organisational work.

It was essential to organise the exchange of products and introduce regular accounting and control—these were tasks for the working class, and the knowledge necessary for their accomplishment had been provided by factory life.

Every factory committee should concern itself not only with the affairs of its own factory, but should also be an organisation nucleus helping arrange the life of the state as a whole.

It was easy to issue a decree on the abolition of private property, but it must and could be implemented only by the workers themselves. Let there be mistakes—they would be the mistakes of a new class creating a new way of life.

There was not and could not be a definite plan for the organisation of economic life.

Nobody could provide one. But it could be done from below, by the masses, through their experience. Instruc-tions would, of course, be given and ways would be indicated, but it was necessary to begin simultaneously from above and from below.

The Soviets would have to become bodies regulating all production in Russia, but in order that they should not become staff headquarters without troops, work in the lower echelons was needed. . . .*

The working-class masses must set about the organisation of control and production on a country-wide scale. Not the organisation of individuals, but the organisation of all the working people, would be a guarantee of success; if they achieved that, if they organised economic life, everything opposing them would disappear of its own accord.

Pravda No. 208,
December 20 (7), 1917
and *Soldatskaya Pravda* No. 104,
December 14, 1917

Collected Works,
Vol. 26, pp. 364-66

---

* Several illegible words were omitted.—*Ed.*

SPEECH ON THE NATIONALISATION
OF THE BANKS DELIVERED AT A MEETING
OF THE ALL-RUSSIA CENTRAL EXECUTIVE
COMMITTEE
DECEMBER 14 (27), 1917[35]

Minutes

The last speaker tried to intimidate us by asserting that we are heading towards an abyss, towards certain destruction. There is, however, nothing new for us in this intimidation. *Novaya Zhizn*, the newspaper that expresses the views of the group to which the speaker[36] belongs, said before the October days that our revolution would bring nothing but disorders and anarchic riots. Talk about our travelling the wrong road is, therefore, a reflection of bourgeois psychology that even disinterested people cannot get rid of. (*Voice from among the internationalists*: "Demagogy!") No, that is not demagogy, it is your constant talk of the axe that is real demagogy.

The measures proposed in the decree are only an effective way of ensuring control.

You speak of the intricacy of the machinery, of its fragility and of the involved nature of the problem—these are elementary truths that everybody is aware of. But if these truths are merely used to put a brake on all socialist undertakings, we say that anyone who takes that line is a demagogue, and a dangerous demagogue at that.

We want to begin an inventory of the vaults, but the learned specialists tell us there is nothing in them but documents and securities. Then what is there bad about representatives of the people checking them?

If what they say is true, why do those same learned

specialists who criticise us not come out with it openly? Whenever the Council makes decisions they declare that they agree with us, but only in principle. This is the way of the bourgeois intelligentsia, of all conciliators, who ruin everything with their constant agreement in principle and disagreement in practice.

If you know so much about all these things and have the experience, why don't you help us, why do we meet with nothing but sabotage from you in our difficult task?

You proceed from a correct scientific theory, but for us theory forms the basis of actions to be undertaken, it gives us confidence in those actions and does not scare the life out of us. Of course it is difficult to make a beginning and we often come up against fragile things; nevertheless we have coped with them, are coping with them and shall continue to cope with them.

If book-learning were to serve no other purpose than that of hampering every new step and instilling eternal fear of the new, it would be useless.

Nobody, with the exception of the utopian socialists, has ever asserted that victory is possible without resistance, without the dictatorship of the proletariat and without seizing the old world in an iron grip.

You accepted this dictatorship in principle, but when that word is translated into Russian, called an "iron grip" and applied in practice, you warn us of the fragility and involved nature of the matter.

You stubbornly refuse to see that the iron hand that destroys also creates. It is an undoubted advantage to us to go over from principles to deeds.

To effect control we have called upon the bankers and together with them have elaborated measures that they agreed to, so that loans could be obtained under full control and properly accounted for. But there are people among the bank employees who have the interests of the people at heart and who have told us: "They are deceiving you, make haste and check their criminal activity that is directly harmful to you." And we did make haste.

We realise that this is an involved measure. None of us, even those who are trained economists, will undertake to carry it out. We shall invite the specialists who are engaged in that work, but only when we have the keys in our own hands. Then we shall even be able to draw advisers from the former millionaires. We invite anybody who wants to work as long as he does not try to reduce every revolutionary enterprise to mere words; that is something we shall not stand for. We use the words "dictatorship of the proletariat" in all seriousness and we shall effect that dictatorship.

We wanted to take the line of agreement with the banks, we gave them loans to finance factories, but they carried out sabotage on an unprecedented scale, and practical experience has forced us to adopt other measures of control.

A comrade from the Left Socialist-Revolutionaries[37] has said that in principle they would vote for the immediate nationalisation of the banks and afterwards work out practical measures in the shortest possible time. But he was wrong in that, because our draft does not contain anything but principles. The Supreme Economic Council is waiting to discuss them, but if the decree is not approved the banks will immediately do everything to further disrupt the economy.

The adoption of the decree is urgent, otherwise opposition and sabotage will ruin us. (*Stormy applause.*)

Pravda No. 216,
December 29 (16), 1917
and *Izvestia* No. 253,
December 16. 1917

Collected Works,
Vol. 26, pp. 388-90

DRAFT DECREE ON THE NATIONALISATION
OF THE BANKS AND ON MEASURES NECESSARY
FOR ITS IMPLEMENTATION

The critical food situation and the threat of famine caused by the profiteering and sabotage of the capitalists and officials, as well as by the general economic ruin, make it imperative to adopt extraordinary revolutionary measures to combat this evil.

To enable all citizens of the state, and in the first place all the working classes, to undertake this struggle under the leadership of their Soviets of Workers', Soldiers' and Peasants' Deputies, and normalise the country's economic life immediately and comprehensively, stopping at nothing and acting in the most revolutionary manner, the following regulations are decreed:

Draft Decree on the Nationalisation
of the Banks and on Measures Necessary
for Its Implementation

1. All joint-stock companies are proclaimed the property of the state.

2. Members of boards and directors of joint-stock companies, as well as all shareholders belonging to the wealthy classes (i.e., possessing property to the value of over 5,000 rubles or an income exceeding 500 rubles per month), shall be obliged to continue to conduct the affairs of these enterprises in good order, observing the law on workers'

control, presenting all shares to the State Bank and submitting to the local Soviets of Workers', Soldiers' and Peasants' Deputies weekly reports on their activities.

3. State loans, foreign and domestic, are annulled (abrogated).

4. The interests of small holders of bonds and all kinds of shares, i.e., holders belonging to the working classes of the population, shall be fully guaranteed.

5. Universal labour conscription is introduced. All citizens of both sexes between the ages of sixteen and fifty-five shall be obliged to perform work assigned to them by the local Soviets of Workers', Soldiers' and Peasants' Deputies, or by other bodies of Soviet power.

6. As a first step towards the introduction of universal labour conscription, it is decreed that members of the wealthy classes (see § 2) shall be obliged to keep, and have entries properly made in, consumer-worker books, or worker budget books, which must be presented to the appropriate workers' organisations or to the local Soviets and their bodies for weekly recording of the performance of work undertaken by each.

7. For the purpose of proper accounting and distribution of food and other necessities, every citizen of the state shall be obliged to join a consumers' society. The food boards, committees of supplies and other similar organisations, as well as the railway and transport unions, shall, under the direction of the Soviets of Workers', Soldiers' and Peasants' Deputies, establish supervision to ensure the observance of the present law. Members of the wealthy classes, in particular, shall be obliged to perform the work to be assigned to them by the Soviets in the sphere of organising and conducting the affairs of the consumers' societies.

8. The railway workers' and employees' unions shall be obliged urgently to draw up and immediately begin to carry into effect emergency measures for the better organisation of transport, particularly as regards the delivery of food, fuel and other prime necessities, and shall be guided in the first place by the instructions and orders of the Soviets of Workers', Soldiers' and Peasants' Deputies and then of the bodies authorised by the latter, and of the Supreme Economic Council.

Similarly, the railway unions, working in conjunction with the local Soviets, shall be responsible for most vigorously combating speculation in food and mercilessly suppressing all profiteering, not hesitating to adopt revolutionary measures.

9. Workers' organisations, unions of office employees and local Soviets shall be obliged immediately to set about switching enterprises which are closing down or are to be demobilised, and also unemployed workers to useful work and the production of necessities, and to search for orders, raw materials and fuel. While under no circumstances postponing either this work or the beginning of the exchange of farm produce for industrial goods pending receipt of special instructions from higher bodies, the local unions and Soviets shall be strictly guided by the orders and instructions of the Supreme Economic Council.

10. Members of the wealthy classes shall be obliged to keep all their monetary possessions in the State Bank and its branches, or in the savings-banks, and shall be entitled to withdraw not more than 100-125 rubles a week (as shall be established by the local Soviets) for living expenses; withdrawals for the needs of production and trade shall be made only on presentation of written certificates of the organs of workers' control.

To supervise the due observance of the present law, regulations will be introduced providing for the exchange of existing currency notes for new currency notes. All the property of persons guilty of deceiving the state and the people shall be confiscated.

11. All offenders against the present law, saboteurs and government officials who go on strike, as well as profiteers, shall be liable to a similar penalty, and also to imprisonment, dispatch to the front, or hard labour. The local Soviets and bodies under their jurisdiction shall urgently decide upon the most revolutionary measures to combat these real enemies of the people.

12. The trade unions and other organisations of the working people, in conjunction with the local Soviets, and with the collaboration of the most reliable persons recommended by Party and other organisations, shall form mobile groups of inspectors to supervise the implementation of the present law, to verify the quantity and quality of

work performed and to bring to trial before the revolutionary courts persons guilty of violating or evading the law.

The workers and office employees of the nationalised enterprises must exert every effort and adopt extraordinary measures to improve the organisation of the work, strengthen discipline and raise the productivity of labour. The organs of workers' control are to present to the Supreme Economic Council weekly reports on the results achieved in this respect. Those found guilty of shortcomings and neglect are to be brought before revolutionary courts.

Written not earlier than
December 14 (27), 1917

Collected Works,
Vol. 26, pp. 391-94

First published in part in
November 1918 in the
magazine *Narodnoye
Khozyaistvo* No. 11

First published in full
in 1949 in the 4th Russian
edition of V. I. Lenin's
Collected Works. Vol. 26

HOW TO ORGANISE COMPETITION?[38]

Bourgeois authors have been using up reams of paper praising competition, private enterprise, and all the other magnificent virtues and blessings of the capitalists and the capitalist system. Socialists have been accused of refusing to understand the importance of these virtues, and of ignoring "human nature". As a matter of fact, however, capitalism long ago replaced small, independent commodity production, under which competition could develop enterprise, energy and bold initiative to any *considerable* extent, by large- and very large-scale factory production, joint-stock companies, syndicates and other monopolies. Under *such* capitalism, competition means the incredibly brutal suppression of the enterprise, energy and bold initiative of the *mass* of the population, of its overwhelming majority, of ninety-nine out of every hundred toilers; it also means that competition is replaced by financial fraud, nepotism, servility on the upper rungs of the social ladder.

Far from extinguishing competition, socialism, on the contrary, for the first time creates the opportunity for employing it on a really *wide* and on a really *mass* scale, for actually drawing the majority of working people into a field of labour in which they can display their abilities, develop their capacities, and reveal talents, which are so abundant among the people and which capitalism crushed, suppressed and strangled by the thousand and million.

Now that a socialist government is in power our task is to organise competition.

The hangers-on and spongers on the bourgeoisie described socialism as a uniform, routine, monotonous and drab barrack system. The lackeys of the money-bags, the lickspittles of the exploiters, the bourgeois intellectual gentlemen used socialism as a bogey to "frighten" the people, who, under capitalism, were doomed to the penal servitude and the barrack-like discipline of arduous, monotonous toil, to a life of dire poverty and semi-starvation. The first step towards the emancipation of the people from this penal servitude is the confiscation of the landed estates, the introduction of workers' control and the nationalisation of the banks. The next steps will be the nationalisation of the factories, the compulsory organisation of the whole population in consumers' societies, which are at the same time societies for the sale of products, and the state monopoly of the trade in grain and other necessities.

Only now is the opportunity created for the truly mass display of enterprise, competition and bold initiative. Every factory from which the capitalist has been ejected, or in which he has at least been curbed by genuine workers' control, every village from which the landowning exploiter has been smoked out and his land confiscated has only now become a field in which the working man can reveal his talents, unbend his back a little, rise to his full height, and feel that he is a human being. For the first time after centuries of working for others, of forced labour for the exploiter, it has become possible to *work for oneself* and moreover to employ all the achievements of modern technology and culture in one's work.

Of course, this greatest change in human history from working under compulsion to working for oneself cannot take place without friction, difficulties, conflicts and violence against the inveterate parasites and their hangers-on. No worker has any illusions on that score. The workers and poor peasants, hardened by dire want and by many long years of slave labour for the exploiters, by their countless insults and acts of violence, realise that it will take time to *break* the resistance of those exploiters. The workers and peasants are not in the least infected with the sentimental illusions of the intellectual gentlemen, of the *Novaya Zhizn* crowd and other slush, who "shouted" themselves hoarse "denouncing" the capitalists and "gesticulated" against them, only to burst into tears and to behave like whipped puppies when it came to *deeds*, to putting threats into action, to carrying out in practice the work of *removing* the capitalists.

The great change from working under compulsion to working for oneself, to labour planned and organised on a gigantic, national (and to a certain extent international, world) scale, also requires—in addition to *"military"* measures for the suppression of the exploiters' resistance—tremendous *organisational*, organising effort on the part of the proletariat and the poor peasants. The organisational task is interwoven to form a single whole with the task of ruthlessly suppressing by military methods yesterday's slave-owners (capitalists) and their packs of lackeys—the bourgeois intellectual gentlemen. Yesterday's slave-owners and their "intellectual" stooges say and think, "We have always been organisers and chiefs. We have commanded, and we want to continue doing so. We shall refuse to obey the 'common people', the workers and peasants. We shall not submit to them. We shall convert knowledge into a weapon for the defence of the privileges of the money-bags and of the rule of capital over the people."

That is what the bourgeoisie and the bourgeois intellectuals say, think, and do. From the point of view of *self-interest* their behaviour is comprehensible. The hangers-on and spongers on the feudal landowners, the priests, the scribes, the bureaucrats as Gogol depicted them, and the "intellectuals" who hated Belinsky, also found it "hard" to part with serfdom. But the cause of the exploiters and of their "intellectual" menials is hopeless. The workers and peasants are beginning to break down their resistance—unfortunately, not yet firmly, resolutely and ruthlessly enough—*and break it down they will*.

"They" think that the "common people", the "common" workers and poor peasants, will be unable to cope with the great, truly heroic, in the world-historic sense of the word, organisational tasks which the socialist revolution has imposed upon the working people. The intellectuals who are accustomed to serving the capitalists and the capitalist state say in order to console themselves: "You cannot do without us." But their insolent assumption has no truth in it; educated men are already making their appearance on the side of the people, on the side of the working people, and are helping to break the resistance of the servants of capital. There are a great many talented organisers among the peasants and the working class, and they are only just beginning to become aware of themselves, to awaken, to stretch out towards great, vital, creative work, to tackle with their own forces the task of building socialist society.

One of the most important tasks today, if not the most important, is to develop this independent initiative of the workers, and of all the working and exploited people generally, develop it as widely as possible in creative *organisational* work. At all costs we must break the old, *absurd,* savage, despicable and disgusting prejudice that only the so-called "upper classes", only the rich, and those who have gone through the school of the rich, are capable of administering the state and directing the organisational development of socialist society.

This is a prejudice fostered by rotten routine, by petrified views, slavish habits, and still more by the sordid selfishness of the capitalists, in whose interest it is to administer while plundering and to plunder while administering. No. The workers will not forget for a moment that they need the power of knowledge. The extraordinary striving after knowledge which the workers reveal, particularly now, shows that mistaken ideas about this do not and cannot exist among the proletariat. But every *rank-and-file* worker and peasant who can read and write, who can judge people and has practical experience, is capable of *organisational* work. Among the "common people", of whom the bourgeois intellectuals speak with such haughtiness and contempt, there are *many* such men and women. This sort of talent among the working class and the peasants is a rich and still untapped source.

The workers and peasants are still "timid", they have not yet become accustomed to the idea that *they* are now the *ruling* class; they are not yet resolute enough. The revolution could not *at one stroke* instil these qualities into millions and millions of people who all their lives had been compelled by want and hunger to work under the threat of the stick. But the Revolution of October 1917 is strong, viable and invincible because it *awakens* these qualities, breaks down the old impediments, removes the worn-out shackles, and leads the working people on to the road of the *independent* creation of a new life.

Accounting and control—this is the *main* economic task of every Soviet of Workers', Soldiers' and Peasants' Deputies, of every consumers' society, of every union or committee of supplies, of every factory committee or organ of workers' control in general.

We must fight against the old habit of regarding the measure of labour and the means of production from the point of view of the slave whose sole aim is to lighten the burden of labour or to obtain at least some little bit *from the bourgeoisie*. The advanced, class-conscious workers have already started this fight, and they are offering determined resistance to the newcomers who flocked to the factory world in particularly large numbers during the war and who now would like to treat the *people's* factory, the factory that has come into the possession of the people, in the old way, with the sole aim of "snatching the biggest possible piece of the pie and clearing out". All the class-conscious, honest and thinking peasants and working people will take their place in this fight by the side of the advanced workers.

Accounting and control, *if* carried on by the Soviets of Workers', Soldiers' and Peasants' Deputies as the supreme state power, or on the instructions, on the authority, of *this* power—widespread, general, universal accounting and control, the accounting and control of the amount of labour performed and of the distribution of products—is the *essence* of socialist transformation, once the political rule of the proletariat has been established and secured.

The accounting and control essential for the transition to socialism can be exercised only by the people. Only the voluntary and conscientious co-operation of the *mass* of the workers and peasants in accounting and controlling *the rich, the rogues, the idlers and the rowdies*, a co-operation marked by revolutionary enthusiasm, can conquer these survivals of accursed capitalist society, these dregs of humanity, these hopelessly decayed and atrophied limbs, this contagion, this plague, this ulcer that socialism has inherited from capitalism.

Workers and peasants, working and exploited people! The land, the banks and the factories have now become the property of the entire people! You *yourselves* must set to work to take account of and control the production and distribution of products—this, and this *alone* is the road to the victory of socialism, the guarantee of its victory, the guarantee of victory over all exploitation, over all poverty and want! For there is enough bread, iron, timber, wool, cotton and flax in Russia to satisfy the needs of everyone, if only labour and its products are properly distributed, if only a *business-like, practical* control over this distribution by the entire people is established, provided only we can defeat the enemies of the people: the rich and their hangers-on, and the rogues, the idlers and the rowdies, *not only* in politics, but also in *everyday economic* life.

No mercy for these enemies of the people, the enemies of socialism, the enemies of the working people! War to the death against the rich and their hangers-on, the bourgeois intellectuals; war on the rogues, the idlers and the rowdies! All of them are of the same brood—the spawn of capitalism, the offspring of aristocratic and bourgeois society; the society in which a handful of men robbed and insulted the people; the society in which poverty and want forced thousands and thousands on to the path of rowdyism, corruption and roguery, and caused them to lose all human semblance; the society which inevitably cultivated in the working man the desire to escape exploitation even by means of deception, to wriggle out of it, to escape, if only for a moment, from loathsome labour, to procure at least a crust of bread by any possible means, at any cost, so as not to starve, so as to subdue the pangs of hunger suffered by himself and by his near ones.

The rich and the rogues are two sides of the same coin, they are the two principal categories of *parasites* which capitalism fostered; they are the principal enemies of socialism. These enemies must be placed under the special surveillance of the entire people; they must be ruthlessly punished for the slightest violation of the laws and regulations of socialist society. Any display of weakness, hesitation or sentimentality in this respect would be an immense crime against socialism.

In order to render these parasites harmless to socialist society we must organise the accounting and control of the amount of work done and of production and distribution by the entire people, by millions and millions of workers and peasants, participating voluntarily, energetically and with revolutionary enthusiasm. And in order to organise this accounting and control, which is *fully within the ability* of every honest, intelligent and efficient worker and peasant, we must rouse their organising talent, the talent that is to be found in their midst; we must rouse among them—and organise on a national scale—*competition* in the sphere of organisational achievement; the workers and peasants must be brought to see clearly the difference between the necessary advice of an educated man and the necessary control by the "common" worker and peasant of the *slovenliness* that is so usual among the "educated".

This slovenliness, this carelessness, untidiness, unpunctuality, nervous haste, the inclination to substitute discussion for action, talk for work, the inclination to undertake everything under the sun without finishing anything, are characteristics of the "educated"; and this is not due to the fact that they are bad by nature, still less is it due to their evil will; it is due to all their habits of life, the conditions of their work, to fatigue, to the abnormal separation of mental from manual labour, and so on, and so forth.

Among the mistakes, shortcomings and defects of our revolution a by no means unimportant place is occupied by the mistakes, etc., which are due to these deplorable—but at present inevitable—characteristics of the intellectuals in our midst, and to the *lack* of sufficient supervision by the *workers* over the *organisational* work of the intellectuals.

The workers and peasants are still "timid"; they must get rid of this timidity, and they *certainly* will get rid of it. We cannot dispense with the advice, the instruction of educated people, of intellectuals and specialists. Every sensible worker and peasant understands this perfectly well, and the intellectuals in our midst cannot complain of a lack of attention and comradely respect on the part of the workers and peasants. Advice and instruction, however, is one thing, and the organisation of *practical* accounting and control is another. Very often the intellectuals give excellent advice and instruction, but they prove to be ridiculously, *absurdly*, shamefully "unhandy" and incapable of *carrying out* this advice and instruction, of exercising *practical control* over the translation of words into deeds.

In this very respect it is utterly impossible to dispense with the help and the *leading role* of the practical organisers from among the "people", from among the factory workers and working peasants. "It is not the gods who make pots"—this is the truth that the workers and peasants should get well drilled into their minds. They must understand that the whole thing now is *practical work*; that the historical moment has arrived when theory is being transformed into practice, vitalised by practice, corrected by practice, tested by practice; when the words of Marx, "Every step of real movement is more important than a dozen programmes",[39] become particularly true—every step in really curbing in practice, restricting, fully registering the rich and the rogues and keeping them under control is worth more than a dozen excellent arguments about socialism. For, "theory, my friend, is grey, but green is the eternal tree of life".[40]

Competition must be arranged between practical organisers from among the workers and peasants. Every attempt to establish stereotyped forms and to impose uniformity from above, as intellectuals are so inclined to do, must be combated. Stereotyped forms and uniformity imposed from above have nothing in common with democratic and socialist centralism. The unity of essentials, of fundamentals, of the substance, is not disturbed but ensured by *variety* in details, in specific local features, in methods of *approach*, in *methods* of exercising control, in *ways* of exterminating and rendering harmless the parasites (the rich and the rogues, slovenly and hysterical intellectuals, etc., etc.).

The Paris Commune gave a great example of how to combine initiative, independence, freedom of action and vigour from below with voluntary centralism free from stereotyped forms. Our Soviets are following the same road. But they are still "timid"; they have not yet got into their stride, have not yet "bitten into" their new, great, creative task of building the socialist system. The Soviets must set to work more boldly and display greater initiative. All "communes"—factories, villages, consumers' societies, and committees of supplies—must *compete* with each other as practical organisers of accounting and control of labour and distribution of products. The programme of this accounting and control is simple, clear and intelligible to all—everyone to have bread; everyone to have sound footwear and good clothing; everyone to have warm dwellings; everyone to work conscientiously; not a single rogue (including those who shirk their work) to be allowed to be at liberty, but kept in prison, or serve his sentence of compulsory labour of the hardest kind; not a single rich man who violates the laws and regulations of socialism to be allowed to escape the fate of the rogue, which should, in justice, be the fate of the rich man. "He who does not work, neither shall he eat"—this is the *practical* commandment of socialism. This is how things should be organised *practically*. These are the *practical* successes our "communes" and our worker and peasant organisers should be proud of. And this applies particularly to the organisers among the intellectuals (*particularly*, because they are *too much, far too much* in the habit of being proud of their general instructions and resolutions).

Thousands of practical forms and methods of accounting and controlling the rich, the rogues and the idlers must be devised and put to a practical test by the communes themselves, by small units in town and country. Variety is a guarantee of effectiveness here, a pledge of success in achieving the single common aim—to *clean* the land of Russia of all vermin, of fleas—the rogues, of bugs—the rich, and so on and so forth. In one place half a score of rich, a dozen rogues, half a dozen workers who shirk their work (in the manner of rowdies, the manner in which many compositors in Petrograd, particularly in the Party printing-shops,[41] shirk their work) will be put in prison. In another place they will be put to cleaning latrines. In a third place they will be provided with "yellow tickets" after they have served their time, so that everyone shall keep an eye on them, as *harmful* persons, until they reform. In a fourth place, one out of every ten idlers will be shot on the spot. In a fifth place mixed methods may be adopted, and by probational release, for example, the rich, the bourgeois intellectuals, the rogues and rowdies who are corrigible will be given an opportunity to reform quickly. The more variety there will be, the better and richer will be our general experience, the more certain and rapid will be the success of socialism, and the easier will it be for practice to devise—for only practice can devise—the *best* methods and means of struggle.

In what commune, in what district of a large town, in what factory and in what village are there *no* starving people, *no* unemployed, *no* idle rich, *no* despicable lackeys of the bourgeoisie, saboteurs who call themselves intellectuals? Where has most been done to raise the productivity of labour, to build good new houses for the poor, to put the poor in the houses of the rich, to regularly provide a bottle of milk for every child of every poor family? It is on these points that *competition* should develop between the communes, communities, producer-consumers' societies and associations, and Soviets of Workers', Soldiers' and Peasants' Deputies. This is the work in which *talented organisers* should come to the fore in practice and be promoted to work in state administration. There is a great deal of talent among the people. It is merely suppressed. It must be given an opportunity to display itself. It *and it alone*, with the support of the people, can save Russia and save the cause of socialism.

Written December 24-27, 1917
(January 6-9, 1918)

First published in *Pravda*
No. 17, January 20, 1929
Signed: *V. Lenin*

Collected Works,
Vol. 26, pp. 404-15

DRAFT DECREE ON CONSUMERS' COMMUNES[42]

1

Preliminary Theses

The drafts put forward by the Commissariat for Food for "supply boards", "delegate committees", etc., and similarly the draft of the Supreme Economic Council for "district economic councils"[43] suggest the need to amalgamate such bodies.

Preliminary theses:

(*Etwa**): ⌐supply and marketing committees?**⌐

The basic unit should be consumers' and producers' (better than purchasing and trading, etc.) volost societies, playing the part both of supply committees and marketing agencies. In case of need, volost boundaries could be made alterable.

In the towns a similar place could perhaps be taken by block committees or committees for sections of blocks.

If we manage to set up such committees, basic units, in the localities, the amalgamation of these committees would provide a network capable of properly organising the supply of the whole population with all essentials, and of organising production on a national scale.

Possibly instead of "societies" these could be Soviets of Workers' and Peasants' Deputies, with the participation of commercial employees, etc., etc.

Every such society or committee or Soviet (or supply and

---

* Roughly.—*Ed.*
** Supply and marketing committees under the Soviets of Workers', Soldiers' and Peasants' Deputies.

marketing committee) would be divided up into sections or departments, according to *goods* marketed and *types of products* supplied, for the general regulation of production and consumption (a department for finance, or for cash receipts and disbursements, should be attached to every supply and marketing committee). With the right of levying income tax and granting interest-free credits to the poor, and also universal labour service, this might be the basic unit of socialist society. The volost banks would then have to be amalgamated with the state savings banks, being transformed into a state-wide accounting department, aggregate of the state's receipts and disbursements accounts.

The transportation of products, and likewise their purchase and sale, would then be permitted *only* from one supply and marketing committee to another, all individual marketing being prohibited. On certificates issued by volost (or generally the "basic", lowest) supply and marketing committees, products could be sold also to individuals from central stores, provided that these transactions are recorded in the books of the volost or other supply and marketing committees (except within small units, or for trifles). No transportation of products would be permitted without certificates from the supply and marketing committee.

This would be the unification of the Commissariats for Agriculture, Trade and Industry, Labour, and Food, and the Supreme Economic Council, and the Commissariats for Finance and Communications.

N.B.:
"Supply and marketing committees": volost, uyezd, gubernia and district. ($\Sigma\Sigma$ = the S.E.C.)
Their departments: Central Textile Board, Central Sugar Board, Central Coal Board, etc. ($\Sigma\Sigma$ = the S.E.C.), Central Bank, etc.
N.B.:
Representatives of the Soviets of Workers', Soldiers' and Peasants' Deputies should superintend the well-to-do quarters in towns (or well-to-do country-house settlements, etc.), i.e., those quarters, etc., where the percentage of workers and peasants is lower than, say, 60 per cent.

2

Draft Decree

The war, brought about by the conflict between capitalists for the division of the spoils of depredation, has resulted in untold ruin. This is intensified by criminal speculation and profiteering, particularly among the wealthy classes, which have brought the tortures of hunger and unemployment to hundreds of thousands and even millions of people. The need to adopt extraordinary measures to aid the starving and to wage merciless war on speculators has induced the workers' and peasants' government to enact the following regulations as a law of the Russian Republic:

Every citizen of the state shall belong to a local (village, volost, hamlet, section of a town, section of a street, etc.) consumers' society.

The grouping of families in the consumers' societies shall be voluntary, except for the proviso that not less than two-thirds of the number of families in each society must belong to the non-affluent classes (i. e., workers, peasants not employing hired labour, and so on).

Apart from the purchase and distribution of products, every consumers' society shall engage in the sale of local products. The boards of the consumers' societies shall set up *committees of supplies*, and no transportation of products shall be permitted without the written sanction of the appropriate committee of supplies.

Existing consumers' societies are hereby nationalised and shall be obliged to admit to membership the whole population of the localities in which they are situated, without exception.

If they so desire private individuals may purchase products in the central stores and not in their local shops, but only on condition that the relevant entry is made in the book of the local consumers' society.

The transportation, purchase and sale of products without a permit from the committees of supplies shall be punishable by the confiscation of the whole of the property of the offender, by imprisonment for a period of not less than six months and by sentence to compulsory labour.

Permits for the transportation or the purchase and sale of products shall be drawn up in duplicate and signed by not less than three members of the board of the committee of supplies concerned, one copy being filed by the board.

Each permit must state from which and to which consumers' society the products are being consigned.

Telegraph offices shall give priority to the telegrams of the committees of supplies.

All committees of supplies shall act under the control and in accordance with the instructions of the local Soviets of Workers', Soldiers' and Peasants' Deputies.

Every individual shall be entitled to acquire at his consumers' society any product, without any restrictions whatsoever, except for such regulations as may be established to limit the import of products from abroad.

Products produced for sale must be delivered to the local committee of supplies at uncontrolled prices, except in cases when fixed prices are established by law. Money received for products sold shall be entered to the account of the owners in the local (village, volost, city, factory or other) branch of the People's Bank.

Every Soviet of Workers', Soldiers' and Peasants' Deputies must appoint a group of inspectors, auditors and instructors to assist the population to establish consumers' societies (committees of supplies) and check their accounts and all their business.

Instructions on keeping the accounts and on the correspondence of the committees of supplies will be issued separately.

Written December 24-27, 1917
(January 6-9, 1918)

First published January 22,
1929 in *Izvestia* No. 18

Collected Works,
Vol. 36, pp. 464-65,
Vol. 26, pp. 416-17

From the DECLARATION OF RIGHTS
OF THE WORKING AND EXPLOITED PEOPLE[44]

The Constituent Assembly resolves:

1. Russia is hereby proclaimed a Republic of Soviets of Workers', Soldiers' and Peasants' Deputies. All power, centrally and locally, is vested in these Soviets.

2. The Russian Soviet Republic is established on the principle of a free union of free nations, as a federation of Soviet national republics.

Its fundamental aim being to abolish all exploitation of man by man, to completely eliminate the division of society into classes, to mercilessly crush the resistance of the exploiters, to establish a socialist organisation of society and to achieve the victory of socialism in all countries, the Constituent Assembly further resolves:

1. Private ownership of land is hereby abolished. All land together with all buildings, farm implements and other appurtenances of agricultural production, is proclaimed the property of the entire working people.

2. The Soviet laws on workers' control and on the Supreme Economic Council are hereby confirmed for the purpose of guaranteeing the power of the working people over the exploiters and as a first step towards the complete conversion of the factories, mines, railways, and other means of production and transport into the property of the workers' and peasants' state.

3. The conversion of all banks into the property of the workers' and peasants' state is hereby confirmed

as one of the conditions for the emancipation of the
working people from the yoke of capital.

4. For the purpose of abolishing the parasitic sections of society, universal labour conscription is hereby
instituted. . . .

Written not later than
January 3 (16), 1918

Published in *Pravda* No. 2 and
Izvestia No. 2, January 4 (17),
1918

Collected Works,
Vol. 26, pp. 423-24

DECLARATION OF THE R.S.D.L.P.
(BOLSHEVIKS) GROUP AT THE CONSTITUENT
ASSEMBLY MEETING
JANUARY 5 (18), 1918[45]

The vast majority of working Russia—workers, peasants and soldiers—have demanded that the Constituent Assembly should recognise the gains of the Great October Revolution, the Soviet decrees on land, peace and workers' control, and above all the power of the Soviets of Workers', Soldiers' and Peasants' Deputies. The All-Russia Central Executive Committee, fulfilling the will of the vast majority of the working classes of Russia, has proposed that the Constituent Assembly should declare itself bound by this will. However, the majority of the Constituent Assembly—in line with the pretensions of the bourgeoisie—has rejected this proposal, thereby challenging the whole of working Russia.

The majority in the Constituent Assembly went to the Party of the Right Socialist-Revolutionaries, the party of Kerensky, Avksentyev and Chernov. This party, which calls itself socialist and revolutionary, is leading the fight of the bourgeois elements against the workers' and peasants' revolution and is in fact a bourgeois and counter-revolutionary party.

The Constituent Assembly, as at present constituted, is the result of the balance of forces obtaining before the Great October Revolution. The present counter-revolutionary majority of the Constituent Assembly, elected on outdated party lists. is a reflection of an earlier period of the revolution and is trying to throw up a roadblock in the way of the workers' and peasants' movement.

The day-long debate has shown that the Party of Right Socialist-Revolutionaries continues, as it did under Kerensky, to lavish the people with promises of all manner of things; actually it has decided to fight against the power of the workers', peasants' and soldiers' Soviets, against the socialist measures, the transfer of land and all implements to the peasants without compensation, the nationalisation of banks, and the repudiation of the state debt.

Refusing for a single moment to cover up the crimes of the enemies of the people, we make this announcement of our withdrawal from the Constituent Assembly, leaving it to Soviet power to take the final decision on the attitude to the counter-revolutionary section of the Constituent Assembly.

Pravda No. 5 (evening edition),
January 19 (6), 1918

Collected Works,
Vol. 26, pp. 429-30

THIRD ALL-RUSSIA CONGRESS OF SOVIETS OF WORKERS', SOLDIERS' AND PEASANTS' DEPUTIES
JANUARY 10-18 (23-31), 1918[46]

From the REPORT ON THE ACTIVITIES OF THE COUNCIL OF PEOPLE'S COMMISSARS
JANUARY 11 (24)

Now I shall deal briefly with the measures which the socialist Soviet Government of Russia has begun to realise. The nationalisation of the banks was one of the first measures adopted for the purpose, not only of wiping the landowners from the face of Russian earth, but also of eradicating the rule of the bourgeoisie and the possibility of capital oppressing millions and tens of millions of the working people. The banks are important centres of modern capitalist economy. They collect fantastic wealth and distribute it over this vast country; they are the nerve centres of capitalist life. They are subtle and intricate organisations, which grew up in the course of centuries; and against them were hurled the first blows of Soviet power which at first encountered desperate resistance in the State Bank. But this resistance did not deter Soviet power. We succeeded in the main thing in organising the State Bank; this main thing is in the hands of the workers and peasants. After these basic measures, which still require a lot of working out in detail, we proceeded to lay our hands on the private banks.

We did not act in the way the compromisers would probably have recommended us to do, i.e., first wait until the Constituent Assembly is convened, then perhaps draft a bill and introduce it in the Constituent Assembly and by that inform the bourgeoisie of our intentions and enable them to find a loophole through which to extricate themselves from this unpleasant thing; perhaps draw them into our company, and then make state laws—that would be a "state act".

That would be the rejection of socialism. We acted quite simply; not fearing to call forth the reproaches of the "educated" people, or rather of the uneducated supporters of the bourgeoisie who were trading in the remnants of their knowledge, we said we had at our disposal armed workers and peasants. This morning they must occupy all the private banks. (*Applause.*) After they have done that, after power is in our hands, only after this, we shall discuss what measures to adopt. In the morning the banks were occupied and in the evening the Central Executive Committee issued a decree: "The banks are declared national property"—state control, the socialisation of banking, its transfer to Soviet power, took place.

There was not a man among us who could imagine that an intricate and subtle apparatus like banking, which grew out of the capitalist system of economy in the course of centuries, could be broken or transformed in a few days. We never said that. And when scientists, or pseudo-scientists, shook their heads and prophesied, we said: you can prophesy what you like. We know only one way for the proletarian revolution, namely, to occupy the enemy's positions—to learn to rule by experience, from our mistakes. We do not in the least belittle the difficulties in our path, but we have done the main thing. The source of capitalist wealth has been undermined in the place of its distribution. After all this, the repudiation of the state loans, the overthrow of the financial yoke, was a very easy step. The transition to confiscation of the factories, after workers' control had been introduced, was also very easy. When we were accused of breaking up production into separate departments by introducing workers' control, we brushed aside this nonsense. In introducing workers' control, we knew that it would take much time before it spread to the whole of Russia, but we wanted to show that we recognise only one road—changes from below ; we wanted the workers themselves, from below, to draw up the new, basic economic principles. Much time will be required for this.

From workers' control we passed on to the creation of a Supreme Economic Council. Only this measure, together with the nationalisation of the banks and railways which will be carried out within the next few days, will make it possible for us to begin work to build up a new socialist economy. We know perfectly well the difficulties that confront us in this work; but we assert that only those who set to work to carry out this task relying on the experience and the instinct of the working people are socialists in deed. The people will commit many mistakes, but the main thing has been done. They know that when they appeal to Soviet power they will get whole-hearted support against the exploiters. There is not a single measure intended to ease their work that was not entirely supported by Soviet power. Soviet power does not know everything and cannot handle everything in time, and very often it is confronted with difficult tasks. Very often delegations of workers and peasants come to the government and ask, for example, what to do with such-and-such a piece of land. And frequently I myself have felt embarrassed when I saw that they had no very definite views. And I said to them: you are the power, do all you want to do, take all you want, we shall support you, but take care of production, see that production is useful. Take up useful work, you will make mistakes, but you will learn. And the workers have already begun to learn; they have already begun to fight against the saboteurs. Education has been turned into a fence which hinders the advance of the working classes; it will be pulled down.

Undoubtedly, the war is corrupting people both in the rear and at the front; people who are working on war supplies are paid far above the rates, and this attracts all those who hid themselves to keep out of the war, the vagabond and semi-vagabond elements who are imbued with one desire, to "grab" something and clear out. But these elements are the worst that has remained of the old capitalist system and are the vehicles of all the old evils; these we must kick out, remove, and we must put in the factories all the best proletarian elements and form them into nuclei of future socialist Russia. This is not an easy task, it will give rise to many conflicts, to much friction and many clashes. We, the Council of People's Commissars, and I personally, have heard complaints and threats from them, but we have remained calm, knowing that now we have a judge to whom we can appeal. That judge is the Soviets of Workers' and Soldiers' Deputies. (Applause.) The word of this judge is indisputable, and we shall always rely upon it.

Capitalism deliberately differentiates the workers in order to rally an insignificant handful of the upper section of the working class around the bourgeoisie. Conflicts with this section are inevitable. We shall not achieve socialism without a struggle. But we are ready to fight, we have started it and we shall finish it with the aid of the apparatus called the Soviets. The Soviet of Workers' and Soldiers' Deputies will easily solve any problem we bring before it. For however strong the group of privileged workers may be, when they are brought before the representative body of all the workers, then this court, I repeat, will be indisputable for them. This sort of adjustment is only just beginning. The workers and peasants have not yet sufficient confidence in their own strength; age-old tradition has made them far too used to waiting for orders from above. They have not yet fully appreciated the fact that the proletariat is the ruling class; there are still elements among them who are frightened and downtrodden and who imagine that they must pass through the despicable school of the bourgeoisie. This most despicable of bourgeois notions has remained alive longer than all the rest, but it is dying and will die out completely. And we are convinced that with every step Soviet power takes the number of people will constantly grow who have completely thrown off the old bourgeois notion that a simple worker and peasant connot administer the state. Well, if he sets to doing it, he can and will learn! (Applause.)

And it will be our organisational task to select leaders and organisers from among the people. This enormous, gigantic work is now on the agenda. There could even be no thought of carrying it out if it were not for Soviet power, a filtering apparatus which can promote people.

Not only have we a state law on control, we have something even far more valuable—attempts on the part of the proletariat to enter into agreements with the manufacturers' associations in order to guarantee the workers' management over whole branches of industry. Such an agreement has begun to be drawn up, and is almost completed, between the leather workers and the all-Russia leather manufacturers' society. I attach very special importance to these agreements,[47] they show that the workers are becoming aware of their strength.

Published in *Pravda* Nos. 8, 9 and 10, January 12, 13 and 14, 1918

Collected Works, Vol. 26, pp. 466-70

DRAFT DECREE ON THE NATIONALISATION OF THE MERCHANT MARINE AND INLAND WATER TRANSPORT[48]

1

Draft Decree

1. The Council of People's Commissars states that the Central Committee[49] and Tsentrovolga* are entirely in agreement concerning the need to nationalise, immediately and without compensation, all sea-going and river vessels used for commercial purposes.

2. The C.P.C. accordingly resolves that such nationalisation shall be carried out immediately, and authorises a special commission consisting of representatives of the Navy Commissariat, two from the C.C., two from Tsentrovolga, and a chairman appointed by the Supreme Economic Council to work out the following main points of a nationalisation decree and to submit it to the Council of People's Commissars within two days.

3. The nationalisation of the entire fleet is decreed.

4. It is incumbent on the crews and subsequently on the unions of ship workers of each basin and sea to maintain order on board their vessels, safeguard them, etc.

5. The C.C. and Tsentrovolga shall be regarded as caretaker central boards of the nationalised fleet, pending a congress and their merger.

If the merger is not achieved on a voluntary basis, it shall be carried out forcibly by the Soviet Government.

6. The central boards shall operate in full subordination to the local and central organs of Soviet power.

---

* The Central Committee of the Volga Fleet.—*Tr.*

Addendum to the Draft

This should be added to the *immediate* decree on nationalisation:
  (α) arrest of all boards of management (house arrest),
  (β) strict liability for damage to vessels, etc.

Written January 18 (31), 1918

First published in 1945
in *Lenin Miscellany XXXV*

Collected Works,
Vol. 26, pp. 505-06

From the SPEECHES AT THE MEETING
OF THE C.P.C.
MARCH 4, 1918[50]

1

I fully agree with Comrade Trutovsky that the tendencies and attempts of which we have heard here are completely at variance with the aims of the workers' and
peasants' government and have nothing in common with
socialism.[51] The aim of socialism is to turn all the means
of production into the property of the whole people, and
that does not at all mean that the ships become the property
of the ship workers or the banks the property of the bank
clerks. If people take such paltry things seriously, then
we must do away with nationalisation, because the whole
thing is preposterous. The task, the aim of socialism, as we
see it, is to convert the land and the industrial enterprises
into the property of the Soviet Republic. The peasant
receives land on condition that he works it properly. If the
river transport workers receive ships, it is on condition that
they take a proprietary interest in them: they must submit
their estimates if only in order to have income and expenditure endorsed, and they must take proper care of the ships. If
they cannot do this, we shall remove them. Seeing that they
have been arguing for three weeks, I would propose removing all of them from the management, because this shows
an utter inaptitude for organisation, a complete failure to
grasp the vital tasks facing the Soviet Republic. It is chaos,
disorganisation, even worse—it borders on sabotage. They
have started a sort of organised crusade in the Union and
come complaining. Meanwhile, the boats on the Volga stand
unrepaired. What is this? What is it—a mad-house? I am

perfectly sure that they realise that if we go on existing in this chaos we shall bring still greater calamities down on our heads. The chief condition with us is discipline and the organised transfer of all property to the people, the transfer of all sources of wealth to the Soviet Republic, and their strictly disciplined disposal. So when we are told that the river transport workers will be private managing proprietors, we obviously cannot agree to it. Soviet power is to do the managing. But you organise a sort of debate preventing unity among all organisations....* If they are dissatisfied, they could have asked for the order to be rescinded. But they are proposing again that it should be decided first whom the ships belong to, so that the ship workers should demand a 140 per cent rise.

2

I fully agree with many things, but as to the make-up of the Board, I think the proposal of the river transport comrades is absolutely unacceptable. For one thing, that is not the question we are dealing with. The question at issue is that the men are not receiving their money. That's simply scandalous, of course. What are we allocating money for? For it to remain on paper? We have heard a thousand complaints, that unless the money is sent, our transport will collapse. If the money was assigned on February 21, and on the 22nd it was not received, then they should have come on the 23rd complaining. We are suffering from a money famine, we are short of currency notes, the treasury cannot print all we need. If we assign money and you unassign it, then actually nothing is sent. You should have come here on February 23, and not March 3. We demanded that these tens of millions should be given. I don't know who is more to blame. I believe the representatives of the Economic Council. We cannot satisfy everybody. While we are supplying Petrograd, Moscow is hungering for currency notes....* If people only wrote assignments and did not take any measures, they should have come here, or called me to the phone or somebody else,

---

* Part of the shorthand report has not been deciphered.—*Ed.*

and complained about it. It is a rare week when I do not receive a complaint about money not being paid out, but from you I never received a single complaint. The people in charge should be made to answer for it, at least reprimanded. Under the ruling of February 21 the congress of river transport workers is obliged to submit the estimates. As regards the composition of the Management Board, I think we should have corrected our decree rather in the vein Comrade Shlyapnikov suggested. Paragraph 3 provides for a Board of seven members. Why this wasn't inserted is incomprehensible. A number of trade union representatives could be included in it. I propose that resolute measures be taken to have this money forwarded immediately by through goods trains. Then notification should be sent in the usual way saying the money has been dispatched. As regards the second point I believe the only Board possible in this instance and most acceptable for everyone, for the Council of People's Commissars—the only possible Board is the one appointed yesterday by the Council of People's Commissars. There are no grounds for changing this. I believe we should put this through. And if it's really true about the 200 rubles salary, which was adopted as definite and made a condition for the nationalisation of transport—if that's a fact, and if demands are made for levelling up with other organisations, then I personally raise the question of cancelling nationalisation. There may come a time shortly when there will be no money at all. We had a single guarantee on the basis of which we wanted to carry out nationalisation, and this is being taken away from us. If that's the case, this measure should be revoked. Unless this is done we shall be taking on another responsibility incurring enormous losses.

First published in 1962 in the
Fifth Russian Edition of the
Collected Works. Vol. 35

Collected Works,
Vol. 42, pp. 63-65

Chapter V

The task of administering the state, which now confronts the Soviet government, has this special feature, that, probably for the first time in the modern history of civilised nations, it deals pre-eminently with economics rather than with politics. Usually the word "administration" is associated chiefly, if not solely, with political activity. However, the very basis and essence of Soviet power, like that of the transition itself from capitalist to socialist society, lies in the fact that political tasks occupy a subordinate position to economic tasks. And now, especially after the practical experience of over four months of Soviet government in Russia, it should be quite clear to us that the task of administering the state is primarily a purely economic task—that of healing the country's wounds inflicted by the war, restoring its productive forces, organising accountancy in and control over production and distribution, raising the productivity of labour—in short, it boils down to the task of economic reorganisation.

This task can be said to fall under two main headings: 1) accounting and control over production and distribution in the broadest, most widespread and universal forms of such accounting and control, and 2) raising the productivity of labour. These tasks can be handled by any form of collective effort or any form of state passing over to socialism only on condition that the basic economic, social, cultural and political preconditions for this have been created in a sufficient degree by capitalism. Without large-scale machine production, without a more or less developed network of railways, postal and telegraph communications, without a more or less developed network of public educational institutions, neither of these tasks can be carried out in a systematic way on a national scale. Russia is in a position when quite a number of these initial preconditions for such a transition actually exist. On the other hand, quite a number of these preconditions are absent in our country, but can be borrowed by it fairly easily from the experience of the neighbouring, far more advanced countries, whom history and international intercourse have long since placed in close contact with Russia.

Chapter VI

The basic aim of every society going over to a socialist system consists in the victory of the ruling class—or rather the class that is growing up to be the ruling class—namely, the proletariat, over the bourgeoisie as described above. And this task is set before us in a substantially new way, quite unlike the way it stood in the course of many decades of the proletariat's world-wide experience of struggle against the bourgeoisie. Now, after the gains of the October Revolution, after our successes in the civil war, victory over the bourgeoisie should stand for something much bigger, albeit more peaceful in form: namely, victory over the bourgeoisie, now that it has been secured politically and made good militarily, should now be achieved in the sphere of organisation of the national economy, in the sphere of organisation of production, in the sphere of country-wide accounting and control. The problem of accounting and control over production was dealt with by the bourgeoisie all the more effectively in proportion as production expanded and the network of national economic institutions embracing tens and hundreds of millions of the population of a large modern state became more ramified. We must handle this task now in a new way, backed by the predominating position of the proletariat, supported by the bulk of the working and exploited masses, making use of those elements of organising talent and technical knowledge which have been accumulated by the preceding society, and nine-tenths, perhaps even ninety-nine hundredths of which belong to a class hostile and opposed to the socialist revolution.

Chapter VII

German imperialism, which has made the greatest advance not only in military power and military techniques, but in big industrial organisations within the framework of capitalism, has incidentally given proof of its economic progressiveness by being the first country to introduce labour conscription. Naturally, in the conditions of capitalist society in general and particularly when the monarchist states are waging an imperialist war, labour conscription is nothing more than a military convict prison for the workers, a new means of enslaving the working and exploited masses, a new system of measures for suppressing all protest on the part of these masses. Nevertheless, there is no question that it is only because of the economic preconditions created by big capitalism that such a reform could be put forward and effected. And now we, amid conditions of appalling post-war economic disorganisation, are obliged to consider the urgency of a similar reform. Naturally, Soviet power, which is passing from a capitalist to a socialist organisation of society, must tackle this problem of labour conscription from the other end, opposite to that of German imperialism. For the capitalists and imperialists of Germany labour conscription meant enslavement of the workers. For the workers and peasant poor in Russia labour conscription should mean, first and foremost, recruitment of the rich and propertied classes for the discharge of their social duties. We should start labour conscription with the rich.

This is necessitated, generally speaking, not only by the fact that the Soviet Republic is a socialist republic. The necessity arises also from the fact that it was precisely the wealthy and propertied classes who, by their resistance, both military and passive (sabotage), mostly prevented Russia from healing the wounds inflicted upon her by the war, hampered the country's economic rehabilitation and progress. That is why accounting and control, which should be now considered a problem of paramount importance in the whole business of state administration, must be applied first of all to the wealthy and propertied classes. It was the members of these classes who enjoyed the tribute they collected from the working people, especially during the war; it was they who used this tribute to evade a task which is the duty of every citizen, namely, that of lending a hand in healing the country's wounds and putting it on its feet again; it was they who used the plundered tribute to retire and entrench themselves behind impregnable walls and offer every possible resistance to the victory of the socialist principle over the capitalist principle of society's organisation. One of the chief weapons of such struggle against the Soviets and against socialism on the part of the wealthy and propertied classes was their possession of considerable hoards of currency notes. The propertied classes in capitalist society derived most of their wealth from the land and other means of production, such as factories, mills, etc., which they owned. The Soviet government had no difficulty, thanks to the support of the workers and the great majority of the peasants, in abolishing the right of the landowners and the bourgeoisie to these basic items of the country's wealth. It was not difficult to decree the abolition of private property in land. It was not difficult to nationalise most of the factories and mills. There is no doubt that the nationalisation of other big industrial enterprises and transport facilities is a problem that will easily be dealt with in the very near future.[53]

Capitalist society, however, has created another form of wealth, which is by no means so easy for the Soviet government to deal with. This is wealth in the form of money, or rather, currency notes. Currency notes during the war were issued in very great numbers. Russia was cut off by a wall of military operations from commerce with a number of countries who had been her largest importers and exporters. The amassment of currency notes in the hands of the wealthy and propertied classes, practically all of whom, directly or indirectly, had speculated on the high prices for military contracts and supplies, is one of the chief means by which the propertied classes amassed wealth and accumulated power over the working people. Today the economic position of Russia, as probably of every capitalist country that has gone through three years of war, is characterised by the fact that enormous amounts of paper money are concentrated in the hands of and hoarded by a comparatively small minority, the bourgeoisie and propertied classes, and this paper money, though greatly depreciated through massive emission, still represents a claim to levy tribute on the working population.

During the transition from capitalist to socialist society it is absolutely impossible to do without currency notes or to replace them with new ones in a short space of time. The Soviet government is now confronted with a difficult task, which nevertheless has to be dealt with at all costs—the task of combating the resistance of the wealthy, a resistance that takes the form of hoarding and concealing the proofs of their claim to levy tribute on the working people. These proofs are currency notes. Naturally, while these currency notes previously gave the right to acquire and purchase the means of production, such as land, factories, mills, etc., their significance today has diminished and even been reduced to naught. The purchase of land has become impossible in Russia after promulgation of the law on the socialisation of the land,[54] while the purchase of factories and mills and similar large-scale means of production and transport has become practically impossible owing to the rapid process of nationalisation and confiscation of all such large enterprises. And so, it becomes more and more difficult and almost impossible for members of the bourgeoisie and propertied classes (including the peasant bourgeoisie) to acquire money for the purchase of the means of production. But in defending their old privileges and trying to retard and obstruct as much as they can the business of socialist reforms within the country, the bourgeoisie are hoarding and concealing the proofs of their claim to a share in the social wealth, their claim to levy tribute on the working people, hoarding and concealing currency notes in order to have a chance, however slender, of maintaining their position and recovering their old privileges in the event of difficulties or crises of a military or commercial nature that might yet beset Russia.

As regards consumer goods, the possibility of buying them with the sums of paper money they have accumulated through speculations during the war remains almost fully with the bourgeoisie and propertied classes, since the problem of proper rationing and distribution of these goods in a country like Russia, with her huge population of small peasants, petty artisans or handicraftsmen, presents tremendous difficulties, and in the prevailing state of economic chaos caused by the war this problem still remains practically unsolved. Thus, the Soviet government is obliged to start the business of accounting and control over production and distribution by an organised struggle against the wealthy and propertied classes who are hoarding vast sums in currency notes and evading state control.

It is estimated that currency notes to the value of about thirty thousand million rubles have been issued in Russia to date. Of this sum probably no less than twenty thousand million, or maybe considerably more, are excess hoards unneeded for trade turnover, which are kept hidden away by members of the bourgeoisie and propertied classes for motives of self-interest—or class self-interest.

The Soviet government will have to combine the introduction of labour conscription with the registration, in the first place, of people belonging to the bourgeoisie and propertied classes; it will have to demand truthful statements (declarations) concerning the amount of currency notes available; it will have to take a number of measures to make sure that this demand will not remain on paper; it will have to consider transitional measures for concentrating all stocks of currency notes in the State Bank or its branches. Unless these measures are taken, the business of accounting and control over production and distribution cannot be effectively carried through.

Dictated between March 23
and 28, 1918

First published in 1962 in the   Collected Works,
Fifth Russian Edition of the   Vol. 42, pp. 71-76
Collected Works. Vol. 36

From THE IMMEDIATE TASKS
OF THE SOVIET GOVERNMENT[55]

The New Phase of the Struggle
Against the Bourgeoisie

The bourgeoisie in our country has been conquered, but it has not yet been uprooted, not yet destroyed, and not even utterly broken. That is why we are faced with a new and higher form of struggle against the bourgeoisie, the transition from the very simple task of further expropriating the capitalists to the much more complicated and difficult task of creating conditions in which it will be impossible for the bourgeoisie to exist, or for a new bourgeoisie to arise. Clearly, this task is immeasurably more significant than the previous one; and until it is fulfilled there will be no socialism.

If we measure our revolution by the scale of West-European revolutions we shall find that at the present moment we are approximately at the level reached in 1793 and 1871. We can be legitimately proud of having risen to this level, and of having certainly, in one respect, advanced somewhat further, namely: we have decreed and introduced throughout Russia the highest *type* of state—Soviet power. Under no circumstances, however, can we rest content with what we have achieved, because we have only just started the transition to socialism, we have *not yet* done the decisive thing in *this* respect.

The decisive thing is the organisation of the strictest and country-wide accounting and control of production and distribution of goods. And yet, we have *not yet* introduced accounting and control in those enterprises and in those branches and fields of economy which we have taken away from the bourgeoisie; and without this there can be no thought of achieving the second and equally essential material condition for introducing socialism, namely, raising the productivity of labour on a national scale.

That is why the present task could not be defined by the simple formula: continue the offensive against capital. Although we have certainly not finished off capital and although it is certainly necessary to continue the offensive against this enemy of the working people, such a formula would be inexact, would not be concrete, would not take into account the *peculiarity* of the present situation in which, in order to go on advancing successfully *in the future*, we must "suspend" our offensive *now*.

This can be explained by comparing our position in the war against capital with the position of a victorious army that has captured, say, a half or two-thirds of the enemy's territory and is compelled to halt in order to muster its forces, to replenish its supplies of munitions, repair and reinforce the lines of communication, build new storehouses, bring up new reserves, etc. To suspend the offensive of a victorious army under such conditions is necessary precisely in order to gain the rest of the enemy's territory, i.e., in order to achieve complete victory. Those who have failed to understand that the objective state of affairs at the present moment dictates to us precisely such a "suspension" of the offensive against capital have failed to understand anything at all about the present political situation.

It goes without saying that we can speak about the "suspension" of the offensive against capital only in quotation marks, i.e., only metaphorically. In ordinary war, a general order can be issued to stop the offensive, the advance can actually be stopped. In the war against capital, however, the advance cannot be stopped, and there can be no thought of our abandoning the further expropriation of capital. What we are discussing is the shifting of the *centre of gravity* of our economic and political work. Up to now measures for the direct expropriation of the expropriators were *in the forefront*. Now the organisation of accounting and control in those enterprises in which the capitalists have already been expropriated, and in all other enterprises, advances *to the forefront*.

If we decided to continue to expropriate capital at the same rate at which we have been doing it up to now, we should certainly suffer defeat, because our work of organising proletarian accounting and control has obviously—obviously to every thinking person—*fallen behind* the work of *directly* "expropriating the expropriators". If we now concentrate all our efforts on the organisation of accounting and control, we shall be able to solve this problem, we shall be able to make up for lost time, we shall *completely* win our "campaign" against capital.

But is not the admission that we must make up for lost time tantamount to admission of some kind of an error? Not in the least. Take another military example. If it is possible to defeat and push back the enemy merely with detachments of light cavalry, it should be done. But if this can be done successfully only up to a certain point, then it is quite conceivable that when this point has been reached, it will be necessary to bring up heavy artillery. By admitting that it is now necessary to make up for lost time in bringing up heavy artillery, we do not admit that the successful cavalry attack was a mistake.

Frequently, the lackeys of the bourgeoisie reproached us for having launched a "Red Guard" attack on capital. The reproach is absurd and is worthy only of the lackeys of the money-bags, because *at one time* the "Red Guard" attack on capital was absolutely dictated by circumstances. Firstly, *at that time* capital put up military resistance through the medium of Kerensky and Krasnov, Savinkov and Gotz (Gegechkori is putting up such resistance even now), Dutov and Bogayevsky. Military resistance cannot be broken except by military means, and the Red Guards fought in the noble and supreme historical cause of liberating the working and exploited people from the yoke of the exploiters.

Secondly, we could not at that time put methods of administration in the forefront in place of methods of suppression, because the art of administration is not innate, but is acquired by experience. At that time we lacked this experience; now we have it. Thirdly, at that time we could not have specialists in the various fields of knowledge and technology at our disposal because those specialists were either fighting in the ranks of the Bogayevskys, or were still able to put up systematic and stubborn passive resistance by way of *sabotage*. Now we have broken the sabotage. The "Red Guard" attack on capital was successful, was victorious, because we broke capital's military resistance and its resistance by sabotage.

Does that mean that a "Red Guard" attack on capital is *always* appropriate, under *all* circumstances, that we have *no* other means of fighting capital? It would be childish to think so. We achieved victory with the aid of light cavalry, but we also have heavy artillery. We achieved victory by methods of suppression; we shall be able to achieve victory also by methods of administration. We must know how to change our methods of fighting the enemy to suit changes in the situation. We shall not for a moment renounce "Red Guard" suppression of the Savinkovs and Gegechkoris and all other landowner and bourgeois counter-revolutionaries. We shall not be so foolish, however, as to put "Red Guard" methods in the forefront at a time when the period in which Red Guard attacks were necessary has, in the main, drawn to a close (and to a victorious close), and when the period of utilising bourgeois specialists by the proletarian state power for the purpose of reploughing the soil in order to prevent the growth of any bourgeoisie whatever is knocking at the door.

This is a peculiar epoch, or rather stage of development, and in order to defeat capital completely, we must be able to adapt the forms of our struggle to the peculiar conditions of this stage.

Without the guidance of experts in the various fields of knowledge, technology and experience, the transition to socialism will be impossible, because socialism calls for a conscious mass advance to greater productivity of labour compared with capitalism, and on the basis achieved by capitalism. Socialism must achieve this advance *in its own way*, by its own methods—or, to put it more concretely, by *Soviet* methods. And the specialists, because of the whole social environment which made them specialists, are, in the main, inevitably bourgeois. Had our proletariat, after capturing power, quickly solved the problem of accounting, control and organisation on a national scale (which was impossible owing to the war and Russia's backwardness), then we, after breaking the sabotage, would also have completely subordinated these bourgeois experts to ourselves by means of universal accounting and control. Owing to the considerable "delay" in introducing accounting and control generally, we, although we have managed to conquer sabotage, have *not yet* created the conditions which would place the bourgeois specialists at our disposal. The mass of saboteurs are "going to work", but the best organisers and the top experts can be utilised by the state either in the old way, in the bourgeois way (i.e., for high salaries), or in the new way, in the proletarian way (i.e., creating the conditions of national accounting and control from below, which would inevitably and of themselves subordinate the experts and enlist them for our work).

Now we have to resort to the old bourgeois method and to agree to pay a very high price for the "services" of the top bourgeois experts. All those who are familiar with the subject appreciate this, but not all ponder over the significance of this measure being adopted by the proletarian state. Clearly, this measure is a compromise, a departure from the principles of the Paris Commune and of every proletarian power, which call for the reduction of all salaries to the level of the wages of the average worker, which urge that careerism be fought not merely in words, but in deeds.

Moreover, it is clear that this measure not only implies the cessation—in a certain field and to a certain degree—of the offensive against capital (for capital is not a sum of money, but a definite social relation); it is also *a step backward* on the part of our socialist Soviet state power, which from the very outset proclaimed and pursued the policy of reducing high salaries to the level of the wages of the average worker.[56]

Of course, the lackeys of the bourgeoisie, particularly the small fry, such as the Mensheviks, the *Novaya Zhizn* people and the Right Socialist-Revolutionaries, will giggle over our confession that we are taking a step backward. But we need not mind their giggling. We must study the specific features of the extremely difficult and new path to socialism without concealing our mistakes and weaknesses, and try to be prompt in doing what has been left undone. To conceal from the people the fact that the enlistment of bourgeois experts by means of extremely high salaries is a retreat from the principles of the Paris Commune would be sinking to the level of bourgeois politicians and deceiving the people. Frankly explaining how and why we took this step backward, and then publicly discussing what means are available for making up for lost time, means educating the people and learning from experience, learning together with the people how to build socialism. There is hardly a single victorious military campaign in history in which the victor did not commit certain mistakes, suffer partial reverses, temporarily yield something and in some places retreat. The "campaign" which we have undertaken against capitalism is a million times more difficult than the most difficult military campaign, and it would be silly and disgraceful to give way to despondency because of a particular and partial retreat.

We shall now discuss the question from the practical point of view. Let us assume that the Russian Soviet Republic requires one thousand first-class scientists and experts in various fields of knowledge, technology and practical experience to direct the labour of the people towards securing the speediest possible economic revival. Let us assume also that we shall have to pay these "stars of the first magnitude"—of course the majority of those who shout loudest about the corruption of the workers are themselves utterly corrupted by bourgeois morals—25,000 rubles per annum each. Let us assume that this sum (25,000,000 rubles) will have to be doubled (assuming that we have to pay bonuses for particularly successful and rapid fulfilment of the most important organisational and technical tasks), or even quadrupled (assuming that we have to enlist several hundred foreign specialists, who are more demanding). The question is, would the annual expenditure of fifty or a hundred million rubles by the Soviet Republic for the purpose of reorganising the labour of the people on modern scientific and technological lines be excessive or too heavy? Of course not. The overwhelming majority of the class-conscious workers and peasants will approve of this expenditure because they know from practical experience that our backwardness causes us to lose thousands of millions, and that we have *not yet* reached that degree of organisation, accounting and control which would induce all the "stars" of the bourgeois intelligentsia to participate voluntarily in *our* work.

It goes without saying that this question has another side to it. The corrupting influence of high salaries—both upon the Soviet authorities (especially since the revolution occurred so rapidly that it was impossible to prevent a certain number of adventurers and rogues from getting into positions of authority, and they, together with a number of inept or dishonest commissars, would not be averse to becoming "star" embezzlers of state funds) and upon the mass of the workers—is indisputable. Every thinking and honest worker and poor peasant, however, will agree with us, will admit, that we cannot immediately rid ourselves of the evil legacy of capitalism, and that we can liberate the Soviet Republic from the duty of paying an annual "tribute" of fifty million or one hundred million rubles (a tribute for our own backwardness in organising *country-wide* accounting and control *from below*) only by organising ourselves, by tightening up discipline in our own ranks, by purging our ranks of all those who are "preserving the legacy of capitalism", who "follow the traditions of capitalism", i.e., of idlers, parasites and embezzlers of state funds (now all the land, all the factories and all the railways are the "state funds" of the Soviet Republic). If the class-conscious advanced workers and poor peasants manage with the aid of the Soviet institutions to organise, become disciplined, pull themselves together, create powerful labour discipline in the course of one year, then in a year's time we shall throw off this "tribute", which can be reduced even before that ... in exact proportion to the successes we achieve in our workers' and peasants' labour discipline and organisation. The sooner we ourselves, workers and peasants, learn the best labour discipline and the most modern technique of labour, using the bourgeois experts to teach us, the sooner we shall liberate ourselves from any "tribute" to these specialists.

Our work of organising country-wide accounting and control of production and distribution under the supervision of the proletariat has lagged very much behind our work of directly expropriating the expropriators. This proposition is of fundamental importance for understanding the specific features of the present situation and the tasks of the Soviet government that follow from it. The centre of gravity of our struggle against the bourgeoisie is shifting to the organisation of such accounting and control. Only with this as our starting-point will it be possible to determine correctly the immediate tasks of economic and financial policy in the sphere of nationalisation of the banks, monopolisation of foreign trade, the state control of money circulation, the introduction of a property and income tax satisfactory from the proletarian point of view, and the introduction of compulsory labour service.

We have been lagging very far behind in introducing socialist reforms in these spheres (very, very important spheres), and this is because accounting and control are insufficiently organised in general. It goes without saying that this is one of the most difficult tasks, and in view of the ruin caused by the war, it can be fulfilled only over a long period of time; but we must not forget that it is precisely here that the bourgeoisie—and particularly the numerous petty and peasant bourgeoisie—are putting up the most serious fight, disrupting the control that is already being organised, disrupting the grain monopoly, for example, and gaining positions for profiteering and speculative trade. We have far from adequately carried out the things we have decreed, and the principal task of the moment is to concentrate all efforts on the businesslike, practical *realisation* of the principles of the reforms which have already become law (but not yet reality).

In order to proceed with the nationalisation of the banks and to go on steadfastly towards transforming the banks into nodal points of public accounting under socialism, we must first of all, and above all, achieve real success in increasing the number of branches of the People's Bank, in attracting deposits, in simplifying the paying in and withdrawal of deposits by the public, in abolishing queues, in catching and *shooting* bribe-takers and rogues, etc. At first we must really carry out the simplest things, properly organise what is available, and then prepare for the more intricate things.

Consolidate and improve the state monopolies (in grain, leather, etc.) which have already been introduced, and by doing so prepare for the state monopoly of foreign trade. Without this monopoly we shall not be able to "free ourselves" from foreign capital by paying "tribute".[57] And the possibility of building up socialism depends entirely upon whether we shall be able, by paying a certain tribute to foreign capital during a certain transitional period, to safeguard our internal economic independence.

We are also lagging very far behind in regard to the collection of taxes generally, and of the property and income tax in particular. The imposing of indemnities upon the bourgeoisie—a measure which in principle is absolutely permissible and deserves proletarian approval—shows that in this respect we are still nearer to the methods of warfare (to win Russia from the rich for the poor) than to the methods of administration. In order to become stronger, however, and in order to be able to stand firmer on our feet, we must adopt the latter methods, we must substitute for the indemnities imposed upon the bourgeoisie the constant and regular collection of a property and income tax, which will bring a *greater* return to the proletarian state, and which calls for better organisation on our part and better accounting and control.[58]

The fact that we are late in introducing compulsory labour service also shows that the work that is coming to the fore at the present time is precisely the preparatory organisational work that, on the one hand, will finally consolidate our gains and that, on the other, is necessary in order to prepare for the operation of "surrounding" capital and compelling it to "surrender". We ought to begin introducing compulsory labour service immediately, but we must do so very gradually and circumspectly, testing every step by practical experience, and, of course, taking the first step by introducing compulsory labour service *for the rich*. The introduction of work and consumers' budget books for every bourgeois, including every rural bourgeois, would be an important step towards completely "surrounding" the enemy and towards the creation of a truly popular accounting and control of the production and distribution of goods.

The Significance of the Struggle
for Country-Wide Accounting and Control

The state, which for centuries has been an organ for oppression and robbery of the people, has left us a legacy of the people's supreme hatred and suspicion of everything that is connected with the state. It is very difficult to overcome this, and only a Soviet government can do it. Even a Soviet government, however, will require plenty of time and enormous perseverance to accomplish it. This "legacy" is especially apparent in the problem of accounting and control—the fundamental problem facing the socialist revolution on the morrow of the overthrow of the bourgeoisie. A certain amount of time will inevitably pass before the people, who feel free for the first time now that the landowners and the bourgeoisie have been overthrown, will understand—not from books, but from their own, *Soviet* experience—will understand and *feel* that without comprehensive state accounting and control of the production and distribution of goods, the power of the working people, the freedom of the working people, *cannot* be maintained, and that a return to the yoke of capitalism is *inevitable*.

All the habits and traditions of the bourgeoisie, and of the petty bourgeoisie in particular, also oppose *state* control, and uphold the inviolability of "sacred private property", of "sacred" private enterprise. It is now particularly clear to us how correct is the Marxist thesis that anarchism and anarcho-syndicalism are *bourgeois* trends, how irreconcilably opposed they are to socialism, proletarian dictatorship and communism. The fight to instil into the people's minds the idea of *Soviet* state control and accounting, and to carry out this idea in practice; the fight to break with the rotten past, which taught the people to regard the procurement of bread and clothes as a "private" affair, and buying and selling as a transaction "which concerns only myself"—is a great fight of world-historic significance, a fight between socialist consciousness and bourgeois-anarchist spontaneity.

We have introduced workers' control as a law, but this law is only just beginning to operate and is only just beginning to penetrate the minds of broad sections of the proletariat. In our agitation we do not sufficiently explain that lack of accounting and control in the production and distribution of goods means the death of the rudiments of socialism, means the embezzlement of state funds (for all property belongs to the state and the state is the Soviet state in which power belongs to the majority of the working people). We do not sufficiently explain that carelessness in accounting and control is downright aiding and abetting the German and the Russian Kornilovs, who can overthrow the power of the working people *only* if we fail to cope with the task of accounting and control, and who, with the aid of the whole of the rural bourgeoisie, with the aid of the Constitutional-Democrats, the Mensheviks and the Right Socialist-Revolutionaries, are "watching" us and waiting for an opportune moment to attack us. And the advanced workers and peasants do not think and speak about this sufficiently. Until workers' control has become a fact, until the advanced workers have organised and carried out a victorious and ruthless crusade against the violators of this control, or against those who are careless in matters of control, it will be impossible to pass from the first step (from workers' control) to the second step towards socialism, i.e., to pass on to workers' regulation of production.

The socialist state can arise only as a network of producers' and consumers' communes, which conscientiously keep account of their production and consumption, economise on labour, and steadily raise the productivity of labour, thus making it possible to reduce the working day to seven, six and even fewer hours. Nothing will be achieved unless the strictest, country-wide, comprehensive accounting and control of *grain* and the *production of grain* (and later of all other essential goods) are set going. Capitalism left us a legacy of mass organisations which can facilitate our transition to the mass accounting and control of the distribution of goods, namely, the consumers' co-operative societies. In Russia these societies are not so well developed as in the advanced countries, nevertheless, they have over ten million members. The Decree on Consumers' Co-operative Societies, issued the other day,[59] is an extremely significant phenomenon, which strikingly illustrates the peculiar position and the specific tasks of the Soviet Socialist Republic at the present moment.

The decree is an agreement with the bourgeois co-operative societies and the workers' co-operative societies which still adhere to the bourgeois point of view. It is an agreement, or compromise, firstly because the representatives of the above-mentioned institutions not only took part in discussing the decree, but actually had a decisive say in the matter, for the parts of the decree which were strongly opposed by these institutions were dropped. Secondly, the essence of the compromise is that the Soviet government has abandoned the principle of admission of new members to co-operative societies without entrance fees (which is the only consistently proletarian principle); it has also abandoned the idea of uniting the whole population of a given locality in a *single* co-operative society. Contrary to this principle, which is the only socialist principle and which corresponds to the task of abolishing classes, the "working-class co-operative societies" (which in this case call themselves "class" societies only because they subordinate themselves to the class interests of the bourgeoisie) were given the right to continue to exist. Finally, the Soviet government's proposal to expel the bourgeoisie entirely from the boards of the co-operative societies was also considerably modified, and only owners of private capitalist trading and industrial enterprises were forbidden to serve on the boards.

Had the proletariat, acting through the Soviet government, managed to organise accounting and control on a national scale, or at least laid the foundation for such control, it would not have been necessary to make such compromises. Through the food departments of the Soviets, through the supply organisations under the Soviets we should have organised the population into a single co-operative society under proletarian management. We should have done this without the assistance of the bourgeois co-operative societies, without making any concession to the purely bourgeois principle which prompts the workers' co-operative societies to remain workers' societies *side by side* with bourgeois societies, *instead of* subordinating these bourgeois co-operative societies entirely to themselves, merging the two together and taking the *entire* management of the society and the supervision of the consumption of the rich *in their own* hands.

In concluding such an agreement with the bourgeois co-operative societies, the Soviet government concretely defined its tactical aims and its peculiar methods of action in the present stage of development as follows: by directing the bourgeois elements, utilising them, making certain partial concessions to them, we create the conditions for further progress that will be slower than we at first anticipated, but surer, with the base and lines of communication better secured and with the positions which have been won better consolidated. The Soviets can (*and should*) now gauge their successes in the field of socialist construction, among other things, by extremely clear, simple and practical standards, namely, in how many communities (communes or villages, or blocks of houses, etc.) co-operative societies have been organised, and to what extent their development has reached the point of embracing the whole population.

**Written between April 13
and 26, 1918**

Published April 28, 1918 in
Pravda No. 83 and in
Supplement to *Izvestia* No. 85
Signed: *N. Lenin*

Collected Works,
Vol. 27, pp. 244-56

BASIC PROPOSITIONS ON ECONOMIC
AND ESPECIALLY ON BANKING POLICY[60]

I. Completion of nationalisation of industry and exchange.

II. Nationalisation of banks and gradual transition to socialism.

III. Compulsory organisation of the population in consumer co-operative societies.

{ + Commodity exchange}

IV. Accounting and control of production and distribution of goods.

V. Labour discipline.

{ + Tax policy}

Compulsory labour service, begun from the top.

The most ruthless measures to combat chaos, disorder and idleness, and the most vigorous and severe measures for raising the discipline and self-discipline of the workers and peasants, are to be regarded as absolutely essential and urgent.

Conversion of state control into a real control for setting up mobile groups of controllers in all spheres of economic life.

Practical conditions concerning the employment of bourgeois intellectuals and saboteurs who express the desire to work with the Soviet government.

Industrial courts for taking account of production, stocks of goods and labour productivity.

Centralisation

(Immediate and categorical.)
1. Completion of nationalisation of industry.
2. Gradual transition to organisation of one and all in consumer co-operatives and commodity exchange.
3. Banking policy.
4. Labour discipline and so forth.
5. Tax policy (finance).

1. Completion of the nationalisation of all factories, railways, means of production and exchange. Categorical and ruthless struggle against the syndicalist and chaotic attitude to nationalised enterprises.[61] Persistent carrying out of centralisation of economic life on a nation-wide scale. Unremitting demand for preliminary plans and estimates, weekly reports and actual increase of labour productivity. Establishment and practical trial of the apparatus for managing the nationalised industries.

Measures for transition to compulsory current accounts or to compulsory keeping of money in the banks.

Compulsory organisation of the population in consumer co-operative societies and measures for transition to this.

Conditions of an agreement with co-operators on gradual transition of their apparatus towards organisation of the whole population in consumer co-operative societies.

Written in April, not earlier
than 8th, 1918

First published in 1933 in
Lenin Miscellany XXI

Collected Works,
Vol. 27, pp. 318-19

THESES ON BANKING POLICY[62]

1. A report to be compiled of what has been received in private banks, including in the report the liquidation of all affairs of each private bank.

(Unanimous.)

On the question of how to draw up the report, the following opinions expressed:

(a) The former staff (the Commissariat for the State Bank having the right to remove some employees) of each private bank will be given an ultimatum requiring them to put in order in a very brief period of time all the affairs of the bank and to draw up a balance sheet in final form, firstly, for December 14, 1917,[63] and, secondly, for the last day of operations.

(b) Private banks, in fulfilling this function of compiling reports and liquidating all affairs of the bank, act exclusively as branches of the united People's Bank of the Russian Republic and only for the purpose of liquidation, without carrying out any new operations.

(Hanecki and Gukovsky and Lenin.)

Special opinion of Spunde:
The balance sheet for 14:XII:1917 should be drawn up by a special commission appointed by us.
No need to draw up another balance sheet.

Further operations, as from 14:XII:1917, to be carried out in the name of the People's Bank.

All private banks, and also the State Bank, to be declared the united People's Bank of the Russian Republic.

2. All the work of compiling reports to be under the supervision of the Commissariat for the State Bank.

The largest possible number of experienced collaborators to be invited, including former employees of the State Bank and private banks.

(Unanimous.)

3. Banking policy, without being confined to nationalisation of the banks, must gradually but steadily be directed towards converting the banks into a single apparatus for accounting and regulation of the socialistically organised economic life of the country as a whole.

> Spunde and Lenin in favour.
> Gukovsky against.
> Hanecki abstains, considers this impossible to carry out.

4. Extraordinary measures for opening the largest possible number of branches of the People's Bank throughout the country.

These branches to be located in towns and villages so as to provide greatest convenience for the public.

Existing branches of former private banks to be used as branches of the People's Bank.

(Unanimous.)

5. Declaration of inviolability of deposits (which, of course, does not diminish the right of the state to levy taxes).

6. Free circulation of cheques.

7. Full preservation of workers' control with regard to withdrawal of money from the banks.

8. Limitation of withdrawals of money for consumer purposes to be retained.

A series of improved facilities for the public to be introduced for the purpose of accelerating deposits of money in the banks and withdrawal of money from the banks, as well as simplification of formalities.

9. Adoption of measures so that the population should keep in the banks all money not absolutely necessary for consumer purposes. Preparation of a law and practical steps for compulsory implementation of this principle.

(Not to be published.)

10. In their activity, all branches of the People's Bank within the bounds of the Federative Russian Soviet Republic are to be guided strictly by the instructions and directives of the central board of management, without having the right to establish any local rules and restrictions. Exceptions are permitted only with the consent of the central board of management.

Written in April, not earlier than 8th, 1918

First published in 1926 in the magazine *Proletarskaya Revolutsia* No. 6

Collected Works, Vol. 27, pp. 222-23

SPEECH AT A JOINT MEETING
OF REPRESENTATIVES OF THE ALL-RUSSIA
CENTRAL COUNCIL OF TRADE UNIONS,
THE CENTRAL COMMITTEE OF THE METALWORKERS'
UNION AND THE SUPREME ECONOMIC COUNCIL
APRIL 11, 1918[64]

From a Newspaper Report

Comrade Lenin urged the complete nationalisation of all trustified enterprises, with the group of capitalists who sponsored the project being enlisted in the service of the state.

Izvestia No. 72,
April 12, 1918

Collected Works,
Vol. 42, p. 88

LETTER ADDRESSED TO THE CONFERENCE OF REPRESENTATIVES OF ENTERPRISES TO BE NATIONALISED[65]

Having heard the statement made by the comrades elected as the workers' delegation at the conference of representatives of large metalworks, and bearing in mind the resolution adopted by the conference, I am able to say that in my opinion the Council of People's Commissars will certainly be unanimously *in favour* of immediate nationalisation if the conference exerts every effort to secure planned and systematic organisation of work and increased productivity.

Hence, it is desirable that the conference:

1) Should immediately elect a Provisional Council to prepare for the amalgamation of the works;

2) Should authorise the Central Committee of the Metalworkers' Union, in agreement with the Supreme Economic Council, to change the form of and to add members to this Provisional Council for the purpose of transforming it into a *Management Board* of a single union (or amalgamation) of all the nationalised works;

3) Should approve, or by means of a resolution legalise, the factory regulations on the model of the Bryansk regulations,[66] for the purpose of creating strict labour discipline;

4) Should nominate candidates from among specialists, engineers and organisers of large-scale production, for the purpose of participating in the management, or authorise the Supreme Economic Council to seek for and appoint such;

5) It is desirable that workers from the best organised works, or those having most experience in managing large-scale production, shall be sent (by the Provisional Council or by the Central Committee of the Metalworkers' Union) to assist in organising affairs properly at the less successful works;

6) By keeping the strictest account and control of all materials with reference to the productivity of labour, we must achieve, and we can achieve, enormous economies in raw materials and labour.

I think that if the conference and the bodies it sets up work energetically, it will be possible for the Council of People's Commissars to pass the nationalisation decree *within the next few days.*

May 17, 1918

V. Ulyanov (Lenin),
**Chairman of the Council of
People's Commissars**

Izvestia No. 99,
May 19, 1918

Collected Works,
Vol. 27, pp. 388-89

COMMENTS ON THE DRAFT "REGULATIONS FOR THE MANAGEMENT OF THE NATIONALISED ENTERPRISES"[67]

Communism requires and presupposes the greatest possible centralisation of large-scale production throughout the country. The all-Russia centre, therefore, should definitely be given the right of direct control over all the enterprises of the given branch of industry. The regional centres define their functions depending on local conditions of life, etc., in accordance with the general production directions and decisions of the centre.

To deprive the all-Russia centre of the right of direct control over all the enterprises of the given industry throughout the country, as follows from the Commission's draft, would be regional anarcho-syndicalism, and not communism.

Written June 2, 1918

First published in 1959 in
Lenin Miscellany XXXVI

Collected Works,
Vol. 42, p. 96

FOURTH CONFERENCE OF TRADE UNIONS AND FACTORY COMMITTEES OF MOSCOW[68]
JUNE 27-JULY 2, 1918

From the REPLY TO THE DEBATE
ON THE CURRENT SITUATION
JUNE 28

I am asked: "Why is not a monopoly introduced on manufactured goods, which are as necessary as grain?" My reply is: "The Soviet government is adopting all measures to this end." You know that there is a tendency to organise, to amalgamate the textile factories, the textile industry. You know that the majority of the people in the leading bodies of this organisation are workers, you know that the Soviet government is preparing to nationalise all branches of industry; you know that the difficulties that confront us in this matter are enormous, and that much effort will be required to do all this in an organised manner. We are not setting to work on this task in the way governments which rely on bureaucrats do. It is quite easy to manage affairs in that way: let one man receive 400 rubles per month; let another get more, a thousand rubles per month—our business is to give orders and the others must obey. That is how all bourgeois countries are administered; they hire officials at high salaries, they hire the sons of the bourgeoisie and entrust the administration to them. The Soviet Republic cannot be administered in this way. We have no officials to manage and guide the work of amalgamating all the textile factories, of registering all their property and stocks, of introducing a monopoly of all articles of primary necessity, and of properly distributing them. We call upon the workers to do this work; we call upon the representatives of the Textile Workers' Union and say to them: "You must form the majority on the collegium of the Central Textile Board, and you are the majority on it, in the same way as you are the majority on the collegiums of the Supreme Economic Council. Comrades, workers, take up this very important state task yourselves. We know that it is more difficult than appointing efficient officials, but we know also that there is no other way of doing it." Power must be placed in the hands of the working class, and the advanced workers must, in spite of all difficulties, learn by their own bitter experience, by their own efforts, by the work of their own hands, how all articles, all textile goods, should be distributed in the interests of the toilers. (*Applause.*)

Hence, the Soviet government is doing all it possibly can in the present circumstances to introduce a state monopoly and to fix prices. It is doing it through the medium of the workers, in conjunction with the workers; it gives them the majority on the management boards, and in every leading centre, be it the Supreme Economic Council or the amalgamated metalworks, or the amalgamated sugar refineries, which were nationalised in a few weeks. This is a difficult road, but, I repeat, we cannot avoid difficulties in the task of getting the workers to adopt a new position, workers who have been accustomed and have been trained by the bourgeoisie for hundreds of years merely to carry out its orders slavishly, to work like convicts, of making them feel that they are the government. We are the owners of industry, we are the owners of the grain, we are the owners of all the wealth of the country. Only when this has deeply penetrated the minds of the working class, when, by their own experience, by their own efforts, they increase their forces tenfold, will all the difficulties of the socialist revolution be overcome.

Brief reports published
June 29, 1918 in *Pravda* No. 131
and *Izvestia* No. 133

Full report published in 1918
in the book: *Minutes of the
Fourth Conference of Factory
Committees and Trade Unions of
Moscow.* A.C.C.T.U. Publishers

Collected Works,
Vol. 27, pp. 487-89

THE DEMOCRATISM AND SOCIALIST NATURE
OF SOVIET POWER

The democratism of Soviet power and its socialist nature
are expressed in the fact

that the supreme state authority is vested in the Soviets,
which are made up of representatives of the working people
(workers, soldiers and peasants), freely elected and remov-
able at any time by the masses hitherto oppressed by
capital;

that the local Soviets freely amalgamate on a basis of
democratic centralism into a single federal union as represented by the Soviet state power of the Russian Soviet
Republic;

that the Soviets concentrate in their hands not only
the legislative power and supervision of law enforcement,
but direct enforcement of the laws through all the members
of the Soviets with a view to a gradual transition to the
performance of legislative functions and state administration by the whole working population.

Taking, further, into consideration,

that any direct or indirect legalisation of the rights of
ownership of the workers of any given factory or any
given trade on their particular production, or of their right
to weaken or impede the orders of the state authority, is
a flagrant distortion of the basic principles of Soviet power
and a complete rejection of socialism. . . .*

Written in the first half of 1918

First published April 22, 1957
in *Pravda* No. 112

Collected Works,
Vol. 42, pp. 100-01

* Here the manuscript breaks off.—*Ed.*

FIFTH ALL-RUSSIA CONGRESS OF SOVIETS OF WORKERS', PEASANTS', SOLDIERS' AND RED ARMY DEPUTIES[69] JULY 4-10, 1918

From the REPLY TO THE DEBATE
JULY 5

When it was said here that the Bolsheviks were yielding, and that their reports contained nothing of practical value, I recalled the words uttered here by one Socialist-Revolutionary, a Maximalist I think he was, to the effect that the Supreme Economic Council is passing from the control of production to its administration. Isn't that statement of practical value? What, then, are those workers doing, who by their own efforts, through their trade unions, have begun to learn from the bosses the business of administering enterprises? You say that it is an easy thing to learn to administer, but every day we in the Supreme Economic Council have to settle thousands of conflicts and incidents which show that the worker has learnt a lot, and we must conclude that the workers are beginning to learn—slowly, to be sure, and with mistakes; but it is one thing to utter fine phrases, and another to see how with every passing month the worker is beginning to find his feet, how he is beginning to lose his timidity and to feel that he is the ruler. Rightly or wrongly, he is acting as the peasant does in an agricultural commune. Time has shown that the worker had to learn to administer industry, and all the rest is just empty talk and not worth a brass farthing. If, after six months of Soviet rule, we are now beginning to find that control is out of date, that is a big step forward.

The cry has been raised here that we are marking time,

or even retreating. Nothing of the kind. You may persuade the kulak of that, but not the ordinary worker; he knows what we mean when we say, let us have better people than the ones you sent, make them learn better than you are learning. And so, when the cry is raised here about concessions, let us ask any worker or peasant what he prefers: to pay in concessions the debt the Germans imposed upon us, or to fight? When we signed the Peace Treaty of Brest,[70] we said of the imperialists that until they were vanquished by an international socialist revolution, we should not be able to defend ourselves in any other way than by retreating. That is unpleasant, but it will remain a fact—and it is better to tell the people so—until we have built up an army, for which we shall need only a few years, not decades, provided we introduce a proper system of bread distribution, so that there will be stocks of grain for the army, gathered and stored. In what uyezd or gubernia have the Left Socialist-Revolutionaries done that? They have done nothing of the kind! And until it is done, we declare that all your cries are just empty talk; whereas when we take a step towards administration by the workers, we take a step forward. My words have been misquoted here. What I said was that it must be a bad party whose sincere members are obliged to stoop to such talk.

We have assigned a thousand million to our Commissariat for Food—isn't that a step forward? Much still remains to be arranged, and you can do it if you only have the desire. But through whom, I do not know. Not through the old officials, surely? Our workers and peasants on the Soviets are learning to do it (*applause*), and so the purchases of textiles and the appropriations are having their effect. Hundreds of times the Council of People's Commissars has discussed through whom to purchase textiles, how to exercise control, and how to get them distributed as quickly as possible. And we know that as the weeks go by measures have been devised for combating profiteering and catching profiteers, and that with every month the workers are getting a firmer mastery of this job—and this success of ours nobody can deny. We are advancing, not marking time. On June 28, we carried out nationalisation[71] to the extent perhaps of several hundred millions, yet you keep on objecting and repeating the talk of the bourgeois intellectuals. Socialism is not a job that can be done in a few months. We are not marking time, but are continuing to move towards socialism, and since the Brest peace we have come closer to it.

Newspaper report published
July 7, 1918 in *Izvestia* No. 140

Published in full in 1918 in the   *Collected Works,*
book *Fifth All-Russia*   Vol. 27, pp. 530-31
Congress of Soviets. Verbatim
Report, All-Russia C.E.C.
Publishers

From the SPEECH AT A CONGRESS
OF CHAIRMEN OF GUBERNIA SOVIETS
JULY 30, 1918

Newspaper Report

Comrades, your job is one of administration, which plays a dominant part in the affairs of the Council of People's Commissars. Quite naturally, many difficulties lie ahead of you. In the majority of gubernia Executive Committees it is evident that the masses are at last beginning to tackle the work of administration themselves. There are certainly bound to be difficulties. One of our greatest shortcomings has been that we still draw too little on the workers for our staffs. But it was never our intention to adapt the old apparatus to the new system of administration, and we do not regret that with the abolition of the old apparatus everything has to be built anew with so much difficulty. The workers and peasants posses greater constructive abilities than might have been expected. It is to the revolution's credit that it swept away the old administrative apparatus. Yet at the same time we must admit that the people's chief shortcoming is their timidity and reluctance to take things into their own hands.

Some of our gubernia Soviets have been inefficient, but now the work is steadily improving. Information has been coming in from many parts of the country stating that the work is progressing without any misunderstandings or conflicts. Although only eight months have elapsed, the Russian revolution has proved that the new class which has taken administration into its own hands is capable of coping with the task. Although it is short-staffed, the administrative apparatus is running more smoothly every day. Our apparatus is still at a stage where no definite results are visible, a fact which the enemy keeps harping on. Nevertheless, quite a lot has already been done. The transfer of land and industry to the working people, the exchange of goods and the organisation of food supply are being carried into effect in face of fantastic difficulties. The working people must be promoted to independent work in building up and running the socialist state. Only practice will teach them that the old exploiting class is finished and done with.

Our chief and most urgent task is administration, organisation and control. This is a thankless and inconspicuous job; but it is in doing this job that the managerial and administrative talents of the workers and peasants will develop more and more effectively.

Izvestia No. 161, July 31, 1918,
Pravda No. 160, August 1, 1918

Collected Works,
Vol. 28, pp. 35-36

From the LETTER TO AMERICAN WORKERS[72]

Let the corrupt bourgeois press shout to the whole world about every mistake our revolution makes. We are not daunted by our mistakes. People have not become saints because the revolution has begun. The toiling classes who for centuries have been oppressed, downtrodden and forcibly held in the vice of poverty, brutality and ignorance cannot avoid mistakes when making a revolution. And, as I pointed out once before, the corpse of bourgeois society cannot be nailed in a coffin and buried.[73] The corpse of capitalism is decaying and disintegrating in our midst, polluting the air and poisoning our lives, enmeshing that which is new, fresh, young and virile in thousands of threads and bonds of that which is old, moribund and decaying.

For every hundred mistakes we commit, and which the bourgeoisie and their lackeys (including our own Mensheviks and Right Socialist-Revolutionaries) shout about to the whole world, 10,000 great and heroic deeds are performed, greater and more heroic because they are simple and inconspicuous amidst the everyday life of a factory district or a remote village, performed by people who are not accustomed (and have no opportunity) to shout to the whole world about their successes.

But even if the contrary were true—although I know such an assumption is wrong—even if we committed 10,000 mistakes for every 100 correct actions we performed, even in that case our revolution would be great and

181

invincible, and so *it will be in the eyes of world history,* because, *for the first time,* not the minority, not the rich alone, not the educated alone, but the real people, the vast majority of the working people, are *themselves* building a new life, are *by their own experience* solving the most difficult problems of socialist organisation.

Every mistake committed in the course of such work, in the course of this most conscientious and earnest work of tens of millions of simple workers and peasants in reorganising their whole life, every such mistake is worth thousands and millions of "flawless" successes achieved by the exploiting minority—successes in swindling and duping the working people. For only *through* such mistakes will the workers and peasants *learn* to build the new life, learn to do *without* capitalists; only in this way will they hack a path for themselves—through thousands of obstacles—to victorious socialism.

Mistakes are being committed in the course of their revolutionary work by our peasants, who at one stroke, in one night, October 25-26 (old style), 1917, entirely abolished the private ownership of land, and are now, month after month, overcoming tremendous difficulties and correcting their mistakes themselves, solving in a practical way the most difficult tasks of organising new conditions of economic life, of fighting the kulaks, providing land for the *working people* (and not for the rich), and of changing to *communist* large-scale agriculture.

Mistakes are being committed in the course of their revolutionary work by our workers, who have already, after a few months, nationalised almost all the biggest factories and plants, and are learning by hard, everyday work the new task of managing whole branches of industry, are setting the nationalised enterprises going, overcoming the powerful resistance of inertia, petty-bourgeois mentality and selfishness, and, brick by brick, are laying the foundation of *new* social ties, of a *new* labour discipline, of a *new* influence of the workers' trade unions over their members.

Mistakes are committed in the course of their revolutionary work by our Soviets, which were created as far back as 1905 by a mighty upsurge of the people. The Soviets of Workers and Peasants are a new *type* of state, a new and higher *type* of democracy, a form of the proletarian dictatorship, a means of administering the state *without* the bourgeoisie and *against* the bourgeoisie. For the first time democracy is here serving the people, the working people, and has ceased to be democracy for the rich as it still is in all bourgeois republics, even the most democratic. For the first time, the people are grappling, on a scale involving one hundred million, with the problem of implementing the dictatorship of the proletariat and semi-proletariat—a problem which, if not solved, makes socialism *out of the question*.

Let the pedants, or the people whose minds are incurably stuffed with bourgeois-democratic or parliamentary prejudices, shake their heads in perplexity about our Soviets, about the absence of direct elections, for example. These people have forgotten nothing and have learned nothing during the period of the great upheavals of 1914-18. The combination of the proletarian dictatorship with the new democracy for the working people—of civil war with the widest participation of the people in politics—such a combination cannot be brought about at one stroke, nor does it fit in with the outworn modes of routine parliamentary democracy. The contours of a new world, the world of socialism, are rising before us in the shape of the Soviet Republic. It is not surprising that this world does not come into being ready-made, does not spring forth like Minerva from the head of Jupiter.

The old bourgeois-democratic constitutions waxed eloquent about formal equality and right of assembly; but our proletarian and peasant Soviet Constitution casts aside the hypocrisy of formal equality. When the bourgeois republicans overturned thrones they did not worry about formal equality between monarchists and republicans. When it is a matter of overthrowing the bourgeoisie, only traitors or idiots can demand formal equality of rights for the bourgeoisie. "Freedom of assembly" for workers and peasants is not worth a farthing when the best buildings belong to the bourgeoisie. Our Soviets have *confiscated* all the good buildings in town and country from the rich and have *transferred all* of them to the workers and peasants for *their* unions and meetings. This is *our* freedom of assembly—for the working people! This is the meaning and content of our Soviet, our socialist Constitution!

That is why we are all so firmly convinced that no matter what misfortunes may still be in store for it, our Republic of Soviets is *invincible*.

It is invincible because every blow struck by frenzied imperialism, every defeat the international bourgeoisie inflict on us, rouses more and more sections of the workers and peasants to the struggle, teaches them at the cost of enormous sacrifice, steels them and engenders new heroism on a mass scale.

We know that help from you will probably not come soon, comrade American workers, for the revolution is developing in different countries in different forms and at different tempos (and it cannot be otherwise). We know that although the European proletarian revolution has been maturing very rapidly lately, it may, after all, not flare up within the next few weeks. We are banking on the inevitability of the world revolution, but this does not mean that we are such fools as to bank on the revolution inevitably coming on a *definite* and early date. We have seen two great revolutions in our country, 1905 and 1917, and we know revolutions are not made to order, or by agreement. We know that circumstances brought *our* Russian detachment of the socialist proletariat to the fore not because of our merits, but because of the exceptional backwardness of Russia, and that *before* the world revolution breaks out a number of separate revolutions may be defeated.

In spite of this, we are firmly convinced that we are invincible, because the spirit of mankind will not be broken by the imperialist slaughter. Mankind will vanquish it. And the first country to *break* the convict chains of the imperialist war was *our* country. We sustained enormously heavy casualties in the struggle to break these chains, but we *broke* them. We are *free from* imperialist dependence, we have raised the banner of struggle for the complete overthrow of imperialism for the whole world to see.

We are now, as it were, in a besieged fortress, waiting for the other detachments of the world socialist revolution to come to our relief. These detachments *exist*, they are *more numerous* than ours, they are maturing, growing, gaining more strength the longer the brutalities of imperialism continue. The workers are breaking away from their social-traitors—the Gomperses, Hendersons, Renaudels, Scheidemanns and Renners. Slowly but surely the workers are adopting communist, Bolshevik tactics and are marching towards the proletarian revolution, which alone is capable of saving dying culture and dying mankind.

In short, we are invincible, because the world proletarian revolution is invincible.

N. Lenin

August 20, 1918

Pravda No. 178,
August 22, 1918

Collected Works,
Vol. 28, pp. 71-75

SIXTH, EXTRAORDINARY, ALL-RUSSIA CONGRESS OF SOVIETS OF WORKERS', PEASANTS', COSSACKS' AND RED ARMY DEPUTIES[74] NOVEMBER 6-9, 1918

From the SPEECH ON THE ANNIVERSARY OF THE REVOLUTION NOVEMBER 6

And so, comrades, when we ask ourselves what big changes we have made over the past year, we can say the following: from workers' control, the working class's first steps, and from disposing of all the country's resources, we are now on the threshold of creating a workers' administration of industry; from the general peasants' struggle for land, the peasants' struggle against the landowners, a struggle that had a national, bourgeois-democratic character, we have now reached a stage where the proletarian and semi-proletarian elements in the countryside have set themselves apart: those who labour and are exploited have set themselves apart from the others and have begun to build a new life; the most oppressed country folk are fighting the bourgeoisie, including their own rural kulak bourgeoisie, to the bitter end.

Furthermore, from the first steps of Soviet organisation we have now reached a stage where, as Comrade Sverdlov justly remarked in opening this Congress, there is no place in Russia, however remote, where Soviet authority has not asserted itself and become an integral part of the Soviet Constitution, which is based on long experience gained in the struggle of the working and oppressed people.

We now have a powerful Red Army instead of being utterly defenceless after the last four years' war, which evoked hatred and aversion among the mass of the exploited and left them terribly weak and exhausted, and which condemned the revolution to a most difficult and drastic period when we were defenceless against the blows of German and Austrian imperialism. Finally, and most important of all, we have come from being isolated internationally, from which we suffered both in October and at the beginning of the year, to a position where our only but firm allies, the working and oppressed people of the world, have at last rebelled. We have reached a stage where the leaders of the West-European proletariat, like Liebknecht and Adler, leaders who spent many months in prison for their bold and heroic attempts to gather opposition to the imperialist war, have been set free under the pressure of the rapidly developing workers' revolutions in Vienna and Berlin. Instead of being isolated, we are now in a position where we are marching side by side, shoulder to shoulder with our international allies. Those are the chief achievements of the past year. I want to say a few words about the road we have covered, about this transitional stage.

At first our slogan was workers' control. We said that despite all the promises of the Kerensky government, the capitalists were continuing to sabotage production and increase dislocation. We can now see that this would have ended in complete collapse. So the first fundamental step that every socialist, workers' government has to take is workers' control. We did not decree socialism immediately throughout industry, because socialism can only take shape and be consolidated when the working class has learnt how to run the economy and when the authority of the working people has been firmly established. Socialism is mere wishful thinking without that. That is why we introduced workers' control, appreciating that it was a contradictory and incomplete measure, but an essential one so that the workers themselves might tackle the momentous tasks of building up industry in a vast country without and opposed to exploiters. And, comrades, everyone who took a direct, or even indirect, part in this work, everyone who lived through all the oppression and brutality of the old capitalist regime, learned a great deal. We know that little has been accomplished. We know that in this extremely backward and impoverished country where innumerable obstacles and barriers were put in the workers' way, it will take them a long time to learn to run industry. But we consider it most important and valuable that the workers have themselves tackled the job, and that we have passed from workers' control, which in all the main branches of industry was bound to be chaotic, disorganised, primitive and incomplete, to workers' industrial administration on a national scale.

The trade unions' position has altered. Their main function now is to send their representatives to all management boards and central bodies, to all the new organisations which have taken over a ruined and deliberately sabotaged industry from capitalism. They have coped with industry without the assistance of those intellectuals who from the very outset deliberately used their knowledge and education—the result of mankind's store of knowledge—to frustrate the cause of socialism, rather than assist the people in building up a socially-owned economy without exploiters. These men wanted to use their knowledge to put a spoke in the wheel, to hamper the workers who were least trained for tackling the job of administration. We can now say that the main hindrance has been removed. It was extremely difficult, but the sabotage of all people gravitating towards the bourgeoisie has been checked. The workers have succeeded in taking this basic step, in laying the foundations of socialism, despite tremendous handicaps. We are not exaggerating and are not afraid to tell the truth. It is true that in terms of our ultimate goal, little has been accomplished. But a great deal, a very great deal, has been done to strengthen the foundations. When speaking of socialism, we cannot say that great sections of workers have laid the foundations in a politically-conscious way in the sense that they have taken to reading books and pamphlets. By political consciousness we mean that they have tackled this formidable task with their own hands and by their own efforts. And they have committed thousands of blunders from each of which they have themselves suffered. But every blunder trained and steeled them in organising industrial administration, which has now been established and put upon a firm foundation. They saw their work through. From now on the work will be different, for now all workers, not just the leaders and advanced workers, but great sections of workers, know that they themselves, with their own hands, are building socialism and have already laid its foundations, and no force in the country can prevent them from seeing the job through.

We may have had great difficulties in industry, where we had to cover a road which to many seemed long, but which was actually short and led from workers' control to workers' administration, yet far greater preparatory work had to be done in the more backward countryside. Anyone who has studied rural life and come into contact with the peasants would say that it was only in the summer and autumn of 1918 that the urban October Revolution became a real rural October Revolution. And the Petrograd workers and the Petrograd garrison soldiers fully realised when they took power that great difficulties would crop up in rural organisational work, and our progress there would have to be more gradual and that it would be the greatest folly to try to introduce socialised farming by decree, for only an insignificant number of enlightened peasants might support us, while the vast majority had no such object in view. We therefore confined ourselves to what was absolutely essential in the interests of promoting the revolution—in no case to endeavour to outrun the people's development, but to wait until a movement forward occurred as a result of their own experience and their own struggle.

Newspaper reports published
November 9, 1918 in *Pravda*
No. 242 and *Izvestia* No. 244

Published in full in 1919 in the
book *Sixth, Extraordinary,*
All-Russia Congress of Soviets.
Verbatim Report

Collected Works,
Vol. 28, pp. 138-41

From the SPEECH DELIVERED
TO A MEETING OF DELEGATES FROM
THE MOSCOW CENTRAL WORKERS' CO-OPERATIVE[75]
NOVEMBER 26, 1918

We must say forthrightly that the workers and poor peasants will do all they can to really promote the ideals of socialism, and if there are people out of step with these ideals, we shall go it alone. We must, however, make use of everyone who can really help us in this most difficult struggle.

When discussing these questions last April the Council of People's Commissars came to an agreement with the co-operators.[76] This was the only meeting that was attended by members of the non-government co-operative movement as well as the Communist People's Commissars.

We came to an agreement with them. This was the only meeting that adopted a decision by a minority, by co-operators, and not by a majority of Communists.

The Council of People's Commissars did this because it thought it necessary to make use of the experience and knowledge of the co-operators and of their apparatus.

You also know that a decree on the organisation of supply was adopted a few days ago[77] and published in Sunday's *Izvestia*, and which allots a considerable role to the co-operatives and the co-operative movement. This is because socialist economic organisation is impossible without a network of co-operative organisations and because there have been a lot of mistakes in this sphere up to now. Some co-operatives have been closed or nationalised even though the Soviets could not cope with distribution and the organisation of Soviet shops.

By the decree everything taken from the co-operatives must be returned to them.

The co-operatives must be denationalised and re-established.

True enough, the decree is cautious towards co-operatives that were closed because counter-revolutionaries had wormed their way into them. We categorically stated that in this respect the work of the co-operatives had to be kept under control, although they must be fully utilised.

All of you well appreciate that one of the proletariat's chief tasks is the immediate and proper organisation of the supply and distribution of food.

Since we do have an apparatus with the necessary experience and which, most important of all, is based on popular initiative, we must set it to fulfilling these tasks. It is particularly important to utilise the initiative of the people who created these organisations. The ordinary people must be drawn into this work, and this is the main task we must set the co-operatives, the workers' co-operatives in particular.

The supply and distribution of food is something everyone understands. Even a man with no book-learning understands. And in Russia most people are still ignorant and illiterate because everything had been done to prevent the working and exploited people from acquiring education.

Yet there are very many live wires among the people who can display tremendous ability, far greater than might be imagined. It is, therefore, the duty of the workers' co-operatives to enlist these people, to nose them out and give them direct work in the supply and distribution of food. Socialist society is one single co-operative.

I do not doubt that popular initiative in the workers' co-operatives will indeed lead to the conversion of the workers' co-operatives into a single Moscow city consumers' commune.

Published in December 1918
as a leaflet and in the journal
Rabochy Mir No. 19

Collected Works,
Vol. 28, pp. 199-200

Kautsky begins his "economic analysis" of industry with the following magnificent argument:

Russia has a large-scale capitalist industry. Cannot a socialist system of production be built up on this foundation? "One might think so if socialism meant that the workers of the separate factories and mines made these their property" (literally appropriated these for themselves) "in order to carry on production separately at each factory" (p. 52).[79] "This very day, August 5, as I am writing these lines," Kautsky adds, "a speech is reported from Moscow delivered by Lenin on August 2, in which he is stated to have declared: 'The workers are holding the factories firmly in their hands, and the peasants will not return the land to the landowners.'[80] Up till now, the slogan: the factories to the workers, and the land to the peasants, has been an anarcho-syndicalist slogan, not a Social-Democratic one" (pp. 52-53).

I have quoted this passage in full so that the Russian workers, who formerly respected Kautsky, and quite rightly, might see for themselves the methods employed by this deserter to the bourgeois camp.

Just think: on August 5, when numerous decrees on the nationalisation of factories in Russia had been issued—and not a single factory had been "appropriated" by the workers, but had *all* been converted into the property of the Republic—on August 5, Kautsky, on the strength of an obviously crooked interpretation of one sentence in my speech, tries to make the German readers believe that in Russia the factories are being turned over to individual groups of workers! And after that Kautsky, at great length, chews the cud about it being wrong to turn over factories to individual groups of workers!

This is not criticism, it is the trick of a lackey of the bourgeoisie, whom the capitalists have hired to slander the workers' revolution.

The factories must be turned over to the state, or to the municipalities, or the consumers' co-operative societies, says Kautsky over and over again, and finally adds:

"This is what they are now trying to do in Russia...." Now! What does that mean? In August? Why, could not Kautsky have commissioned his friends Stein or Axelrod, or any of the other friends of the Russian bourgeoisie, to translate at least one of the decrees on the factories?

"...How far they have gone in this direction, we cannot yet tell. At all events, this aspect of the activity of the Soviet Republic is of the greatest interest to us, but it still remains entirely shrouded in darkness. There is no lack of decrees...." (That is why Kautsky ignores their *content*, or conceals it from his readers!) "But there is no reliable information as to the effect of these decrees. Socialist production is impossible without all-round, detailed, reliable and rapidly informative statistics. The Soviet Republic cannot possibly have created such statistics yet. What we learn about its economic activities is highly contradictory and can in no way be verified. This, too, is a result of the dictatorship and the suppression of democracy. There is no freedom of the press, or of speech" (p. 53).

This is how history is written! From a "free" press of the capitalists and Dutov men Kautsky would have received information about factories being taken over by the workers.... This "serious savant" who stands above classes is magnificent, indeed! About the countless facts which show that the factories are being turned over to the Republic *only*, that they are managed by an organ of Soviet power, the Supreme Economic Council, which is constituted mainly of workers elected by the trade unions, Kautsky refuses to say a single word. With the obstinacy of the "man in the muffler", he stubbornly keeps repeating one thing: give me peaceful democracy, without civil war, without a dictatorship and with good statistics (the Soviet Republic has created a statistical service in which the best statistical experts in Russia are employed, but, of course, ideal statistics cannot be obtained so quickly). In a word, what Kautsky demands is a revolution without revolution, without fierce struggle, without violence. It is equivalent to asking for strikes in which workers and employers do not get excited. Try to find the difference between this kind of "socialist" and common liberal bureaucrat!

Written October-not later than
November 10, 1918

Published in pamphlet form in
1918 by Kommunist
Publishers. Moscow

Collected Works,
Vol. 28, pp. 315-17

TELEGRAM TO THE SOVIET OF COMMUNES
OF THE NORTHERN REGION

Zinoviev, Smolny, Petrograd
Northern Region Food Committee, Economic Council,
Petrokomprod
Gubernia Food Committee, Optosoyuz

Copies to Trudosoyuz, Gubernia Food Committees
Olonets, Cherepovets, Novgorod, Pskov Economic Councils

According to information received, notwithstanding the
decree of November 21, local co-operatives are being
nationalised and closed, their goods requisitioned and no
help is being given in restoring their legitimate activity.[81]
Everybody who causes dislocation of supply upsets the
organisation of the Soviet Republic's rear. The present is
an instruction immediately to cease attempts to infringe
and evade the decree of November 21, to restore the closed
and nationalised co-operatives, to return their goods, and
without fail to include the co-operatives in the distributive
system, on an equal footing with state shops. The co-
operative machinery should be made use of in all possible
ways in the business of purchasing supplies and distribution, and representatives of the co-operative movement
should be drawn into co-operative commissions of the
food supply organisations. Infringement and evasion of
the decree will be punished. This telegram is to be com-

municated for information and action to all Executive
Committees and food supply organisations of the Northern
Region. To be published in the local newspapers.

Ulyanov (Lenin),
Chairman, Defence Council

Written December 25, 1918

Published in *Petrogradskaya*
Pravda No. 285, December 27,
1918

Collected Works,
Vol. 35, p. 376

Points from the Economic Section
of the Programme

The Russian Communist Party, developing the general tasks of the Soviet government in greater detail, at present formulates them as follows.

In the Economic Sphere

The present tasks of Soviet power are:

(1) to continue steadily and finish the expropriation of the bourgeoisie and the conversion of the means of production and distribution into the property of the Soviet Republic, i.e., the common property of all working people, which has in the main been completed.

(2) To pay particularly great attention to the development and strengthening of comradely discipline among the working people and to stimulate their initiative and sense of responsibility in every field. This is the most important if not the sole means of completely overcoming capitalism and the habits formed by the rule of the private ownership of the means of production. This aim can be achieved only by slow, persistent work to re-educate the masses; this re-education has not only become possible now that the masses have seen that the landowner, capitalist and merchant have really been eliminated, but is actually taking place in thousands of ways through the practical experience of the workers and peasants themselves. It is extremely important in this respect to work for the further

organisation of the working people in trade unions; never before has this organisation developed as rapidly anywhere in the world as under Soviet power, and it must be developed until literally all working people are organised in properly constituted, centralised and disciplined trade unions.

8.[83] This same task of developing the productive forces calls for the immediate, extensive and comprehensive employment in science and technology of the specialists who have been left us as our heritage by capitalism, although, as a rule, they are imbued with a bourgeois world outlook and habits. The Party, in close alliance with the trade union organisations, must continue its former line—on the one hand, there must not be the slightest political concession to this bourgeois section of the population, and any counter-revolutionary attempts on its part must be ruthlessly suppressed, and, on the other hand, there must be a relentless struggle against the pseudo-radical but actually ignorant and conceited opinion that the working people are capable of overcoming capitalism and the bourgeois social system without learning from bourgeois specialists, without making use of their services and without undergoing the training of a lengthy period of work side by side with them.

Although the ultimate aim of the Soviet government is to achieve full communism and equal remuneration for all kinds of work, it cannot, however, introduce this equality straightaway, at the present time, when only the first steps of the transition from capitalism to communism are being taken. For a certain period of time, therefore, we must retain the present higher remuneration for specialists in order to give them an incentive to work no worse, and even better, than they have worked before; and with the same object in view, we must not reject the system of paying bonuses for the most successful work, particularly organisational work.

It is equally necessary to surround the bourgeois specialist with a comradely atmosphere created by working hand in hand with the masses of rank-and-file workers led by politically-conscious Communists in order to promote mutual understanding and friendship between workers by hand and brain whom capitalism kept apart.

The mobilisation of the entire able-bodied population by the Soviet government, with the trade unions participating, for certain public works must be much more widely and systematically practised than has hitherto been the case.

In the sphere of distribution, the present task of Soviet power is to continue steadily replacing trade by the planned, organised and nation-wide distribution of goods. The goal is the organisation of the entire population in a single system of consumers' communes that can distribute all essential products most rapidly, systematically, economically and with the least expenditure of labour by strictly centralising the entire distribution machinery.

To achieve this object it is particularly important in the present period, when there are transitional forms based on different principles, for the Soviet food supply organisations to make use of the co-operative societies, the only mass apparatus for systematic distribution inherited from capitalism.

Being of the opinion that in principle the only correct policy is the further communist development of this apparatus and not its rejection, the R.C.P. must systematically pursue the policy of making it obligatory for all members of the Party to work in the co-operatives and, with the aid of the trade unions, direct them in a communist spirit, develop the initiative and discipline of the working people who belong to them, endeavour to get the entire population to join them, and the co-operatives themselves to merge into one single co-operative that embraces the whole of the Soviet Republic. Lastly, and most important, the dominating influence of the proletariat over the rest of the working people must be constantly maintained, and everywhere the most varied measures must be tried with a view to facilitating and bringing about the transition from petty-bourgeois co-operatives of the old capitalist type to consumers' communes led by proletarians and semi-proletarians.

(6) It is impossible to abolish money at one stroke in the first period of transition from capitalism to communism. As a consequence, the bourgeois elements of the population continue to use privately-owned currency notes— these tokens by which the exploiters obtain the right to

receive public wealth—for the purpose of speculation, profit-making and robbing the working population. The nationalisation of the banks is insufficient in itself to combat this survival of bourgeois robbery. The R.C.P. will strive as speedily as possible to introduce the most radical measures to pave the way for the abolition of money, first and foremost to replace it by savings-bank books, cheques, short-term notes entitling the holders to receive goods from the public stores, and so forth, to make it compulsory for money to be deposited in the banks, etc. Practical experience in paving the way for, and carrying out, these and similar measures will show which of them are the most expedient.

(7) In the sphere of finance, the R.C.P. will introduce a graduated income-and-property tax in all cases where it is feasible. But these cases cannot be numerous since private property in land, the majority of factories and other enterprises has been abolished. In the epoch of the dictatorship of the proletariat and of the state ownership of the principal means of production, the state finances must be based on the direct appropriation of a certain part of the revenue from the different state monopolies to meet the needs of the state. Revenue and expenditure can be balanced only if the exchange of commodities is properly organised, and this will be achieved by the organisation of consumers' communes and the restoration of the transport system, which is one of the major immediate objects of the Soviet government.

Published February 27, 1919
in *Pravda* No. 45

Collected Works,
Vol. 29, pp. 135-38

EIGHTH CONGRESS OF THE R.C.P.(B.)[84]
MARCH 18-23, 1919

1

From the REPORT OF THE CENTRAL
COMMITTEE
MARCH 18

Take the question which engaged our attention most of all, namely, the transition from workers' control to workers' management in industry. Following the decrees and decisions passed by the Council of People's Commissars and local Soviet authorities—all of which contributed to our political experience in this field—actually the only thing left for the Central Committee to do was to sum up. In a matter like this it was scarcely able to give a lead in the true sense of the word. One has only to recall how clumsy, immature and casual were our first decrees and decisions on the subject of workers' control of industry. We thought that it was an easy matter; practice showed that it was necessary to build, but we gave no answer whatever to the question as to *how* to build. Every nationalised factory, every branch of nationalised industry, transport, and particularly railway transport—that most striking example of highly centralised capitalist machinery built on the basis of large-scale engineering, and most vital for the state—all embodied the concentrated experience of capitalism, and created immense difficulties for us.

We are still far from having overcome these difficulties. At first we regarded them in an entirely abstract way, like revolutionary preachers, who had absolutely no idea of how to set to work. There were lots of people, of course, who accused us—and all the socialists and Social-Democrats are accusing us today—of having undertaken this task without knowing how to finish it. But these accusations are ridiculous, made by people who lack the spark of life. As if one can set out to make a great revolution and know beforehand how it is to be completed! Such knowledge cannot be derived from books and our decision could spring only from the experience of the masses. And I say that it is to our credit that amidst incredible difficulties we undertook to solve a problem with which until then we were only half familiar, that we inspired the proletarian masses to display their own initiative, that we nationalised the industrial enterprises, and so forth. I remember that in Smolny we passed as many as ten or twelve decrees at one sitting. That was an expression of our determination and desire to stimulate the spirit of experiment and initiative among the proletarian masses. We now have experience. Now, we have passed, or are about to pass, from workers' control to workers' management of industry. Instead of being absolutely helpless as we were before, we are now armed with experience, and as far as this is possible, we have summed it up in our programme. We shall have to discuss this in detail when we deal with the question of organisation. We would not have been able to do this work had we not had the assistance and collaboration of the comrades from the trade unions.

Published March 20 and 21,
1919 in *Pravda* Nos. 60 and 61

Collected Works,
Vol. 29, pp. 154-55

DRAFT THIRD CLAUSE OF THE GENERAL POLITICAL SECTION OF THE PROGRAMME
(For the Programme Commission
of the Eighth Party Congress)[85]

Bourgeois democracy confined itself to proclaiming formal rights equally applicable to all citizens, e.g., the right of assembly, of association, of the press. At best all legislative restrictions on these points were abolished in the most democratic bourgeois republics. But, in reality, both administrative practices and particularly the economic bondage of the working people always made it impossible for them, under bourgeois democracy, to make any wide use of these rights and liberties.

By contrast, proletarian or Soviet democracy, instead of the formal proclamation of rights and liberties, guarantees them in practice first and foremost to those classes of the population who were oppressed by capitalism, i.e., the proletariat and the peasantry. For this purpose, the Soviet power expropriates from the bourgeoisie premises, printing presses and stocks of paper, and places them at the entire disposal of the working people and their organisations.

The task of the Russian Communist Party is to draw ever wider masses of working people into the exercise of their democratic rights and liberties, and to extend the material possibilities for this.

Written not later than
March 20, 1919

First published April 22, 1956
in *Pravda* No. 113

Collected Works,
Vol. 36, p. 505

From SPEECHES ON GRAMAPHONE RECORDS[86]

Communication on the Wireless Negotiations
With Béla Kun

I knew Comrade Béla Kun very well when he was still a prisoner of war in Russia; and he visited me many times to discuss communism and the communist revolution. Therefore, when news of the Hungarian communist revolution[87] was received, and in a communication signed by Comrade Béla Kun at that, we wanted to speak to him and ascertain exactly how the revolution stood. The first communication we received about it gave us some grounds for fearing that, perhaps, the so-called socialists, traitor-socialists, had resorted to some deception, had got round the Communists, the more so that the latter were in prison. And so, the day after the first communication about the Hungarian revolution was received, I sent a wireless message to Budapest, asking Béla Kun to come to the apparatus, and I put a number of questions to him of such a nature as to enable me to make sure that it was really he who was speaking. I asked him what real guarantees there were for the character of the government and for its actual policy[88] Comrade Béla Kun's reply was quite satisfactory and dispelled all our doubts. It appears that the Left Socialists had visited Béla Kun in prison to consult him about forming a government. And it was only these Left Socialists, who sympathised with the Communists, and also people from the Centre who formed the new government, while the Right Socialists, the traitor-socialists, the irreconcilables and incorrigibles, so to speak, left the Party, and not a single worker followed them. Later communications showed that the policy of the Hungarian Government was most firm and so communist in trend that while we began with workers' control of industry and only gradually began to socialise industry, Béla Kun, with his prestige, his conviction that he was backed by vast masses, could at once pass a law which converted all the industrial undertakings in Hungary that were run on capitalist lines into public property. Two days later we became fully convinced that the Hungarian revolution had at once, with extraordinary rapidity, taken the communist road. The bourgeoisie voluntarily surrendered power to the Communists of Hungary. The bourgeoisie demonstrated to the whole world that when a grave crisis supervenes, when the nation is in danger, the bourgeoisie is unable to govern. And there is only one government that is really a popular government, a government that is really beloved of the people—the government of the Soviets of Workers', Soldiers' and Peasants' Deputies.

Long live Soviet power in Hungary!

Delivered at the end of
March 1919

Published in 1924 in the
magazine *Molodaya Gvardia*
No. 2-3

Collected Works,
Vol. 29, pp. 242-43

MESSAGE OF GREETINGS TO THE BAVARIAN SOVIET REPUBLIC[89]

We thank you for your message of greetings, and on our part whole-heartedly greet the Soviet Republic of Bavaria. We ask you insistently to give us more frequent, definite information on the following. What measures have you taken to fight the bourgeois executioners, the Scheidemanns and Co.; have councils of workers and servants been formed in the different sections of the city; have the workers been armed; have the bourgeoisie been disarmed; has use been made of the stocks of clothing and other items for immediate and extensive aid to the workers, and especially to the farm labourers and small peasants; have the capitalist factories and wealth in Munich and the capitalist farms in its environs been confiscated; have mortgage and rent payments by small peasants been cancelled; have the wages of farm labourers and unskilled workers been doubled or trebled; have all paper stocks and all printing-presses been confiscated so as to enable popular leaflets and newspapers to be printed for the masses; has the six-hour working day with two- or three-hour instruction in state administration been introduced; have the bourgeoisie in Munich been made to give up surplus housing so that workers may be immediately moved into comfortable flats; have you taken over all the banks; have you taken hostages from the ranks of the bourgeoisie; have you introduced higher rations for the workers than for the bourgeoisie; have all the workers been mobilised for defence and for ideological propaganda in the neighbouring villages? The most urgent and most extensive implementation of these and similar measures, coupled with the initiative of workers', farm labourers' and—acting apart from them—small peasants' councils, should strengthen your position. An emergency tax must be levied on the bourgeoisie, and an actual improvement effected in the condition of the workers, farm labourers and small peasants at once and at all costs.

With sincere greetings and wishes of success.

Lenin

Written April 27, 1919

First published in *Pravda*
No. 111, April 22, 1930

Collected Works,
Vol. 29, pp. 325-26

FIRST ALL-RUSSIA CONGRESS ON ADULT EDUCATION
MAY 6-19, 1919

From the Speech DECEPTION
OF THE PEOPLE WITH SLOGANS OF FREEDOM
AND EQUALITY[90]
MAY 19

We know perfectly well that we have to contend against world capital; we know perfectly well that at one time it was the task of world capital to create freedom, that it overthrew feudal slavery, that it created bourgeois freedom. We know perfectly well that this was epoch-making progress. And yet we say that we are opposing capitalism in general, republican capitalism, democratic capitalism, free capitalism; and, of course, we know that it will raise the standard of liberty against us. But to this we have our answer, and we deemed it necessary to give this answer in our programme—all freedom is deception if it runs counter to the emancipation of labour from the yoke of capital.

But, perhaps, this is not the case? Perhaps there is no contradiction between freedom and the emancipation of labour from the yoke of capital? Take the West-European countries that you have visited, or at least have read about. Every book you read describes their system as the freest system. And now, these civilised countries of Western Europe—France and Britain—and America have raised this standard, are marching against the Bolsheviks "in the name of freedom". Only the other day—we now get French newspapers but rarely because we are completely surrounded, but we do get wireless information, because, after all, they cannot blockade the air, and we

208

intercept foreign wireless messages—the other day I had the opportunity of reading a wireless message that was sent out by the predatory government of France to the effect that in fighting the Bolsheviks and supporting their opponents, France was remaining true to her "lofty ideals of freedom". We hear this sort of thing at every step, it is the general tone of their polemics against us.

But what do they mean by freedom? By freedom these civilised Frenchmen, Englishmen and Americans mean, say, freedom of assembly. The constitution should contain the clause: "Freedom of assembly for all citizens." "This," they say, "is the substance, this is the principal manifestation of freedom. But you Bolsheviks have violated freedom of assembly."

To this we answer: indeed, the freedom that you British, French and American gentlemen preach is a deception if it runs counter to the emancipation of labour from the yoke of capital. You have forgotten a detail, you civilised gentlemen. You have forgotten that your freedom is inscribed in a constitution which *sanctions private property*. That is the whole point.

In your constitution you have freedom side by side with private property. The fact that you recognise freedom of assembly, of course, marks vast progress compared with the feudal system, with medievalism, with serfdom. All socialists admitted this when they took advantage of the freedom of bourgeois society to teach the proletariat how to throw off the yoke of capitalism.

But your freedom is only freedom on paper, but not in fact. By that I mean that the large halls that are to be found in big cities—like this hall, for example—belong to the capitalists and landowners, and are sometimes called "Assembly Rooms for the Gentry". You may freely assemble in these halls, citizens of the Russian Democratic Republic, but remember that they are private property and, pardon me for saying so, you must respect private property, otherwise you will be Bolsheviks, criminals, murderers, robbers and mischief-makers. But we say: "We shall change all this. We shall first convert these Assembly Rooms into premises for workers' organisations and then begin to talk about freedom of assembly." You accuse us of violating freedom. But we say that all freedom is deception if it is not subordinated to the task of emancipating labour from the yoke of capital. The freedom of assembly inscribed in the constitutions of all bourgeois republics is a deception because in order to assemble in a civilised country, which after all has not abolished winter, has not changed its climate, it is necessary to have premises in which to assemble, and the best of these premises are private property. First, we shall confiscate the best premises and then begin to talk about freedom.

Published in 1919 in the
pamphlet: N. Lenin, *Two Speeches
at the First All-Russia Congress on
Adult Education
(May 6-19, 1919)*, Moscow

Collected Works,
Vol. 29, pp. 352-54

5. More than anything else I should like to state the following to the American public:

Compared to feudalism, capitalism was an historical advance along the road of "liberty", "equality", "democracy" and "civilisation". Nevertheless capitalism was, and remains, a system of *wage-slavery*, of the enslavement of millions of working people, workers and peasants, by an insignificant minority of modern slave-owners, landowners and capitalists. Bourgeois democracy, as compared to feudalism, has changed the form of this economic slavery, has created a brilliant screen for it but has not, and could not, change its essence. Capitalism and bourgeois democracy are wage-slavery.

The gigantic progress of technology in general, and of means of transport in particular, and the tremendous growth of capital and banks have resulted in capitalism becoming mature and overmature. It has outlived itself. It has become the most reactionary hindrance to human progress. It has become reduced to the absolute power of a handful of millionaires and multimillionaires who send whole nations into a bloodbath to decide whether the German or the Anglo-French group of plunderers is to obtain the spoils of imperialism, power over the colonies, financial "spheres of influence" or "mandates to rule", etc.

During the war of 1914-18 tens of millions of people were killed or mutilated for that reason and for that reason alone. Knowledge of this truth is spreading with indomitable force and rapidity among the working people of all countries, the more so because the war has everywhere caused unparalleled ruin, and because interest on war debts has to be paid *everywhere*, even by the "victor" nations. What is this interest? It is a tribute of thousands of millions to the millionaire gentlemen who were kind enough to allow tens of millions of workers and peasants to kill and maim one another to settle the question of the division of profits by the capitalists.

The collapse of capitalism is inevitable. The revolutionary consciousness of the masses is everywhere growing; there are thousands of signs of this. One small sign, unimportant, but impressive to the man in the street, is the novels written by Henri Barbusse (*Le Feu, Clarté*) who was a peaceful, modest, law-abiding petty bourgeois, a philistine, a man in the street, when he went to the war.

The capitalists, the bourgeoisie, can at "best" put off the victory of socialism in one country or another at the cost of slaughtering further hundreds of thousands of workers and peasants. But they cannot save capitalism. The *Soviet Republic* has come to take the place of capitalism, the Republic which gives power to the working people and only to the working people, which entrusts the proletariat with the guidance of their liberation, which abolishes private property in land, factories and other means of production, because this private property is the source of the exploitation of the many by the few, the source of mass poverty, the source of predatory wars between nations, wars that enrich only the capitalists.

The victory of the world Soviet republic is certain.

A brief illustration in conclusion: the American bourgeoisie are deceiving the people by boasting of the liberty, equality and democracy of their country. But neither this nor any other bourgeoisie nor any government in the world can accept, it is afraid to accept, a contest with our government on the basis of real liberty, equality and democracy; let us suppose that an agreement ensured our government and any other government freedom to exchange ... pamphlets published in the name of the government in any language and containing the text of the laws of the given country, the text of its constitution, and an explanation of its superiority over the others.

Not one bourgeois government in the world would dare conclude such a peaceful, civilised, free, equal, democratic treaty with us.

Why? Because all of them, with the exception of Soviet governments, keep in power by the oppression and deception of the masses. But the great war of 1914-18 exposed the great deception.

Lenin

July 20, 1919

Pravda No. 162,
July 25, 1919

Collected Works,
Vol. 29, pp. 517-19

What we need is not only organisational work on a scale involving millions; we need organisational work on the smallest scale and this makes it possible for women to work as well. Women can work under war conditions when it is a question of helping the army or carrying on agitation in the army. Women should take an active part in all this so that the Red Army sees that it is being looked after, that solicitude is being displayed. Women can also work in the sphere of food distribution, on the improvement of public catering and everywhere opening dining-rooms like those that are so numerous in Petrograd.

It is in these fields that the activities of working women acquire the greatest organisational significance. The participation of working women is also essential in the organisation and running of big experimental farms and should not take place only in isolated cases. This is something that cannot be carried out without the participation of a large number of working women. Working women will be very useful in this field in supervising the distribution of food and in making food products more easily obtainable. This work can well be done by non-Party working women and its accomplishment will do more than anything else to strengthen socialist society.

We have abolished private property in land and almost completely abolished the private ownership of factories; Soviet power is now trying to ensure that all working people, non-Party as well as Party members, women as well as men, should take part in this economic development. The work that Soviet power has begun can only make progress when, instead of a few hundreds, millions and millions of women throughout Russia take part in it. We are sure that the cause of socialist development will then become sound. Then the working people will show that they can live and run their country without the aid of the landowners and capitalists. Then socialist construction will be so soundly based in Russia that no external enemies in other countries and none inside Russia will be any danger to the Soviet Republic.

Pravda No. 213, September 25, 1919

Collected Works, Vol. 30, pp. 45-46

From ECONOMICS AND POLITICS
IN THE ERA OF THE DICTATORSHIP
OF THE PROLETARIAT

2

In Russia, the dictatorship of the proletariat must inevitably differ in certain particulars from what it would be in the advanced countries, owing to the very great backwardness and petty-bourgeois character of our country. But the basic forces—and the basic forms of social economy—are the same in Russia as in any capitalist country, so that the peculiarities can apply only to what is of lesser importance.

The basic forms of social economy are capitalism, petty commodity production and communism. The basic forces are the bourgeoisie, the petty bourgeoisie (the peasantry in particular) and the proletariat.

The economic system of Russia in the era of the dictatorship of the proletariat represents the struggle of labour, united on communist principles on the scale of a vast state and making its first steps—the struggle against petty commodity production and against the capitalism which still persists and against that which is newly arising on the basis of petty commodity production.

In Russia, labour is united communistically insofar as, first, private ownership of the means of production has been abolished, and, secondly, the proletarian state power is organising large-scale production on state-owned land and in state-owned enterprises on a national scale, is distributing labour-power among the various branches of economy and the various enterprises, and is distributing among the working people large quantities of articles of consumption belonging to the state.

We speak of "the first steps" of communism in Russia (it is also put that way in our Party Programme adopted in March 1919), because all these things have been only partially effected in our country, or, to put it differently, their achievement is only in its early stages. We accomplished instantly, at one revolutionary blow, all that can, in general, be accomplished instantly; on the first day of the dictatorship of the proletariat, for instance, on October 26 (November 8), 1917, the private ownership of land was abolished without compensation for the big landowners—the big landowners were expropriated. Within the space of a few months practically all the big capitalists, owners of factories, joint-stock companies, banks, railways, and so forth, were also expropriated without compensation. The state organisation of large-scale production in industry and the transition from "workers' control" to "workers' management" of factories and railways—this has, by and large, already been accomplished; but in relation to agriculture it has only just begun ("state farms", i.e., large farms organised by the workers' state on state-owned land). Similarly, we have only just begun the organisation of various forms of co-operative societies of small farmers as a transition from petty commodity agriculture to communist agriculture.* The same must be said of the state-organised distribution of products in place of private trade, i.e., the state procurement and delivery of grain to the cities and of industrial products to the countryside.

October 30, 1919

Pravda No. 250 and *Izvestia* No. 250, November 7, 1919 Signed: *N. Lenin*   *Collected Works,* Vol. 30, pp. 108-09

---

* The number of "state farms" and "agricultural communes" in Soviet Russia is, as far as is known, 3,536 and 1,961 respectively, and the number of agricultural artels is 3,696. Our Central Statistical Board is at present taking an exact census of all state farms and communes. The results will begin coming in in November 1919.

From the **SPEECH AT A JOINT SESSION OF THE ALL-RUSSIA CENTRAL EXECUTIVE COMMITTEE, THE MOSCOW SOVIET OF WORKERS' AND RED ARMY DEPUTIES, THE ALL-RUSSIA CENTRAL COUNCIL OF TRADE UNIONS, AND FACTORY COMMITTEES, ON THE OCCASION OF THE SECOND ANNIVERSARY OF THE OCTOBER REVOLUTION NOVEMBER 7, 1919**

It is particularly important for us to understand the development that has taken place in this period, because there is development along the same lines all over the world. The industrial workers and other working people do not take their first steps with their real leaders; the proletariat themselves are now taking over the administration of state, political power, and at their head we see everywhere leaders who are destroying the old prejudices of petty-bourgeois democracy, old prejudices the vehicles of which in our country are the Mensheviks and Socialist-Revolutionaries, and throughout Europe are the representatives of bourgeois governments. Previously this was an exception, now it has become the general rule. Two years ago, in October, the bourgeois government in Russia—their alliance or coalition with the Mensheviks and Socialist-Revolutionaries—was smashed, but we know how, in carrying on our work, we had subsequently to reorganise every branch of administration in such a way that genuine representatives, revolutionary workers, the vanguard of the proletariat, really took in hand the organisation of state power. That was in October, two years ago, when the work went on at terrific pressure; nevertheless we know, and we must say it, that this work is not finished even now. We know how those who formerly ran the state resisted us, how officials at first tried refusing to administrate, but this gross sabotage was stopped in a few weeks by the proletarian government. It showed that not the slightest impression could be made on it by such refusal; and after we had put an end to this gross sabotage this same enemy tried other methods.

Time and again it has happened that supporters of the bourgeoisie have been found even at the head of workers' organisations; we had to get down to the business of making the fullest use of the workers' strength. Take, for example, what we experienced when the railway administration, the railway proletariat were headed by people who led them along the bourgeois, and not the proletarian path. We know that in all spheres, wherever we could get rid of the bourgeoisie, we did so, but at what a price! In each sphere we gained ground inch by inch, and promoted the best of our workers, those who had gone through the hard school of organising the administration. Viewed from the side, all this is, perhaps, not very difficult, but actually, if you go into the matter, you will see with what difficulty the workers, who had been through all the stages of the struggle, asserted their rights, how they set things going—from workers' control to workers' management of industry, or how on the railways, beginning from the notorious Vikzhel,* they got an efficient organisation working; you will see how representatives of the working class are gradually making their way into all our organisations and strengthening them by their activity. Take the co-operatives, for example, where we see huge numbers of workers' representatives. We know that formerly they consisted almost entirely of non-working-class people. Furthermore, in the old co-operatives, there were people steeped in the views and interests of the old bourgeois society. In this respect the workers had to wage a long

---

* Vikzhel—All-Russia Executive Committee of the Railwaymen's Trade Union.—*Ed.*

struggle before they could take power into their own hands and subordinate the co-operatives to their interests, before they could carry on more fruitful work.

Brief newspaper report
published in *Izvestia* No. 251,
November 9, 1919

Published in full in *Pravda*   *Collected Works,*
No. 251, November 9, 1919   Vol. 30, pp. 129-31

NINTH CONGRESS OF THE R.C.P.(B.)
MARCH 29-APRIL 5, 1920[92]

From the SPEECH ON THE CO-OPERATIVES
APRIL 3

That is why Comrade Chuchin is wrong when he advocates immediate nationalisation. It would be a good thing, but it is impossible, for we are dealing with a class which is least susceptible to our influence and which certainly cannot be nationalised. We have not even nationalised all the industrial enterprises. By the time an order of the chief administrations and central boards reaches the localities it becomes absolutely ineffective; it is completely lost in a sea of documents, because of lack of roads and telegraph, etc. It is therefore impossible to speak of the nationalisation of the co-operatives as yet. Comrade Milyutin is wrong in principle too. He feels that his position is weak and thinks that he can simply withdraw this point. But in that case, Comrade Milyutin, you are undermining your own resolution, you are issuing a certificate to the effect that the resolution of the minority is right; for the spirit of your resolution—to subordinate them to the volost executive committees (that is exactly what is said in the first clause—"take measures")—is a Cheka spirit, wrongly introduced into an economic issue. The other resolution says that the first thing to do is to increase the number of Communists, to intensify communist propaganda and agitation—that a basis must be created. There is nothing grandiloquent here, no immediate promises of a land flowing with milk and honey. But if there are Communists in the localities, they will know what has to be done, and there will be no need for Comrade Chuchin to explain where counter-revolutionaries should be taken to. Secondly, an organ must be created. Create an organ and test it in action, check whether production is increasing—that is what the resolution of the minority says. First of all create a basis, and then—then we shall see. What has to be done will follow from this of itself. We have enough decrees saying that counter-revolutionaries should be handed over to the Cheka, and if there is no Cheka, to the Revolutionary Committee. We need less of this fist-shaking. We must adopt the resolution of the minority, which lays down a basic line of policy.

Brief newspaper report
published in *Pravda* No. 11,
April 4, 1920

Published in full in 1920 in the   *Collected Works,*
book *Ninth Congress of the*   Vol. 30, pp. 483-84
Russian Communist Party.
Verbatim Report

INTERNATIONAL WORKING WOMEN'S DAY

The gist of Bolshevism and the Russian October Revolution is getting into politics the very people who were most oppressed under capitalism. They were downtrodden, cheated and robbed by the capitalists, both under the monarchy and in the bourgeois-democratic republics. So long as the land and the factories were privately owned this oppression and deceit and the plunder of the people's labour by the capitalists were inevitable.

The essence of Bolshevism and the Soviet power is to expose the falsehood and mummery of bourgeois democracy, to abolish the private ownership of land and the factories and concentrate all state power in the hands of the working and exploited masses. They, these masses, get hold of politics, that is, of the business of building the new society. This is no easy task: the masses are downtrodden and oppressed by capitalism, but there is no other way—and there can be no other way—out of the wage-slavery and bondage of capitalism.

But you cannot draw the masses into politics without drawing in the women as well. For under capitalism the female half of the human race is doubly oppressed. The working woman and the peasant woman are oppressed by capital, but over and above that, even in the most democratic of the bourgeois republics, they remain, firstly, deprived of some rights because the law does not give them equality with men; and secondly—and this is the main thing—they remain in "household bondage", they continue to be "household slaves", for they are overburdened with the drudgery of the most squalid, backbreaking and stultifying toil in the kitchen and the family household.

No party or revolution in the world has ever dreamed of striking so deep at the roots of the oppression and inequality of women as the Soviet, Bolshevik revolution is doing. Over here, in Soviet Russia, no trace is left of any inequality between men and women under the law. The Soviet power has eliminated all there was of the especially disgusting, base and hypocritical inequality in the laws on marriage and the family and inequality in respect of children.

This is only the first step in the liberation of woman. But none of the bourgeois republics, including the most democratic, has dared to take even this first step. The reason is awe of "sacrosanct private property".

The second and most important step is the abolition of the private ownership of land and the factories. This and this alone opens up the way towards a complete and actual emancipation of woman, her liberation from "household bondage" through transition from petty individual housekeeping to large-scale socialised domestic services.

This transition is a difficult one, because it involves the remoulding of the most deep-rooted, inveterate, hidebound and rigid "order" (indecency and barbarity would be nearer the truth). But the transition has been started, the thing has been set in motion, we have taken the new path.

And so on this international working women's day countless meetings of working women in all countries of the world will send greetings to Soviet Russia, which has been the first to tackle this unparalleled and incredibly hard but great task, a task that is universally great and truly liberatory. There will be bracing calls not to lose heart in face of the fierce and frequently savage bourgeois reaction. The "freer" or "more democratic" a bourgeois country is, the wilder the rampage of its gang of capitalists against the workers' revolution, an example of this being the democratic republic of the United States of North America. But the mass of workers have already awakened. The dormant, somnolent and inert masses in America, Europe and even in backward Asia were finally roused by the imperialist war.

The ice has been broken in every corner of the world.

Nothing can stop the tide of the peoples' liberation from the imperialist yoke and the liberation of working men and women from the yoke of capital. This cause is being carried forward by tens and hundreds of millions of working men and women in town and countryside. That is why this cause of labour's freedom from the yoke of capital will triumph all over the world.

March 4, 1921

Published March 4, 1921 in a
Supplement to *Pravda* No. 51
Signed: *N. Lenin*

Collected Works,
Vol. 32, pp. 161-63

4. My last observation concerns the points of the theses
which speak of the need to increase the output of agricultural produce and the importance of modern machines
(*des machines modernes*), particularly threshing machines
(*les batteuses*), tractor ploughs (*les charrues à trac-
teur*), etc.

All these statements in the theses are undoubtedly correct and necessary from the practical point of view. I
think, however, that we should not confine ourselves to
the ordinary capitalist technique, but should take a step
beyond that. A few words should have been said about
the need for planned and complete electrification of the
whole of France, and to show that it is absolutely impossible to do this *for the benefit of the workers and peasants*
unless bourgeois rule is overthrown and power is seized
by the proletariat. French literature contains no little data
on the importance of electrification for France. I know
that a small part of this data is quoted in the plan for the
electrification of Russia that was drawn up by order of
our government, and that since the war considerable
progress has been made in France towards the technical
solution of the problem of electrification.

In my opinion it is extremely important both from the
theoretical and from the practical propaganda point of
view to say in the theses (and generally to enlarge on it
in our communist literature) that modern advanced technology imperatively calls for *the electrification of the*

226

whole country—and of a number of neighbouring countries—under a single plan; that this is quite feasible at the present time; that agriculture, and particularly the peasantry, stand to gain most from this; that as long as capitalism and private ownership of the means of production exist, the electrification of a whole country, or a series of countries, firstly, cannot be carried out speedily and according to plan, and secondly, *cannot benefit* the workers and peasants. Under capitalism, electrification will inevitably lead to increased *oppression* of the workers *and peasants* by the *big banks*. Even before the war not a "narrow-minded Marxist", but none other than Lysis—who is now patriotically licking the boots of the capitalists—had proved that France was actually governed by a *financial oligarchy.*

France possesses splendid opportunities for electrification. After the victory of the proletariat in France, the *small peasants* particularly will benefit *enormously* from electrification carried out according to plan and unhindered by the private property of big landowners and capitalists. If the capitalists remain in power, however, electrification cannot possibly be planned and rapid; and in so far as it is carried out at all, it will be a means of imposing new fetters on the peasants, a new means of enslaving the peasants to the "financial oligarchy" which is robbing them today.

These are the few observations I am able to make on the French agrarian theses, which on the whole are, in my opinion, quite correct.

December 11, 1921

First published in 1922 in
The Communist International
No. 20
Signed: *A Russian Communist*

Collected Works,
Vol. 33, pp. 136-37

NOTES

1 The *"Draft and Explanation of a Programme for the Social-Democratic Party"* was written by Lenin in 1895-96 while he was in prison in St. Petersburg. Nadezhda Krupskaya and Anna Ulyanova-Yelizarova recall that the text was written in milk in the space between the lines of a book.

In this work Lenin searchingly analysed the essence of capitalism in Russia and advanced the basic tasks of the proletarian class struggle.   p. 7

2 The peasant unrest in Russia in 1902 brought Lenin round to the conclusion that it was necessary to write a pamphlet for the peasants. In this pamphlet he used simple language to explain to the peasants the objectives of the workers' party and why the peasant poor had to align themselves with the workers.

Published in Geneva in May 1903, with the Draft Programme of the R.S.D.L.P. as a supplement, the pamphlet was smuggled into Russia where it was widely distributed. It was studied at underground Social-Democratic and workers' study-circles, and penetrated into the countryside and into the Army and Navy.

p. 10

3 An international meeting to mark three anniversaries—the 25th anniversary of Marx's death, the 60th anniversary of the 1848 revolution and Paris Commune day—was held in Geneva on March 5 (18), 1908. It was addressed by 2,000 people.

On behalf of the R.S.D.L.P., Lenin made a speech in which he spoke of the significance of the Paris Commune. The article "Lessons of the Commune" is a verbatim record of this speech. It was printed on March 23, 1908 in *Zagranichnaya Gazeta* No. 2 —organ of a group of Russian émigrés in Geneva (published in March-April 1908).   p. 13

4 *Proudhonism*, named after the French anarchist Pierre Joseph Proudhon, was a variety of petty-bourgeois socialism which became widespread in France and some other countries in the 1860s. Proudhon stigmatised big capitalist ownership from a petty-bour-

geois standpoint and dreamed of perpetuating small private ownership. He was opposed to the revolutionary class struggle of the proletariat, denouncing even strikes and trade unions. Proudhonist theories were later adopted by exponents of so-called anarcho-syndicalism and are also used by Right-wing socialists.

p. 13

5 See K. Marx, "Second Address of the General Council of the International Working Men's Association on the Franco-Prussian War" (Marx and Engels, *Selected Works*, Vol. I, Moscow, 1962, pp. 491-98). p. 14

6 This is a reference to a speech by Arthur Schmid on November 30, 1916 at a meeting of Swiss Left-wing Social-Democrats. This meeting examined the question of drawing up a draft resolution for the pending extraordinary congress of the Swiss Social-Democratic Party, which was being called to discuss the attitude of socialists to militarism and war. p. 24

7 The *Aarau decision*—a decision calling for a mass revolutionary struggle against war passed at a congress of the Swiss Social-Democratic Party held in Aarau on November 20-21, 1915. p. 25

8 Lenin began to write his *Letters From Afar* while in emigration in Switzerland, as soon as he was informed of the February Revolution in Russia and the composition of the bourgeois Provisional Government and of the Executive Committee of the Petrograd Soviet of Workers' and Soldiers' Deputies. In these letters he analysed the revolutionary developments in Russia and showed that Bolshevik tactics were well-founded. He wrote four letters in the period from March 7 to 12 (20 to 25), 1917. Considerably abridged and with some changes, the first letter, "The First Stage of the First Revolution", was printed by the Bolshevik newspaper *Pravda* in Petrograd on March 21-22 (April 3-4). The other letters were not published in 1917. The fifth letter, begun by Lenin on the eve of his departure from Switzerland for Russia, was not completed. The ideas contained in it were later developed in his works *Letters on Tactics* and *The Tasks of the Proletariat in Our Revolution*. p. 27

9 The *agrarian programme of the 104* was the land reform bill signed by 104 members of the First State Duma and submitted by a group of peasant deputies, so-called Trudoviks, at a sitting of the Duma on May 23 (June 5), 1906. In this bill the Trudoviks demanded the setting up of a "national land fund" that would include land belonging to the state, the royal family, the churches, the nobility and other big owners of land. Some compensation was envisaged for alienated privately-owned land (surpluses over and above the "labour norm" were subject to alienation). Allotted and small privately-owned plots of land would be temporarily in the possession of their owners. The bill envisaged the subsequent gradual transfer of this land to the national fund. p. 28

10 "*Farewell Letter to the Swiss Workers*" was written by Lenin in mid-March 1917. It was debated and adopted on March 26 (April 8) at a meeting of Bolsheviks who were departing for Russia.

While living as an émigré in Switzerland, Lenin was active in the political struggle, first in the Berne and then in the Zurich Social-Democratic organisation, against that party's Right wing. The numerous documents the Lefts issued against opportunism in their party were drawn up in close co-operation with Lenin. p. 29

11 On November 9 (22), 1906, aiming to set up in the countryside a reliable mainstay in the person of the kulaks, the tsarist government issued a decree regulating the peasants' withdrawal from the communes and the establishment of their proprietary rights on the allotted lands. After it was passed this decree became known as the law of June 14, 1910. Under this law, named after P. A. Stolypin, then Chairman of the Council of Ministers, the peasant was free to leave the commune and use the land allotted to him as private property or sell it. The rural community was obliged to provide peasants leaving the commune with an allotment of land in one place (an *otrub*, homestead). The Stolypin agrarian reform accelerated the development of capitalism in agriculture, speeded up the stratification of the peasantry and intensified the class struggle in the countryside. p. 30

12 The work *The Tasks of the Proletariat in Our Revolution. Draft Platform for the Proletarian Party* was written by Lenin on April 10 (23), 1917 during the preparations for the Seventh All-Russia Bolshevik Conference (see the following note). It was typed and circulated among Party members before and at the conference. p. 31

13 *The Seventh (April) All-Russia Conference of the R.S.D.L.P.(B.)* was held in Petrograd on April 24-29 (May 7-12), 1917. It was attended by 131 delegates with deciding vote and 18 with deliberative vote from 78 Party organisations. This was the first legally-held Party conference.

Its significance was that it charted the ways and means of turning the bourgeois-democratic revolution into a socialist revolution and advanced a plan for placing all power in the hands of the Soviets. Essentially, this conference played the role of a Party Congress. p. 33

14 The reference is to Lenin's article "Impending Debacle", which was published on May 14 (27), 1917 in *Pravda* No. 57 (*Collected Works*, Vol. 24, pp. 395-97). p. 38

15 *Rech* (Speech)—a daily newspaper, the central organ of the Constitutional-Democratic Party, a leading party of the liberal-monarchist bourgeoisie in Russia. Its publication was started in 1906, and it was closed on October 26 (November 8), 1917 by the Military Revolutionary Committee of the Petrograd Soviet. Subsequently (until August 1918) it was published under various names: *Nasha Rech, Svobodnaya Rech, Vek, Novaya Rech* and *Nash Vek*. p. 38

16 Here Lenin uses a quotation from the "Resolution on the Current Situation" adopted by the Seventh (April) All-Russia Conference

of the R.S.D.L.P.(B.). The resolution was written by Lenin (see pp. 36-37 of this book).   p. 39

17 This is a reference to the statements by a delegation of Donets workers to the Economic Department of the Petrograd Soviet of Workers' and Soldiers' Deputies on acts of sabotage by owners of mines and iron and steel plants who were out to suppress revolutionary-minded workers by hunger. The statements described the unbearable condition of the miners and steelworkers.

Novaya Zhizn (New Life)—a Menshevik daily newspaper which was published from April 18 (May 1), 1917 to July 1918.   p. 41

18 *Resolution on Measures to Cope with Economic Disorganisation* was written by Lenin for the pending conference of factory committees of Petrograd (see the following note). It was published on behalf of the Party Central Committee in the Moscow Bolshevik newspaper *Sotsial-Demokrat* on May 25 (June 7), 1917, and on June 2 (15) in *Pravda* as a draft resolution suggested by the Organising Bureau set up to convene the conference. As such it was passed at the conference by an overwhelming majority of votes.
                                                                           p. 45

19 *Shop (factory) committees* were proletarian class organisations which sprang up in March 1917, immediately after the February revolution. They drew up and presented economic demands to factory owners, established an eight-hour working day without waiting for official permission, controlled the hire and dismissal of workers, set up workers' militia detachments, combated sabotage by entrepreneurs, obtained raw materials and fuel for the factories where they were set up in order to enable them to operate uninterruptedly, and so forth. These committees were active in the October Revolution. In 1918 they were integrated with the trade unions, becoming the lower organs of the latter.

The First Petrograd Conference of Factory Committees was held on May 30-June 3 (June 12-16), 1917. It debated the state of industry, control and regulation of production in Petrograd, the tasks of factory committees and their role in the trade union movement, and so on.   p. 48

20 *Izvestia (News) of the Petrograd Soviet of Workers' and Soldiers' Deputies*—a daily newspaper whose publication was started on February 28 (March 13), 1917. On August 1 (14) it became the organ of the Central Executive Committee and began to be published as *Izvestia of the Central Executive Committee and the Petrograd Soviet of Workers' and Soldiers' Deputies*; on September 29 (October 12) its name was changed to *Izvestia of the Central Executive Committee of the Soviets of Workers' and Soldiers' Deputies*. Throughout this period it was in the hands of the Mensheviks and Socialist-Revolutionaries and attacked the Bolshevik Party.

After the October Socialist Revolution the composition of the *Izvestia* editorial board was changed and the newspaper became an official organ of Soviet power.   p. 51

21 *Rabochaya Gazeta* (Workers' Gazette)—a Menshevik daily news-

paper published in Petrograd from March 7 (20) to November 30 (December 13), 1917.   p. 51

²² *Yedinstvo* (Unity)—a Menshevik newspaper published in Petrograd. Four issues were put out in May-June 1914. In the period from March to November 1917 it was published daily. In December 1917-January 1918 it was printed under the name *Nashe Yedinstvo*.
                                                                     p. 51

²³ *Vestnik Finansov, Promyshlennosti i Torgovli* (The Financial, Industrial and Commercial Herald)—a weekly journal of the Ministry for Finance; it was published in St. Petersburg from November 1883 to 1917.   p. 53

²⁴ *The Impending Catastrophe and How to Combat It* was written by Lenin in mid-September 1917 while he was residing illegally in Helsingfors.

In this work Lenin advanced a number of programme propositions. The measures of the proletarian government in the building of a new, socialist life, charted by Lenin on the eve of the October Socialist Revolution, have been applied in the U.S.S.R. and other countries of the socialist camp.   p. 55

²⁵ *Dyen* (The Day)—a daily liberal-bourgeois newspaper whose publication was begun in St. Petersburg in 1912. After the revolution of February 1917 it passed into the hands of the Mensheviks. It was closed on October 26 (November 8), 1917 by the Military Revolutionary Committee of the Petrograd Soviet.   p. 62

²⁶ Lenin refers to his article "Introduction of Socialism or Exposure of Plunder of the State?", which was published on June 9 (22), 1917 in *Pravda* No. 77 (*Collected Works*, Vol. 25, pp. 68-69).   p. 70

²⁷ The reference is to Lenin's article "Paper Resolutions" published in the second issue of the Bolshevik newspaper *Rabochy* on August 26 (September 8), 1917 (*Collected Works*, Vol. 25, pp. 261-64).   p. 71

²⁸ *Svobodnaya Zhizn* (Free Life)—a Menshevik daily newspaper published in Petrograd from September 2 (15) to 8 (21) instead of the newspaper *Novaya Zhizn*, which was closed by the Provisional Government.   p. 80

²⁹ *Birzhevka—Birzheviye Vedomosti* (Stock-Exchange Records)—a bourgeois newspaper founded in 1880. It was published in St. Petersburg. At the end of October 1917 it was closed by the Military Revolutionary Committee of the Petrograd Soviet.   p. 81

³⁰ During the Franco-Prussian war of 1870-71, the Germans surrounded the French army at Sedan, and Emperor Napoleon III, who was there, signed the capitulation.   p. 96

³¹ Lenin's *"Draft Regulations on Workers' Control"* were the basis for the draft law on workers' control which was drawn up later. On November 14 (27), 1917, the All-Russia Central Executive Committee examined this draft law and issued the decree which is known as "Regulations on Workers' Control". The decree helped develop workers' initiative and establish control over production

and distribution of goods. Workers' control played an important part in protecting the enterprises against the plunder by capitalists and in training workers for production management after the nationalisation of industry. p. 100

[32] *The Committee of Salvation (Committee of Public Safety)* was set up on October 25 (November 7), 1917 by the Moscow City Council to wage armed struggle against Soviet power. It headed the counter-revolutionary revolt of officer cadets which began on October 28 (November 10). The revolt was crushed on November 2 (15) and the Committee of Public Safety capitulated to the Moscow Military Revolutionary Committee. p. 102

[33] These theses were written by Lenin in connection with the drafting of a decree for the nationalisation of urban real estate by the Council of People's Commissars. The draft was approved by the meeting of the Council of People's Commissars on November 23 (December 6), 1917, and on August 20, 1918 the corresponding decree was endorsed at a meeting of the All-Russia Central Executive Committee. p. 105

[34] After the October Revolution, the board of the Urals Mining Societies stopped remitting money to the Urals plants, owing to which they faced extreme difficulties. The workers received no pay for several months and were starving. The Urals Regional Soviet of Workers', Peasants' and Soldiers' Deputies delegated one of its members, V. Vorobyov, to Petrograd to inform the Council of People's Commissars of the situation in the Urals and settle the wages question. Vorobyov met Sverdlov and told him in detail about the situation in the Urals. Sverdlov suggested that Vorobyov should go to Lenin with him and report on the situation in the Urals industry and the feeling among the workers. After their conversation Lenin handed to Vorobyov the note we publish in this book.

On December 23, 1917 (January 5, 1918), the Council of People's Commissars adopted a decision on the urgent remittance of 50 million rubles to the Urals branch of the State Bank.

In December 1917, the Urals Regional Executive Committee closed down the bureau of the Urals mining industry conference in Yekaterinburg (now Sverdlovsk), and late in December 1917 or early in 1918, the largest Urals enterprises were nationalised. p. 106

[35] Lenin delivered this speech at the meeting of the All-Russia Central Executive Committee on December 14 (27), 1917 in connection with a discussion of the Decree on the Nationalisation of the Banks.

Practical measures for the nationalisation of the banks were taken immediately after the victory of the October Socialist Revolution. The first step in this direction was the taking over of the State Bank, which had refused to pay out money on the orders of the Council of People's Commissars.

By the order of the Council of People's Commissars, a number of employees in the Ministry of Finance, notably the manager of the State Bank, were dismissed and the Chief Commissar of the State Bank was appointed to replace the manager. High bank officials replied by going on strike. Despite this, the bank was soon opened and, supported by junior employees, resumed its work. In mid-December 1917, Soviet power established control over all payments by private banks as a transitional measure pending their nationalisation. On the morning of December 14 (27), the government ordered workers' detachments and Red Guard units to seize all banks and credit institutions in Petrograd. That same day, the All-Russia Central Executive Committee adopted the decrees "On the Nationalisation of the Banks" and "On the Inspection of Steel Safes in Banks". Both decrees were published in *Izvestia TsIK* No. 252, on December 15 (28)   p. 110

[36] Lenin refers to B. V. Avilov's statement: "By such a primitive approach to the matter and the desire to settle everything with a single blow of the axe, you will only undermine the delicate credit organism."   p. 110

[37] *The Left Socialist-Revolutionaries* were organisationally formed as a party in November 1917. Until then, they had existed as the Left wing of the petty-bourgeois Socialist-Revolutionary Party (S.R.s). After the victory of the October Revolution, the Left S.R.s, striving to maintain their influence among the peasants, co-operated with the Bolsheviks for some time and their representatives joined the Council of People's Commissars. However, the Left S.R.s disagreed with the Bolsheviks on the basic questions of socialist construction and opposed the dictatorship of the proletariat. Being opposed to the signing of the Brest Peace Treaty (see Note 70), they withdrew from the Council of People's Commissars in March 1918, but continued to take part in the collegia of the Commissariats and local organs of power. In July 1918, the Central Committee of the Left S.R.s organised in Moscow the assassination of the German Ambassador Mirbach and an armed revolt against Soviet power in order to frustrate the Brest Peace Treaty and involve Soviet Russia in a war against Germany. When the revolt had been suppressed, the Fifth All-Russia Congress of Soviets (see Note 69) decided to expel from the Soviets the Left Socialist-Revolutionaries who shared the adventurist views of their leadership. Having lost all support among the masses, the Party of Left Socialist-Revolutionaries launched an armed struggle against Soviet power. Some of the S.R.s stood for collaboration with the Bolsheviks and were later admitted into the Communist Party.   p. 112

[38] The article *"How to Organise Competition?"* and the *"Draft Decree on Consumers' Communes"*, which follows it in this book, were written by Lenin during his four-day leave in Finland from December 24 to 27, 1917 (January 6-9, 1918). The views and propositions expounded by Lenin in this article were later developed in his work *The Immediate Tasks of the Soviet Government* (part of which is included in this book, pp. 151-63) and other writings.   p. 117

[39] Marx, Letter to Wilhelm Bracke of May 5, 1875 (Marx and Engels, *Selected Correspondence*, Moscow, 1965, pp. 296-97).   p. 124

[40] A quotation from Goethe's *Faust*, Part One, Scene 4.   p. 124

[41] Lenin has in mind a group of printing workers who for a long time were under the influence of the Mensheviks and the Right S.R.s who headed the yellow Union of Printing Workers. After the October Revolution, this union launched a struggle against Soviet power and instigated strikes in Moscow, Petrograd and some other cities. The Bolsheviks had their groups in all big printing shops and founded the Red Union of Printers, after which the yellow union's influence diminished. p. 125

[42] Lenin's *"Draft Decree on Consumers' Communes"* was particularised by the People's Commissariat for Food and published in *Izvestia TsIK* on January 19 (February 1), 1918. The draft was fiercely opposed by the bourgeois co-operators, who demanded that co-operatives be independent of the organs of Soviet power. Deeming it necessary to use the co-operative machinery to normalise trade and the distribution of products among the population, the Council of People's Commissars had to make certain concessions to the co-operators. As a result of the talks held in March and early April 1918 between representatives of the Supreme Economic Council and of co-operatives and food organisations a decree was drafted and was discussed on April 9 and 10 at the meetings of the Council of People's Commissars. The draft was adopted with Lenin's addenda and amendments by the Council of People's Commissars and endorsed by the All-Russia C.E.C. on April 11. The resolution proposed by the Bolshevik group and adopted by the C.E.C. said that "the Decree on Consumers' Co-operatives is a compromise decision suffering from substantial shortcomings" and that the C.E.C. "approves the Decree on Consumers' Co-operatives as a transitional measure" (*Izvestia VTsIK* No. 72, April 12, 1918). On April 13, the decree was published in *Pravda* No. 71.

Lenin gave his assessment of the decree in his work *The Immediate Tasks of the Soviet Government* (see pp. 151-63 of this book). p. 127

[43] Lenin has in mind the directive of the People's Commissariat for Food to the local Soviets on organising the food supply machinery, the Commissariat's project for a Commissariat for Supply, and also the Supreme Economic Council's project for district economic councils.

Since the old food supply organs were sabotaging the decrees of Soviet power, on December 22, 1917 (January 4, 1918) the People's Commissariat for Food gave a directive to the local Soviets to take food supply in their hands and organise their own food supply machinery with the support of the delegate organisations, formed under food supply organs, from consumer gubernias and armies (delegates' committees). At the same time, the People's Commissariat for Food drafted a project on its reorganisation into a Commissariat for Supply which would be in charge of supplying the population not only with foodstuffs, but with all commodities, while private trade would be greatly reduced. According to the project, local bodies of the Commissariat for Supply were to become supply departments under the Soviets (supply offices). p. 127

⁴⁴ The draft "*Declaration of Rights of the Working and Exploited People*" was submitted at the meeting of the All-Russia Central Executive Committee on January 3 (16), 1918. It was adopted as a basis and referred to a Co-ordinating Commission for final adjustment. The Declaration was adopted by the All-Russia C.E.C. and on January 4 (17) published in *Izvestia TsIK*. On January 5 (18), the Declaration was read out by Y. M. Sverdlov on behalf of the All-Russia C.E.C. at the first sitting of the Constituent Assembly and submitted for its approval. The counter-revolutionary part of the Constituent Assembly voted against the motion to discuss it. On January 12 (25), the Declaration was endorsed by the Third All-Russia Congress of Soviets.   p. 131

⁴⁵ When the counter-revolutionary majority of the Constituent Assembly refused to discuss the Declaration of Rights of the Working and Exploited People, the Bolsheviks and the Left S.R.s asked for the sitting to be interrupted for discussion in their groups. Lenin spoke at the sitting of the Bolshevik group. He suggested that the declaration of the Bolshevik group which he had written should be read out at the sitting of the Constituent Assembly and that the Bolsheviks should then leave the Assembly. This proposal was adopted by the group.

After the Bolsheviks' departure, the Left S.R.s motioned to put immediately to the vote the question of the attitude to the peace policy pursued by Soviet power. When the Right wing of the Constituent Assembly rejected this proposal, the Left S.R.s also left the session hall.

Soon after the departure of the Bolsheviks and the Left S.R.s, the People's Commissar for the Navy, P. Y. Dybenko, who was entrusted with guarding the Taurida Palace, ordered the guard to close the sitting of the Constituent Assembly. On learning this, Lenin gave the following instruction: "The comrades soldiers and sailors on guard duty in the Taurida Palace must refrain from any acts of violence in respect of the counter-revolutionary section of the Constituent Assembly, freely allowing everyone to leave the Taurida Palace, but allowing no one in without a special pass. Chairman of the Council of People's Commissars, *V. Ulyanov (Lenin)*" (*Collected Works*, Fifth Russ. Ed., Vol. 50, p. 26).

The Constituent Assembly ended its sittings on the night of January 5 (18), 1918.

On the night of January 6 (19), the All-Russia Central Executive Committee adopted a decree on the dissolution of the Constituent Assembly, which was published in *Pravda* and *Izvestia TsIK* on January 7 (20), 1918.   p. 133

⁴⁶ *The Third All-Russia Congress of Soviets of Workers', Soldiers' and Peasants' Deputies* was held in Petrograd from January 10 to 18 (23 to 31), 1918.

Lenin delivered a report on the work of the Council of People's Commissars. The Congress approved Lenin's Declaration of Rights of the Working and Exploited People, which later formed the basis of the Constitution of the Soviet state. The Congress adopted a resolution fully endorsing the policy of the All-Russia Central Executive Committee and the Council of People's Commissars and expressing complete confidence in them.

The Congress also approved the basic provisions of the Law on the Socialisation of Land (see Note 54). p. 135

[47] Lenin refers to the talks between the All-Russia Leather Workers' Union and their employers for wider workers' representation in the Central Leather Committee and its remoulding on democratic lines. As a result of these talks, the Central Committee and the district committees were reorganised in early 1918, and the workers got two-thirds of the votes. On April 6, 1918, a telegram signed by Lenin was sent to all Soviets on the need to democratise the local organs of the leather industry and to fulfil exactly the instructions issued by the Central and district committees for the leather industry. p. 139

[48] The question of the nationalisation of the merchant marine and inland water transport was discussed at a meeting of the Council of People's Commissars on January 18 (31), 1918. It heard three reports: one from Tsentrovolga, another from the Central Committee of the All-Russia Seamen's and River Transport Workers' Union, and a third from the Supreme Economic Council. Lenin's draft was approved as a decision of the Council of People's Commissars "On Seamen and River Transport Workers".

In the manuscript of the draft decree, Lenin noted after Point 4: "add §3 from Obolensky", and after Point 5: "++§1 from Comrade Obolensky's resolution".

Paragraph 3 of the Council of People's Commissars' draft resolution proposed by N. Osinsky (V. V. Obolensky) said: "Prior to settling the question of nationalising the merchant fleet all marine and river freight and passenger vessels should be sequestered and compulsory repair of these vessels should be carried out at the shipowners' expense and under control of the shipbuilding workers' organisations."

Paragraph 1 said: "It should be suggested to the Central Committee of the All-Russia Seamen's and River Transport Workers' Union and to Tsentrovolga that they unite at the forthcoming congress of seamen and river transport workers and immediately enter into business contacts." p. 140

[49] The reference is to the Central Committee of the All-Russia Seamen's and River Transport Workers' Union. p. 140

[50] On March 4, 1918, the Council of People's Commissars discussed the question of forming a Collegium for Water Transport Management in accordance with the Council of People's Commissars resolution "On the Management of the Marine and River Merchant Fleet and Water Communications" adopted on February 27, 1918, and also the question of wage payments to the workers in the Volga and Mariinskaya system backwaters. According to the resolution of the Council of People's Commissars, the management of water transport was transferred to the jurisdiction of the Supreme Economic Council with the Department of Water Communications formed under

it. The Department's Collegium was to consist of representatives of the Supreme Economic Council, the Council of People's Commissars, the Water Transport Workers' Union and the regional economic council.   p. 142

51 The reference is to the proposal made by the Central Committee of the All-Russia Seamen's and River Transport Workers' Union to concentrate the management of water transport in the union's hands. The Council of People's Commissars rejected the anarcho-syndicalist demands of the water transport workers. On Lenin's suggestion, the Council of People's Commissars decreed to form immediately a collegium on the basis of §3 of the Council of People's Commissars decision of February 27, to increase temporarily the number of trade union representatives in the collegium and to take steps for the immediate despatch of banknotes to pay the wages of the workers in the Volga and Mariinskaya system backwaters. The main points of the Council of People's Commissars resolution were written by Lenin.   p. 142

52 The "Original Version of the Article 'The Immediate Tasks of the Soviet Government'" was dictated by Lenin to a stenographer on March 23-28, 1918. His work on the article was apparently connected with the preparation for the discussion in the Central Committee of the R.C.P.(B.) of the plan for the development of socialist construction. As early as March 31, the meeting of the Party Central Committee, attended by Lenin, "stated that the period of winning power has ended and main construction is on" and that therefore "it is necessary to draw efficient, experienced, business people to the work". Since the meeting revealed different views, it was decided to convene the Plenary Meeting of the Central Committee to reach a common point of view. On April 4, 1918, at the meeting of the leading C.C. members with the "Left" Communists' group, Lenin put forward, as a counteraction to the "Theses on the Current Situation" proposed by the "Left" Communists, his programme and slogans for new construction, which were fiercely attacked by the "Left" Communists in the press. In his opening speech at the C.C. Plenary Meeting on April 7, Lenin again stressed that the revolution was going through "a new period". The Central Committee entrusted Lenin with "working out the theses on the current situation and submitting them to the C.C." In connection with this decision, Lenin wrote his work, *The Immediate Tasks of the Soviet Government.*

Most of the chapters of the original version of the article (including those published in *Miscellanies V, VI* and *VII*) were first found in 1962, when V. I. Lenin's *Collected Works* (Fifth Russian edition) were being prepared for printing.   p. 145

53 The Decree on the Nationalisation of Large-Scale Industry was adopted by the Council of People's Commissars on June 28, 1918, and on June 30 it was published in *Izvestia VTsIK* No. 134. This decree nationalised all large industrial enterprises and completed the socialisation of the basic means of production. It was preceded by measures on the nationalisation of the banks, large metallurgical works, the sugar, coal and oil industries, water

transport, etc. Announcing the transfer of large-scale industry to the ownership of the state, the Council of People's Commissars left the nationalised enterprises temporarily, pending their transfer to the jurisdiction of Soviet economic organs, in "gratuitous tenant use by the former owners" who were responsible for the safety and normal work of the enterprises. All workers and technical personnel were declared to be in the service of Soviet power. The Supreme Economic Council undertook to elaborate urgently and send to all nationalised enterprises detailed instructions on the organisation of their management.

Owing to the organisational work of the Communist Party and the activity of the working masses, nationalisation was carried out promptly, despite enormous difficulties. By August 31, 1918, there were already over 3,000 nationalised enterprises.

This decree also announced the nationalisation of all private railways and communal enterprises (water supply, gas works, communal transport, etc.) which were transferred to the local Soviets.
p. 148

54 The reference is to the *Basic Law on the Socialisation of Land* adopted on January 18 (31), 1918 by the Third All-Russia Congress of Soviets and approved by the All-Russia Central Executive Committee on January 27 (February 9), 1918. This law confirmed the abolition of all land property and transferred the disposal of land to Soviet power. p. 149

55 In the manuscript, Lenin's *The Immediate Tasks of the Soviet Government* was called *Theses on the Tasks of the Soviet Government at the Present Moment.* Lenin's Theses were discussed at the meeting of the Party Central Committee on April 26, 1918. The Central Committee unanimously approved them and directed that they should be published as articles in *Pravda* and *Izvestia VTsIK* and also put out as separate pamphlets.

The Central Committee empowered Lenin to make a report on the immediate tasks of the Soviet government at a meeting of the All-Russia Central Executive Committee and to prepare a summary of the Theses in the form of a resolution.

In *The Immediate Tasks of the Soviet Government*, Lenin outlined a plan of socialist construction, clarified the key problems of transition from capitalism to socialism, and elaborated the principles of the Soviet state's economic policy. Many of the propositions contained in this work are fully applicable in the conditions of socialist society. p. 151

56 On November 18 (December 1), 1917, on Lenin's suggestion, the Council of People's Commissars adopted a decision "On the Remuneration of People's Commissars and Senior Government Employees". According to the decision, which had been drafted by Lenin, the maximum monthly pay of a People's Commissar was fixed at 500 rubles plus 100 rubles for each disabled member of his family, which amounted roughly to a worker's average monthly wage. Another decision adopted by the Council on January 2 (15), 1918, following the inquiry by People's Commissar for Labour A. G. Shlyapnikov, and likewise drafted by Lenin, explained

that the decision of November 18, 1917 did not prohibit payment to specialists exceeding the fixed top limit. The Council of People's Commissars thereby sanctioned higher remuneration to experts in science and technology. p. 155

⁵⁷ The Soviet Government established control over foreign trade in the first days of its existence. Initially, this control was exercised by the Petrograd Military Revolutionary Committee, which considered applications for the export and import of goods and supervised customs activities. Under the decree of the Council of People's Commissars adopted on December 29, 1917 (January 11, 1918), the powers of control over foreign trade were vested in the People's Commissariat for Trade and Industry. This control and customs inspection, however, were not enough to safeguard the national economy against foreign capital. State monopoly in foreign trade was what Lenin proposed as early as December 1917, and the relevant decree was adopted by the Council of People's Commissars on April 22, 1918. p. 159

⁵⁸ In the early months of Soviet power impositions and special taxes were one of the main sources of budget revenue, particularly in the localities. As the positions of Soviet power consolidated, a transition to regular taxation became possible, a progressive income tax and a property tax being the main instrument for shifting the burden of taxation on to the propertied social groups. The First All-Russia Congress of Representatives of Soviets' Financial Departments, held in Moscow between May 17 and 21, 1918, approved Lenin's proposal to introduce a tax on income and property, and set up a special commission to draft the requisite statute on the basis of Lenin's theses.

A decree which laid down a strict system of income and property taxation was adopted by the Council of People's Commissars on June 17, 1918. p. 159

⁵⁹ See note 42. p. 161

⁶⁰ This document was written by Lenin below the following text of the "Theses on Banking Policy" drafted by the People's Commissariat for Finance: "1. Not monopolisation, but nationalisation of the banking system. Further and more radical nationalisation of industry and exchange, provided the grass-root workers are organised for the purpose. 2. Continued regulation of issues for consumption. 3. Free cheque circulation and introduction [Lenin changed "introduction" to "preservation".—*Ed.*] of the right to control the cheque circulation of private enterprises. 4. Compulsory current accounts, provided the technical side of the business is previously thought out. 5. Nationalisation of foreign trade and protectionism."

Lenin wrote the title "Basic Propositions on Economic and Especially on Banking Policy" above the text of the "Theses". p. 164

⁶¹ This demand was vital, since the nationalisation process was complicated by the fact that workers of some enterprises and certain trade unions tended to regard their nationalised enterprises and industries as their own property. Lenin denounced those anarcho-

syndicalist tendencies. See Lenin's speech at a discussion of the Volga River transport in the Council of People's Commissars on March 4, 1918 (pp. 142-44 of this book). p. 165

62 The *"Theses on Banking Policy"* were drawn up by Lenin at a meeting with the leading officials of the People's Commissariat for Finance and the State Bank held in March-April 1918. p. 166

63 The decrees "On the Nationalisation of the Banks" and "On the Inspection of Steel Safes in Banks" were approved by the All-Russia Central Executive Committee on December 14 (27), 1917 (see Note 35). p. 166

64 *The Joint Meeting of Representatives of the All-Russia Central Council of Trade Unions, the Central Committee of the Metalworkers' Union and the Supreme Economic Council* discussed a proposal sponsored by a group of capitalists to set up a trust ("The National Company"). The trust was to include plants producing steam engines, railway cars, ships, rails, heavy machinery and also a considerable number of Donbas mines and iron and steel works in the Urals and the South. The project envisaged the transfer to the trust of large tracts of farmland to organise its own agricultural production. The trust was intended to have a basic capital of 1,500 million rubles and to employ 300 thousand workers. This project of bourgeois businessmen was an attempt to prevent the nationalisation of a vital branch of industry. The Soviet state was assigned a secondary role: only 33 per cent of the basic capital was to be held by the state, the bulk belonging to private capitalists. Moreover, the state was to contribute its share in cash, which meant financing the whole trust.

The talks went on from November 1917 to April 1918. The Soviet Government rejected the monopolists' attempts to preserve capitalist property, but expressed readiness to employ bourgeois specialists in Soviet economy. On April 18, the Council of People's Commissars turned down the project and decided to nationalise the plants. This decision was supported by the conference of representatives of engineering works, held between May 12 and 18, 1918 (see pp. 170-71 of this book). p. 169

65 *The Conference of Representatives of Enterprises to Be Nationalised* was held in Moscow from May 12 to 18, 1918. Each enterprise was represented by a delegation of six: three workers, two engineers and one office employee.

Prior to the conference, the problems of the nationalisation of the country's largest works were discussed at economic department and trade union levels, as well as in the Council of People's Commissars. The participants in the discussion turned down the project for the association of the largest engineering works into a state-capitalist joint-stock company (see the previous note) sponsored by the capitalists and bourgeois specialists, and spoke in favour of their nationalisation. The conference approved the nationalisation line by a majority vote on May 17.

The audience burst into applause when Lenin's letter was read at the morning sitting on May 18. On Lenin's motion, the confer-

ence elected a provisional committee to supervise the amalgamation of state metallurgical works under the Supreme Economic
Council and approved the Committee Statute and rules for managing the nationalised enterprises.   p. 170

[66] *The Bryansk regulations*—the Provisional Regulations of Internal
Management drawn up by the factory trade union committee and
the workers' management of the nationalised Bryansk Rail-Roll-
ing, Ironmaking and Machine Works in Bezhitsa (now the Krasny
Profintern Works). On May 9, 1918 they were published as an
order, over the signatures of the factory committee members and
the director of the works.

The Regulations were drawn up on the basis of the Statute on
Labour Discipline adopted by the All-Russia Central Council of
Trade Unions. These Regulations served to consolidate one-man
management in production and improve discipline. They also provided for strict control over labour productivity and held workers
responsible for waste.   p. 170

[67] The draft, *"Regulations for the Management of the Nationalised
Enterprises"*, drawn up by the Supreme Economic Council, was
discussed on May 28 and 30, 1918, at a sitting of the Organisation
of Production Section of the First All-Russia Congress of Economic
Councils (held in Moscow from May 26 to June 4, 1918). The main
reporter was the author of the draft, G. D. Veinberg, member of
the Presidium of the Supreme Economic Council, and his co-
reporters were the "Left" Communist V. M. Smirnov and V. N.
Andronnikov, an industrialist from the Urals. After a lengthy
discussion, the section, pressed by the "Left" Communists, adopted
the Regulations, which ran counter to the Party and state policy.
When Lenin was informed of the action by the "Left" Communists and read the Regulations adopted by the section he suggested that they be examined by the Conciliation Board specially
set up on June 2 and including Lenin (from the Council of People's Commissars) and Rykov and Veinberg (from the Supreme
Economic Council). The Conciliation Board revised the Regulations in accordance with Lenin's notes published here. Despite
opposition from the "Left" Communists, the Congress approved the
Conciliation Board's Draft Regulations by a majority vote.
Under the Regulations, the nationalised enterprise was to be
managed by the factory administration, two-thirds of whose members were appointed by the Regional Economic Council or the
Supreme Economic Council (if the enterprise was subordinated
directly to the central board). The S.E.C. had the right to allow
the regional (or all-Russia) trade union association to nominate
half the candidates. A third of the administration members was
elected by the unionised workers of the enterprise. Engineering
and commercial personnel were to form a third of the administration's membership.   p. 172

[68] The *Fourth Conference of Trade Unions and Factory Committees
of Moscow* was held from June 27 to July 2, 1918. The questions
on the agenda included: food supply, aggravated by the situation
at the time; general military training and mobilisation; labour

242

discipline; the Labour Exchange activities; rules of the factory committees. Lenin made a report on the vital question of food supply. The resolution passed by the conference on Lenin's report was also drafted by Lenin. p. 173

[69] *The Fifth All-Russia Congress of Soviets* opened in Moscow on July 4, 1918. There were 773 Bolsheviks out of the total of 1,164 delegates with the right to vote.

Y. M. Sverdlov reported on the activities of the All-Russia Central Executive Committee and V. I. Lenin, on the work of the Council of People's Commissars. A heated discussion of these reports ended in the Congress carrying, by a majority vote, a resolution motioned by the Communist group and expressing "total approval of the home and foreign policies of the Soviet Government". The Congress turned down a resolution drafted by the Left Socialist-Revolutionaries, who demanded a vote of non-confidence in the government, abrogation of the Peace Treaty of Brest, and a change in the home and foreign policies.

The setback at the Congress spurred the Left Socialist-Revolutionaries on to open action: they organised a counter-revolutionary revolt in Moscow on July 6. This caused a break in the Congress's regular work, which was resumed on July 9. The participants were informed of the July 6-7 events and gave full approval to the resolute steps taken by the government to suppress the revolt.

In a resolution on the food question adopted following the report by A. D. Tsyurupa, People's Commissar for Food, the Congress reaffirmed the stability of state monopoly in grain, pointed to the need to suppress the kulaks' opposition, and approved the setting up of Poor Peasants' Committees. At its final sitting on July 10, the Congress heard a report on the organisation of the Red Army and unanimously adopted a resolution of the Communist group on priority measures for organising and strengthening the Red Army on the basis of military conscription.

The Congress approved the first Constitution of the Russian Federation, which gave the force of law to the achievements of Soviet people. p. 176

[70] The reference is to the peace treaty between Soviet Russia and the countries of the Quadruple Alliance (Germany, Austria-Hungary, Bulgaria and Turkey) signed at Brest-Litovsk on March 3, 1918, and ratified on March 15 by the Fourth, Extraordinary, All-Russia Congress of Soviets. The terms were extremely harsh for Soviet Russia. Under the treaty, Germany and Austria-Hungary gained control over Poland, almost the whole of the Baltic region and a part of Byelorussia. The Ukraine was taken from Soviet Russia and turned into a satellite state depending on Germany. Turkey got Kars, Batum (now Batumi) and Ardahan.

The Treaty of Brest, nevertheless, granted a respite which was used by the Soviet Government to demobilise the old demoralised army and build up the new Red Army, embark on socialist construction and muster forces for the forthcoming struggle against internal counter-revolutionaries and foreign interventionists. The treaty promoted the peace campaign, the growth of revolutionary sentiment in the armies and among the people at large in the belligerent countries.

The conclusion of the treaty met with a strong opposition from Trotsky and the anti-Party group of "Left" Communists. It was only due to Lenin's tremendous effort that the treaty was signed. It was annulled by the All-Russia Central Executive Committee on November 13, 1918, when the November Revolution in Germany did away with the monarchist regime there.   p. 177

[71] See Note 53.   p. 177

[72] To deliver the *Letter to American Workers* to the United States was a very difficult business, since Soviet Russia at that time was the object of military intervention and blockade by the capitalist countries. The whole thing was organised by M. M. Borodin, a Bolshevik who had returned from the United States a short while before. The letter was personally delivered to the U.S.A. by P. I. Travin (Sletov). He also took there the Constitution of the Russian Federation and the text of the Soviet Note to President Wilson demanding an end to the intervention. These documents were published in the American press with the help of the well-known American Socialist and journalist John Reed.

In December 1918, the letter was published in English (abridged) in the journal *The Class Struggle* (New York) and the weekly *The Revolutionary Age* (Boston), both organs of the Left wing of the American Socialist Party. Lenin's letter attracted such great public interest that it was reprinted from *The Class Struggle* in a large number of copies. Later the letter was repeatedly printed in the socialist and bourgeois press in the United States and Western Europe. In 1934, it was published as a booklet in New York.

The "Letter to American Workers" was of great help for the American Left Socialists, the working-class and the communist movement in the United States and Europe. It helped the politically-conscious workers to understand the nature of imperialism and appreciate the great revolutionary transformations taking place in Soviet Russia. Lenin's appeal to the workers of America gave fresh impetus to their protest movement against the armed intervention in Soviet Russia.   p. 181

[73] Lenin refers to his report on fighting the famine at the joint meeting of the All-Russia Central Executive Committee, the Moscow Soviet of Workers', Peasants' and Red Army Deputies and the trade unions, which took place on June 4, 1918.   p. 181

[74] The *Sixth, Extraordinary, All-Russia Congress of Soviets of Workers', Peasants', Cossacks' and Red Army Deputies* was held in Moscow from November 6 to 9, 1918. It was attended by 1,296 delegates, 1,260 of whom were Communists.

Lenin was elected honorary chairman of the Congress. At the first sitting on November 6, Lenin delivered his report on the first anniversary of the October Revolution, and then messages of greetings were addressed by the Congress to the workers, peasants and soldiers of all nations and their leaders fighting for peace and socialism, and to the Red Army. On Sverdlov's motion, the Congress appealed to the governments waging war against Soviet Russia to start peace negotiations.

At its second sitting on November 8, the Congress heard Lenin's report on the international situation and unanimously passed the resolution on the report, drafted by Lenin. Following the report by People's Commissar for Justice D. I. Kursky, the Congress carried a decree on revolutionary law. At its final sitting on November 9, the Congress discussed the military situation and problems of Soviet construction. It was decided to merge the Poor Peasants' Committees, which had fulfilled their functions by that time, with the volost and village Soviets.

The Congress elected the new All-Russia Central Executive Committee consisting of 207 members and 39 alternate members. The Congress reviewed the work of the Soviet Government in its first year and outlined a programme of action for the immediate future.
p. 186

75 *The Meeting of Delegates from the Moscow Central Workers' Co-operative* was held on November 26-27, 1918. The meeting heard and discussed the reports of the Board and the Auditing Committee, and a report on the distribution of food in Moscow. A new Board was elected.
p. 190

76 See Note 42.
p. 190

77 The draft of the decree *"On the Organisation of Supply"* was discussed at a meeting of the Council of People's Commissars on November 12, 1918 and was finally approved on November 21. Three days later, it was published in *Izvestia VTsIK*. Lenin took an active part in drafting the décree.
p. 190

78 Lenin began to write *The Proletarian Revolution and the Renegade Kautsky* in early October 1918, immediately after he had read Kautsky's pamphlet, *The Dictatorship of the Proletariat*, in which the author distorted Marxism and denied the necessity for the socialist revolution and the dictatorship of the proletariat. While still working on his book, Lenin wrote an article, "The Proletarian Revolution and the Renegade Kautsky" (published in *Pravda* on October 11, 1919), and proposed to have it published abroad to make known his position on the questions raised by Kautsky. The article was published in German in Berne in 1918 and in Vienna in 1919, and in Italian in Milan also in 1919.

Lenin's pamphlet *The Proletarian Revolution and the Renegade Kautsky* was published in 1919 in Britain, France and Germany.
p. 192

79 Here and below Lenin quotes Kautsky's booklet *Die Diktatur des Proletariats*, Vienna, 1918.
p. 192

80 The reference is to Lenin's speech at a public meeting in the Butyrsky District of Moscow on August 2, 1918.
p. 192

81 The decree *"On the Organisation of Supply"*, passed by the Council of People's Commissars on November 21, 1918 (see Note 77), envisaged expansion of the co-operatives' activities, de-nationalisation and de-municipalisation of co-operative shops and storehouses.

It obliged the Poor Peasants' Committees and the local Soviets to establish regular control over the activities of the co-operatives to prevent the kulaks and other counter-revolutionaries from taking them over.   p. 195

[82] Lenin raised the question of a revision of the Party Programme (adopted by the Second Congress of the R.S.D.L.P. in 1903) immediately after the February Revolution of 1917. This question was also raised at the Seventh (April) All-Russia Conference of the R.S.D.L.P. (Bolsheviks) and the Sixth Party Congress, which worked from July 26 to August 3 (August 8-16), 1917.

After the victory of the October Revolution and the implementation of the first Party Programme, a revision became a pressing necessity. In March 1919, a commission headed by Lenin was set up by the Seventh Party Congress to draw up the final Draft Programme.

In February 1919, the Commission finished work on the Draft Programme of the R.C.P.(B.), whose main principles were formulated by Lenin. It was published in *Pravda* on February 25-27. In its foreword to the Draft, the commission noted that the new programme differed considerably from the old one and that it reflected "not only the results of Marxist study of the latest, imperialist, stage of capitalism, but also the lessons of the world war and a year's experience of the proletariat who has won state power". The Draft was widely discussed by the local Party organisations, approved by most of them and recommended for endorsement, with some changes and additions.   p. 197

[83] This point of the draft of the economic section of the Programme was originally placed third; Lenin later recast it and made it point eight, under which number it was included in the Party Programme.
                                                                         p. 198

[84] *The Eighth Congress of the R.C.P.(B.)* was held in Moscow from March 18 to 23, 1919. It was attended by 301 delegates with deciding vote and 102 with deliberative vote, representing the total of 313,766 Party members.

Lenin made a report on the work of the Central Committee and reports on the main issues on the agenda: the Party Programme, Party work in the countryside, and military affairs.

The Congress adopted the new Party Programme, whose main principles were formulated by Lenin. The new Programme outlined the tasks of the Communist Party for the entire period of transition from capitalism to socialism and ideologically armed the Party and the working class for building a socialist society.

The Congress turned down Bukharin's proposal to leave out from the new Programme the description of simple commodity production and pre-monopoly capitalism. This description was necessary to correctly determine the Party line with regard to the working peasants and the capitalist elements. The Congress also rejected the anti-Bolshevik views of Bukharin and Pyatakov who proposed to strike out the Programme clause on the right of nations to self-determination.

Of major importance for socialism in Russia was the Congress decision on changing the Party policy of neutralising the middle peasants to that of establishing a stable alliance with them.

Considerable attention was given to military issues. The majority of the delegates censured the position of members of the so-called military opposition, who rejected the services of tsarist military experts and argued against the centralisation of the Army and the introduction of strict discipline there. The Congress pointed out certain mistakes and shortcomings in the work of the Republic's Revolutionary Military Council; for instance, R.M.C. Chairman Trotsky was sharply criticised for violating the Party line of observing the class principle in Army enlistment and for belittling the role of Party leadership in the Army.

The Congress hailed the founding, in early March 1919, of the Third, Communist, International and subscribed to its platform.

p. 201

[85] The *"Draft Third Clause of the General Political Section of the Programme"* was written by Lenin on the suggestion of the Programme Commission of the Eighth Party Congress. The draft was approved by the Commission, and included, with only slight changes, in the final text of the Programme (see *The C.P.S.U. in Resolutions of Congresses, Conferences and Central Committee Plenary Meetings*, Part I, Moscow, 1954, Russ. ed., p. 414).

p. 203

[86] The recording of Lenin's speeches was undertaken by *Tsentropechat* (the Central Agency of the All-Russia Central Executive Committee for the Supply and Distribution of Periodicals). Sixteen speeches of Lenin were recorded between 1919 and 1921.

p. 204

[87] The Hungarian Soviet Republic was established on March 21, 1919. The government included Communists and Social-Democrats, who concluded an agreement uniting their parties into the Socialist Party of Hungary. The unification, however, was accomplished quite mechanically, without breaking away with reformists, and this later told on the Party's political line.

On March 26, the Hungarian Soviet Government passed decrees on the nationalisation of industrial enterprises, transport, and banks. On April 2, it adopted the decree on the monopoly of foreign trade, and on April 3, the law on the land reform. Under the latter law, all estates exceeding 57 hectares were confiscated and turned into large state farms managed practically by the former stewards. Poor peasants hoped to get land from the Soviet government but their hopes were frustrated. This hindered the establishment of a close alliance between the proletariat and the peasants and weakened Soviet government in Hungary.

The victory of the proletarian dictatorship in Hungary was not to the taste of the imperialist Entente, which organised military intervention in Soviet Hungary. The attack spurred on the counter-revolutionaries at home to fresh activity. Betrayal by the Right Social-Democrats, who struck a deal with international imperialism, facilitated the fall of the Hungarian Soviet Republic.

Soviet Russia was unable to render any support to the Hungarian Republic, since in the summer of 1919 it was blockaded by the Entente troops. On August 1, 1919, the Soviet government was overthrown in Hungary by the joint forces of foreign imperialist intervention and internal counter-revolution.   p. 204

88 In a radio message sent on March 23, 1919, Lenin asked Béla Kun: "Please inform us what real guarantees you have that the new Hungarian Government will actually be a communist, and not simply a socialist, government, i.e., one of social-traitors.... So that I may be certain that the answer has come to me from you personally, I ask you to indicate in what sense I spoke to you about the National Assembly when you last visited me in the Kremlin" (*Collected Works*, Vol. 29, p. 227).   p. 204

89 An attempt of the Bavarian counter-revolutionaries to seize power in Munich on April 13, 1919 met with fierce resistance on the part of the workers and ended in their victory. In the night of April 13, a meeting of revolutionary factory committees and Soldiers' Soviets formed a Council of Action which elected a new Soviet government—the Executive Committee with leader of Bavarian Communists Eugene Levine at its head. The new government began to disarm the bourgeoisie, build up a Red Army, nationalise the banks, effect control over enterprises and normalise the food situation. The home and international situation of the Bavarian Republic was extremely serious. The first difficulties that arose in the Soviet Republic made the so-called independent Social-Democrats, who had also entered the government, throw off their mask. They ousted the Communists from the leading government posts in late April. This had a stimulating effect on the counter-revolution. On May 1, white-guard troops entered Munich and captured the city after three days of heavy fighting.   p. 206

90 *The First All-Russia Congress on Adult Education* took place in Moscow from May 6 to 19, 1919. It was attended by some 800 delegates. Lenin greeted the participants at the opening sitting, and delivered a speech, "Deception of the People with Slogans of Freedom and Equality" at the last sitting on May 19.   p. 208

91 The article gives answers to the questions put to Lenin by the United Press Agency. The fifth, last, question, the answer to which is given in this book, was: "What else would you care to bring to the notice of American public opinion?" In October 1919, a Left Socialist journal, *The Liberator*, carried an article, "A Statement and a Challenge". In a note to the article, the editors wrote that the United Press Agency sent Lenin's answers to the newspapers but excluded the answer to the fifth question as "purely Bolshevist propaganda".   p. 211

92 *The Ninth Congress of the R.C.P.(B.)* was held in Moscow from March 29 to April 5, 1920. It was attended by 715 delegates representing 611,978 Party members. Problems of economic construction were pivotal at the Congress. Lenin outlined the tasks of the Party in this field in the report he made on behalf of the Central Committee, as well as in his reports on the economic build-up and on the co-operatives. Particular attention of the Congress was drawn to

the necessity for a single economic plan with the electrification of the economy as its backbone. The Congress called upon Party members to strain every effort to restore the national economy, which was utterly dislocated at the time, and outlined a number of measures to stimulate popular initiative and constructive effort.

The Congress defined the role and place of the trade unions in the Soviet state system and gave a resolute rebuff to the anarcho-syndicalist elements who demanded "independence" for the trade unions and counterposed them to the Communist Party and the Soviet Government. The Congress clarified the problem of industrial management and censured the anti-Party propositions of the "democratic centralism" group and all those who opposed centralised state control of the economy and renounced the principle of one-man management in industry.   p. 221

B

Barbusse, Henri (1873-1935)—a well-known French writer and public figure; member of the French Communist Party since 1923. Barbusse's revolutionary, anti-militarist views shaped under the influence of the imperialist world war, in which he took part, and the October Socialist Revolution. A friend of the Soviet state since its first days, he took an active part in the movement against the anti-Soviet armed intervention of 1918-20.

In the 1920s-30s, he played a prominent role in the anti-war and anti-fascist movement of progressive writers and artists in France and the rest of the world.—212.

*Bazarov, V. (Rudnev, V. A.)** (1874-1939)—took part in the Social-Democratic movement from 1896. In 1905-07, he contributed to various Bolshevik publications. In 1917, a Menshevik-internationalist, an editor of the semi-Menshevik newspaper *Novaya Zhizn;* opposed the October Revolution; in 1919 was associated with the Menshevik journal *Mysl* (Thought). Since 1921 worked in the State Planning Commission; during the last years of his life translated fiction and philosophical literature.—51, 52.

Belinsky, V. G. (1811-1848)— a Russian revolutionary democrat, literary critic and publicist, materialist philosopher. Belinsky had a major influence on the development of Russian social and aesthetic thought.—119.

Bernatsky, M. V. (b. 1876)—a professor of political economy; from September 1917 Finance Minister in the bourgeois Provisional Government, and the counter-revolutionary governments of Denikin and Wrangel. Later a white émigré. —63.

Blanc, Louis (1811-1882)—a French petty-bourgeois socialist and historian. Denying that class contradictions under capitalism are irreconcilable, he opposed a proletarian revolution and advocated conciliation with the bourgeoisie. During the 1848 revolution was a member of the provisional government and head of the commission for "the study of the labour problem"; his conciliatory tactics helped the bourgeoisie divert the attention of the workers from the revolutionary struggle. Elected to the National Assembly in February 1871, Blanc sided with the opponents of the Paris Commune.—52.

The Bobrinskys, Al. A., An. A., V. A.—Russian counts, big landlords and owners of sugar refineries, reactionary politicians.—65.

Bogayevsky, M. P. (1881-1918)— a leader of the counter-revolutionary Don Cossacks. From June 18, 1917 to January 29, 1918, was Deputy Ataman of General Kaledin's Don Army and in early January 1918 became a member of the counter-revolutionary "Don government".—153.

Briand, Aristide (1862-1932)—a French statesman and diplomat. In 1913, 1915-17, 1921-22 —Prime Minister; in 1924 was France's delegate to the League of Nations. French Foreign

---

* Real names are given in brackets in italics.

Minister from 1926 to 1931.—95.

Bublikov, A. A. (b. 1875)—an engineer, sided with the big merchants and industrialists; member of the bourgeois Progressist Party. At the State Conference in Moscow in August 1917 he advocated a coalition between the bourgeoisie and the Mensheviks. Left Russia after the October Revolution.—72.

C

Chernov, V. M. (1876-1925)—a leader of the Socialist-Revolutionary Party. In May-August 1917, Minister for Agriculture in the bourgeois Provisional Government; instigated severe repressions against peasants who had seized landed estates. Organised anti-Soviet revolts after the October Revolution. In 1920, he went abroad and continued his anti-Soviet activities.—73, 79, 87, 133.

Chuchin, F. G. (1883-1942)—joined the Bolshevik Party in 1904. In 1917 became member of the Tomsk Soviet of Soldiers' Deputies and of the Siberian Regional Bureau of the R.S.D.L.P.(B). In 1918-19 engaged in underground activity on the territory seized by the insurgent Czechoslovak corps and Kolchak's troops. Was a delegate to the Ninth Party Congress. From 1923 engaged in research and lectured at Moscow's higher educational establishments.—221.

D

Dan (Gurvich), F. I. (1871-1947) a Menshevik leader. In 1917,

member of the Executive Committee of the Petrograd Soviet and of the Presidium of the Central Executive Committee (first convocation); supported the bourgeois Provisional Government. After the October Revolution engaged in anti-Soviet activities. Early in 1922 was banished as an enemy of the Soviet state.—87.

Dutov, A. I. (1864-1921)—a tsarist colonel, Ataman of the Orenburg Cossack army. Soon after the October Revolution, he organised, jointly with the Mensheviks and Socialist-Revolutionaries, the Committee of Salvation of the Homeland and Revolution which seized power in Orenburg in mid-November. On January 18 (31), 1918, Dutov was driven from the town by the Red Guard. In 1918-19 commanded the Orenburg detached Cossack army of Kolchak. In March 1920, following Kolchak's rout, crossed the Chinese frontier with the remnants of his units.—152, 193.

Dzerzhincsky, F. E. (1877-1926) —an outstanding leader of the Communist Party and the Soviet state. A member of the Party since 1895, he was an organiser of the Social-Democratic Party in Poland and Lithuania. After the October Revolution, Chairman of the All-Russia Extraordinary Commission for the Struggle Against Counter-revolution, Sabotage and Profiteering (All-Russia Cheka). In 1921 was appointed People's Commissar for Railways, while retaining the posts of Chairman of the Cheka and People's Commissar for Internal Affairs; as of 1924, Chairman of the Supreme Economic Council. In June

1924, elected alternate member of the Political Bureau of the Central Committee of the Russian Communist Party (Bolsheviks) and member of the Organising Bureau of the Party's Central Committee.— 106.

G

Gegechkori, Y. P. (b. 1879)—a Menshevik; since November 1917 chairman of the Transcaucasian counter-revolutionary government (Transcaucasian Commissariat), then Foreign Minister and Deputy Chairman of the Georgian Menshevik government. Following the establishment of Soviet power in Georgia in 1921, a white émigré.—153, 154.

Gogol, N. V. (1809-1852)—great Russian writer.—119.

Gompers, Samuel (1850-1924)— a prominent leader of the American trade-union movement, one of the founders of the American Federation of Labour and its permanent chairman since 1895. Pursued a policy of collaboration with the capitalists, opposed the revolutionary struggle of the working class. A social-chauvinist during the First World War. Was hostile to the October Revolution and the Soviet state.—185.

Gotz, A. R. (1882-1940)—a leader of the Socialist-Revolutionary Party. In 1917, member of the Executive Committee of the Petrograd Soviet of Workers' and Soldiers' Deputies, later Deputy Chairman of the All-Russia Central Executive Committee. After the October Revolution engaged in anti-Soviet activities.—153.

Guchkov, A. I. (1862-1936)—a big capitalist, organiser and leader of the Octobrist Party which upheld the interests of the big bourgeoisie and landowners. Following the February revolution of 1917, Minister for the Army and Navy in the first bourgeois Provisional Government. After the October Revolution engaged in anti-Soviet activity; subsequently a white émigré. —27.

Gukovsky, I. E. (1871-1921)—a Bolshevik, took up revolutionary activity in 1898. After the October Socialist Revolution, People's Commissar for Finance of the R.S.F.S.R. and then plenipotentiary of the R.S.F.S.R. in Estonia.—166, 167.

Gvozdyov, K. A. (b. 1883)—a Menshevik. In 1917, member of the Executive Committee of the Petrograd Soviet, Deputy Minister and, since September 1917, Minister for Labour in the bourgeois Provisional Government.—93.

H

Hanecki (Fürstenberg), Y. S. (1879-1937)—a prominent figure in the Polish and Russian revolutionary movement, member of the Social-Democratic Party from 1896. In 1917, member of the Bureau of the Central Committee of the R.S.D.L.P.(B.) Abroad. After the October Revolution worked in the People's Commissariat for Finance, then engaged in diplomatic work, was member of the Board of the People's Commissariat for Trade and of the Presidium of the Supreme Economic Council.

Since 1935, director of the State Museum of the Revolution—166, 167.

Henderson, Arthur (1863-1935)—a leader of the Labour Party and the British trade union movement. During the First World War a social-chauvinist. In 1919, one of the organisers of the Berne (Second) International; since 1923, chairman of the Executive Committee of the so-called Labour and Socialist International. Was on a number of British bourgeois governments.—185.

Hindenburg, Paul (1847-1934)—a German military leader and statesman. During World War I Commander-in-Chief of the German Army on the Eastern Front, then Chief of the General Staff. From 1925 to 1934, President of the Weimar Republic. In 1933 he empowered Hitler to form a new government, thus officially handing over all power to the nazis.—78.

K

Kautsky, Karl (1854-1938)—a leader of the German Social-Democratic Party and of the Second International, who abandoned Marxism and became an ideologist of Centrism (Kautskyism), the most dangerous and harmful variety of opportunism. During the First World War Kautsky stood on Centrist positions, using internationalist phrases to conceal his social-chauvinism. After the October Revolution became an outspoken enemy of the proletarian revolution and the dictatorship of the working class, the Bolshevik Party and the Soviet state. —192, 193, 194.

Kerensky, A. F. (b. 1881)—a Socialist-Revolutionary. Following the February revolution of 1917 was Minister for Justice, Minister for War and Navy and later Chairman of the bourgeois Provisional Government and Supreme Commander-in-Chief. After the October Socialist . Revolution engaged in anti-Soviet activities; since 1918, in emigration. —27, 63, 66, 68, 72, 80, 81, 82, 83, 88, 93, 102, 133-34, 153, 187.

Kievsky, Y.—see *Pyatakov G. L.*

Kornilov, L. G. (1870-1918)—a tsarist general, monarchist. In July 1917, was appointed Supreme Commander-in-Chief of the Russian Army. In August 1917 headed a counter-revolutionary revolt; was one of the organisers and later head of the whiteguard Volunteer Army. Killed in the field near Yekaterinodar.—63, 67, 78, 88, 94, 102, 103, 161.

Krasnov, P. N. (1869-1947)—a tsarist general. At the end of October 1917 commanded the Cossack troops dispatched by Kerensky against Petrograd during the anti-Soviet revolt. In 1918-19 headed the white Cossack army on the Don. In 1919 fled abroad where he continued his anti-Soviet activities; later collaborated with the nazis. Was taken prisoner and sentenced to death by the Military Board of the Supreme Court of the U.S.S.R.—153.

Kun, Béla (1886-1939)—a prominent leader of the Hungarian and international working-class movement, one of the founders and leaders of the Hungarian Communist Party. During the First World War, a prisoner of war in Russia, he joined the Bolshevik Party. In 1918, chairman of the Federation of Foreign Groups of the R.C.P.(B.). In the autumn of 1918 returned to Hungary. In the Hungarian Soviet Republic, established in March 1919, Kun acted as the virtual head of government, officially holding the posts of People's Commissar for Foreign Affairs and board member of the People's Commissariat for War. Following the suppression of Soviet power in Hungary went first to Austria, then to Russia. Was a member of the Presidium of the All-Russia Central Executive Committee, representative of the R.C.P.(B.) Central Committee in the C.C. of the Russian Young Communist League, member of the Presidium of the Executive Committee of the Comintern. —204, 205.

L

Lenin (Ulyanov), V. I. (1870-1924).—166, 167, 169, 192.
Lensch, Paul (1873-1926)—a German Social-Democrat. At the outbreak of the First World War adopted a social-chauvinist stand. After the war editor-in-chief of *Deutsche Allgemeine Zeitung*, organ of the Ruhr industrial magnates. In 1922 was expelled from the Social-Democratic Party of Germany at the demand of its rank-and-file members.—87.
Liebknecht, Karl (1871-1919)—an outstanding leader of the German and international working-class movement; a leader of the Left wing of the German Social-Democratic Party. In 1916 was sentenced to hard labour for his anti-

militarist propaganda. During the November 1918 revolution in Germany together with Rosa Luxemburg headed the revolutionary vanguard of the German workers. Was one of the founders of the Communist Party of Germany and a leader of the Berlin workers' uprising in January 1919. After the suppression of the uprising was brutally murdered by counter-revolutionaries.—187.
Lvov, G. Y. (1861-1925)—a Russian prince, big landowner, Constitutional-Democrat. From March to July 1917, Chairman of the bourgeois Provisional Government and Minister for the Interior. After the October Revolution a white émigré; helped organise the foreign military intervention against Soviet Russia.—27.
Lysis (Letailleur), Eugène— a French bourgeois economist, author of several works on financial and political subjects. —227.

M

Marx, Karl (1818-1883).—13, 18, 124.
Milyukov, P. N. (1859-1943)— a leader of the Cadet Party, an ideologist of the Russian imperialist bourgeoisie, historian and publicist. In 1917, Minister for Foreign Affairs in the first bourgeois Provisional Government; pursued the policy of "war to a victory". After the October Revolution helped organise the foreign military intervention against Soviet Russia, became a leader of the white émigrés.—27, 63, 88.
Milyutin, V. P. (1884-1938)— joined the Social-Democratic

movement in 1903, member of the Bolshevik Party from 1910. After the October Revolution was appointed People's Commissar for Agriculture. In 1918-21, Deputy Chairman of the Supreme Economic Council, later engaged in other important economic and government work; was elected alternate member of the Party's Central Committee and member of the Central Control Commission.—221.

N

Nekrasov, N. V. (b. 1879)—a Deputy to the Third and Fourth Dumas from Tomsk Gubernia, Cadet. In 1917, Minister for Railways, Minister without portfolio and Minister for Finance in the bourgeois Provisional Government. Left the Cadet Party in the summer of 1917. Following the October Revolution worked in the Central Union of Cooperative Societies.—63.

Nikitin, A. M. (b. 1876)—a Menshevik, lawyer; from July 1917, Minister for Posts and Telegraphs, Minister for the Interior in the last bourgeois Provisional Government.—93.

P

Palchinsky, P. I. (d. 1930)—an engineer, organiser of the Produgol Syndicate; was closely connected with banking circles. In 1917, Deputy Minister for Trade and Industry in the bourgeois Provisional Government; organised sabotage by industrialists, actively opposed democratic organisations. Headed the defence of the

Winter Palace on October 25 (November 7), 1917. Following the October Revolution, one of the instigators of sabotage in Soviet industry.—78, 79, 80.

Peshekhonov, A. V. (1867-1933) —a liberal Narodnik in the 1890s. From 1906 a leader of the petty-bourgeois Popular Socialist Party. In 1917, Minister for Food Supplies in the bourgeois Provisional Government. After the October Revolution fought against Soviet power; from 1922 a white émigré.—78, 80, 95.

Plekhanov, G. V. (1856-1918)— an outstanding leader of the Russian and international working-class movement, first propagandist of Marxism in Russia. In 1883, in Geneva, founded the Emancipation of Labour group, the first Russian Marxist organisation. In 1883-1903 wrote a number of works which played an important part in the defence and dissemination of the materialist world-outlook. After the Second Congress of the R.S.D.L.P. adopted a conciliatory attitude towards opportunism, and then sided with the Mensheviks; a social-chauvinist during the First World War. After his return to Russia following the February revolution of 1917 headed the Unity group, the extreme Right wing of the Menshevik defencists; opposed the Bolsheviks and was against a socialist revolution, as he considered Russia immature for a transition to socialism. He took a negative stand with regard to the October Revolution but did not take part in the struggle against Soviet power.

Lenin highly valued Plekhanov's philosophic works and his role in spreading Marxism in Russia; at the same time he sharply criticised Plekhanov for his deviations from Marxism and his serious political mistakes.—62, 87, 88.

Potresov, A. N. (1869-1934)—a Menshevik leader. A social-chauvinist during the First World War. In 1917 was editor of the newspaper *Dyen* (The Day), which unleashed a malicious campaign against the Bolsheviks. After the October Revolution went abroad; wrote articles attacking Soviet Russia for Kerensky's weekly *Dni* (Days).—62.

Prokopovich, S. N. (1871-1955)— a bourgeois economist and publicist. In 1917, Minister for Food Supplies in the bourgeois Provisional Government. After the October Revolution fought against Soviet power; was banished from the U.S.S.R. for his counter-revolutionary activities.—63, 93.

Pyatakov, G. L. (1890-1937)— a member of the Bolshevik Party from 1910. From 1914 till 1917 lived in emigration in Switzerland, later in Sweden; opposed Lenin on the question of the right of nations to self-determination. Held a number of responsible posts after the October Revolution. Repeatedly opposed the Party's Leninist policy, for which he was expelled from the Party. —20, 21.

R

Renaudel, Pierre (1871-1935)—a reformist leader of the French Socialist Party. From 1914 to 1919 and in 1924, a member of the Chamber of Deputies. A social-chauvinist during the First World War. In 1927 withdrew from the leadership of the Socialist Party, and was expelled from it in 1933; later he organised a small non-socialist group.—185.

Renner, Karl (1870-1950)—an Austrian politician, leader and theoretician of the Austrian Right-wing Social-Democrats. A social-chauvinist during the First World War. In 1919-20, Austrian Chancellor, from 1945 to 1950, President of Austria.—185.

Rolovich (Rokhovich, G. Y.)— a member of the Central Food Committee in 1917.—80, 81.

S

Savinkov, B. V. (1879-1925)—a leader of the Socialist-Revolutionary Party and of its "fighting organisation". After the October Revolution instigated several counter-revolutionary revolts, helped organise the military intervention against the Soviet Republic.— 153, 154.

Scheidemann, Philipp (1865-1939)—a leader of the extreme Right opportunist wing of the German Social-Democratic Party. During the November 1918 revolution in Germany was a member of the so-called Council of People's Representatives, which served the interests of the counter-revolutionary bourgeoisie. In February-June 1919, head of the coalition government of the Weimar Republic; was one of the organisers of the brutal suppression of the German working-class movement in 1918-21.—87, 185, 206.

Schmid, Arthur (b. 1889)—a Swiss bourgeois economist,

member of the Swiss Socialist Party. During the First World War a teacher of commercial science. In 1917-20, a member of the Zurich Cantonal Council, later national counsellor, secretary of the Socialist Party cantonal organisation and editor of its newspaper. From 1947, member of the Consultative Council of the Swiss National Bank.—24.

Shingaryov, A. I. (1869-1918)—a doctor, member of the Cadet Party. In 1917, was Minister for Agriculture in the first, and Minister for Finance in the second bourgeois Provisional Governments.—63, 96.

Shlyapnikov, A. G. (1885-1937)—a member of the R.S.D.L.P. from 1901. After the October Revolution was People's Commissar for Labour, later engaged in military, trade union and economic activities. In 1920-22 organised and led the anti-Party Workers' Opposition group. In 1933 was expelled from the Party.—106, 144.

Shulgin, V. V. (b. 1878)—a landowner, rabid monarchist and nationalist. After the October Revolution was one of the organisers of the white-guard Volunteer Army, helped counter-revolutionary generals Alexeyev, Denikin and Wrangel; later fled abroad where he continued to oppose Soviet power. In the 1920s he ceased all political activity.—43.

Skobelev, M. I. (1885-1939)—a Menshevik active in the Social-Democratic movement from 1903. In 1917, Deputy Chairman of the Petrograd Soviet, Deputy Chairman of the Central Executive Committee (first convocation); from May to August 1917, Minister for Labour in the bourgeois Provisional Government. After the October Revolution broke with the Mensheviks, worked in the co-operative movement, then in the People's Commissariat for Foreign Trade. In 1922 joined the R.C.P.(B.), held responsible economic posts; in 1936-37 worked in the All-Union Radio Committee.—38, 39, 41, 66, 79.

Smith-Falkner, Maria Natanovna (*Smith, M.*) (b. 1878)—an economist and statistician; took part in the revolutionary movement from 1897. After the February 1917 revolution contributed for some time to the semi-Menshevik newspaper *Novaya Zhizn* (New Life), was a member of the Mezhrayontsi group. In July 1918 joined the Bolshevik Party. After the October Revolution worked at various research institutions; Corresponding Member of the U.S.S.R. Academy of Sciences from 1939.—81.

Spunde, A. P. (1892-1962)—joined the Bolshevik Party in 1909. In 1917, member of the Bureau of the Perm and Urals Regional Committee of the R.S.D.L.P.(B.). After the October Revolution, Deputy Chief Commissar of the State Bank in Petrograd, then engaged in Party and government work in various cities. In 1926-30, board member of the State Bank, board member of the People's Commissariat for Finance and of the People's Commissariat for Railways.—166, 167.

Stein (Rubinstein), A. (1881-1948)—a Menshevik. In 1906 emigrated to Germany. At the beginning of the First World War, together with Kautsky and Bernstein, published the weekly *Sozialistische Auslands-politik* (Socialist Foreign Policy). In 1917 joined the Centrist Independent Social-Democratic Party of Germany. Took an active part in the smear campaign against the October Revolution and the Bolsheviks unleashed by the German Centrists.—193.

Struve, P. B. (1870-1944)—a bourgeois economist and publicist, a Cadet Party leader. A leading exponent of "legal Marxism" in the 1890s, came out with "amendments" to and "criticism" of Marx's economic and philosophic teaching; endeavoured to adapt Marxism and the working-class movement to the interests of the bourgeoisie. One of the ideologists of Russian imperialism. After the October Revolution a rabid enemy of Soviet power, member of Wrangel's counter-revolutionary government, white émigré. —51, 86.

Sverdlov, Y. M. (1885-1919)—an outstanding leader of the Communist Party and the Soviet state. On November 8(21), 1917, was elected Chairman of the All-Russia Central Executive Committee.—186.

T

Taylor, Frederick Winslow (1856-1915)—an American engineer, founder of the system of labour organisation aimed at the maximum utilisation of the working day and rational utilisation of means of production and implements of labour. Under capitalism his system is used to intensify the exploitation of the working people.—15-17.

Tereshchenko, M. I. (b. 1888)—an owner of big sugar refineries in Russia, millionaire; Finance Minister and then Minister for Foreign Affairs in the bourgeois Provisional Government in 1917, actively pursued the imperialist policy of "war to victory". White émigré after the October Revolution; one of the organisers of the counter-revolution and military intervention against the Soviet state.—63, 65, 72, 82.

Tolstoy, L. N. (1828-1910)—great Russian writer.—21.

Trutovsky, V. Y. (1889-1937)—a member of the Left Socialist-Revolutionary Party and of its Central Committee. In December 1917 was appointed People's Commissar of Municipal and Local Self-government. In March 1918 withdrew from the Council of People's Commissars in connection with the signing of the Brest Peace Treaty.—142.

Tsereteli, I. G. (1882-1959)—a Menshevik leader. After the February revolution of 1917, member of the Executive Committee of the Petrograd Soviet and of the Central Executive Committee (first convocation). In May 1917 became Minister for Posts and Telegraphs in the bourgeois Provisional Government; subsequently was Minister for the Interior. After the October Revolution was one of the leaders of the Georgian counter-revolutionary Menshevik government. A white émigré after the establishment of Soviet power in Georgia.—79, 88, 93.

V

Vorobyov, V. A. (b. 1896)—a member of the Bolshevik

Party from 1914. From September 1917 till the end of 1918, editor of the newspaper *Uralsky Rabochy* (Urals Worker); member of the Urals Regional Party Committee and of the Executive Committee of the Urals Regional Soviet. In 1920-22 was on the staff of the Central Committee of the R.C.P.(B.). In 1927 was expelled from the Party for his splitting activity; was reinstated in 1928.—106.

Z

Zinoviev (Radomyslsky), G. Y. (1883-1936)—joined the R.S.D.L.P. in 1901.

After the October Revolution Chairman of the Petrograd Soviet, member of the Political Bureau of the Party's Central Committee, Chairman of the Comintern Executive Committee.

Repeatedly opposed the Party's Leninist policy; vacillated during the preparation for and the carrying out of the October Revolution; was against an armed uprising; in 1925 he was one of the organisers of the "New Opposition" and in 1926 one of the leaders of the anti-Party Trotsky-Zinoviev bloc. In November 1927 was expelled from the Party for his splitting policy; was twice reinstated and expelled again for his anti-Party activity.—195.